AN IRISH JO

Also by Gerry Adams

A Pathway to Peace
An Irish Voice
Before the Dawn
Cage Eleven
Falls Memories
Free Ireland: Towards a Lasting Peace
Selected Writings
The Politics of Irish Freedom
The Street and Other Stories

GERRY ADAMS

An Irish Journal

BRANDON

First published in 2001 by
Brandon
an imprint of Mount Eagle Publications
Dingle, Co. Kerry, Ireland

10 9 8 7 6 5 4 3 2 1

Copyright © Gerry Adams 1997, 1998, 1999, 2000, 2001
Chronology, Biographies, Glossary and Index copyright © Brandon 2001

The author has asserted his moral rights.

ISBN 0 86322 282 X

"Mother's Day" was first published in *Mothers – Memories from Famous Daughters and Sons*, compiled by UNICEF Ireland (O'Brien Press, Dublin 1999).

"The State We Are In" was first published in *The Border: Personal Reflections from Ireland, North and South*, edited by Paddy Logue (Oak Tree Press, Dublin 1999).

This book is sold subject to the condition that it shall not, by way of trade or otherwise, be lent, resold, hired out or otherwise circulated without the publisher's prior consent in any form of binding or cover other than that in which it is published and without a similar condition being imposed on the subsequent purchaser.

Cover design: id communications, Tralee
Cover photograph: Kit de Fever
Typesetting by Red Barn Publishing, Skeagh, Skibbereen
Printed by The Guernsey Press, Channel Islands

CONTENTS

Introduction	7
An Irish Journal	9
Chronology	270
Biographies	273
Glossary	275
Index	279

Cleaky
1947–2000

INTRODUCTION

This book is a gathering up of pieces I have written since August 1997. Most of these were published in the Irish American newspaper *An Irish Voice*, and for this I remain indebted to Niall O'Dowd and Debbie McGoldrick. Others appeared elsewhere in bits and pieces of other publications; Richard and Caroline Newcombe of Creators Syndicate did manage to place one or two somewhere or other, including the *Boston Herald*, on a fairly regular basis. Some didn't appear anywhere. This is their first public outing. Other bits I can't find.

Some of these days I must get myself properly organised. That way at least I may have some possibility of retaining some shadow of a relationship with ever-patient publisher Steve MacDonogh.

Getting published is a big part of what writing is about. The creation of pieces which deal with contemporary issues forces the writer into acquiescing to the need for a discipline of regular production to meet newspaper deadlines. Reproduced in book form like this, these articles provide a diary of sorts of the period involved. Hopefully they also present an insight into matters of interest to the reader.

This is my second such venture. *An Irish Journal* takes up where *An Irish Voice*, published in 1997, left off. At that time I noted, in reading over the text, "I am reminded of developments and non-developments and other events I had forgotten in the twists and turns of the situation over this period."

So it is with *An Irish Journal*. This book begins five months after a Labour government was returned in Britain and two months after the IRA had announced a second cessation, and it ends as the peace process faces a real crisis. But these years and these articles are not only about the peace process. These were difficult times for my family also, especially for my sister Margaret and her husband Mickey. Their daughter Deirdre's husband Terry Enright was assassinated, and then a year or so later their two sons Liam and Miceál were killed in a car crash. *Go ndéana Dia trócaire ar a anamacha.*

The peace process is, however, a spinal element of these terrible times and of what I was involved with. Reading over these pages I was struck by the sheer slowness of it all. The old Unionist catch cry "Not an inch" is entirely appropriate. It almost makes "process" a bad word. Yet there can be no gainsaying the progress which has been made or the need to continue to inch ahead.

As I write these lines even that appears a daunting task at this time. It is just after Christmastide and I am minded of another Christmas twenty years ago. Then a hunger strike in Armagh Women's Prison and in the H-Blocks of Long Kesh had come to an end. There was a deal which had the capacity to resolve the issues at the core of the prison protests which had endured for over five years at that time. But it was not to be. Those within the British establishment who clung to the old agenda, including maybe some of those who created that agenda, had their way, and despite the best efforts of the protesting prisoners and their leaders, the deal was reneged upon and a second hunger strike started.

The rest is history. Could it be that history will be repeated? I hope not. By the time you get to read these lines, that much might be clear. Or at least we will know whether the rolling crisis which is gathering momentum at this time in the process has been averted. We will know whether another deal has been reneged upon.

On a lighter note, spring will have sprung once again. I will have planted more trees. Indeed, for the first time I will have planted wild roses. I have a few dozen young wild roses all ready for planting out if they have not been devastated by this Christmas's snow. It is good to have worries like that to focus on. It makes the other bits bearable. Or at least puts them in context. Things could be worse. Somewhere else they probably are.

That at least is what Richard Gerard McAuley always says. Without Richard there would not be *An Irish Journal*. Thanks, RG. And thanks, Colette. For everything.

Neither will it be possible for those who are trying to prevent change to have their way. Yes, they can slow it down. Yes, they can dilute or frustrate or delay the changes which are needed if there is to be peace and justice on this island. But they cannot stop the changes. Why not?

Because for them to succeed would mean the rest of us giving up. And we are not going to do that. We are not going to ever again acquiesce to the old agenda. Those days are gone.

Gerry Adams
Belfast, January 2001

22 September 1997

That Was the Week That Was

On 17 September, the Ulster Unionist Party joined the multi-party talks at Stormont. The Democratic Unionist Party and the UK Unionist Party boycotted the talks.

It was an historic week. There is no doubt about that. A week of historic days. But still, for all the history that we are making we have yet to begin the talking which is required if we are to make the peace. That is because the Unionists have still to make their way into the negotiations with the rest of us.

There are two sides to that. On the one hand all the parties in the negotiating room, including the two governments, share a common objective of getting the Unionists in, and on the other hand there is considerable difference about the best way to achieve this. One view is that David Trimble has nowhere else to go; that his tediously aggressive posturing – which includes staging an "indictment" of Sinn Féin, seeking our ejection from the process, and similar noisy protestations – is his ticket into the substantive talks and that we should put up with it. So we do. The other view is that his behaviour is unacceptable, deeply hurtful to those who have suffered because of British, Unionist or Loyalist violence, and that he is going to continue with this type of playacting indefinitely. Or at least until the two governments tell him that enough is enough.

And that is where we all are at this time.

One thing can be said with absolute certainty: the Unionist leaders have yet to come to the decision that they should make peace with the rest of us. And it is important to stress that this is about the rest of us, by which I mean both governments and all the other parties, and not about some special problem which Unionists have with Sinn Féin, though of course they have that as well. But the reality is that David Trimble has yet to engage with anyone, except on a merely tactical basis.

Look back over the last year to before Sinn Féin arrived into the talks building. The big achievement of that period was the unequivocal restoration of the IRA cessation of August 1994. There is no comparable initiative on the Unionist side or worthy response to it, despite the widespread desire among a very large

Unionist constituency for its leaders to engage in real talks. On the contrary, the Unionist response to the IRA cessation was to withdraw from the process.

I do not doubt that David Trimble's grandstanding tactics are popular with sections of his support base. That's politics for you. But we should note the difference between making politics and making peace. Anyone can grandstand, and, given half a chance, most politicians will. But how many can lead instead of playing to the gallery?

Those who say Mr Trimble is behaving as he does because of the threat from rival Unionists Ian Paisley and Bob McCartney are making excuses for him. The Ulster Unionist Party (UUP) is well able to take care of itself, and anyone who is genuinely committed to peace will not let party politicking hold back progress. Because that is all this inter-Unionist rivalry is: politicking. And the Unionist leaders are all big boys now and well able for it.

In my opinion Mr Trimble has a strategy which includes engaging in these talks in his own time and on his own terms with everyone except Sinn Féin, and his objective, at this time anyway, is to subvert the peace talks and to reduce their potential and their capacity to usher in real change. That is what this is all about. About change. Which is what Unionism is afraid of. Which is why the UUP is adopting its current tactical approach.

Today Mr Trimble led his party into the negotiating room. There has been a massive media focus on this because Sinn Féin is in that room. But Mr Trimble never said a word during what he had billed as his confrontation with Sinn Féin. He remained silent. Instead, his colleague Ken Maginnis read a tediously long "indictment" of our party, during which he indicted the new Labour government in London, the Irish government, John Hume and us. Then David Trimble, Ken Maginnis and Jeffrey Donaldson left the room and sent in some junior people to listen to the responses of the indicted ones.

For our part, the Sinn Féin delegation welcomed the attendance of UUP and the smaller Loyalist parties. Looking at it from their point of view, today was a big step, but it was a big step for us as well. Among our delegation was Councillor Sean McManus, whose son was shot to death by a UDR officer. He

22 September 1997

listened patiently to former UDR officer Maginnis describing Sinn Féin as "a monstrous deceit" and "an evil mafia" in the course of a rambling invective of untrue allegations against his namesake Martin McGuinness and myself. Afterwards, in a press conference, Sean extended the hand of friendship to Mr Maginnis and his party. He did so because our party is here to make peace.

David Trimble may yet surprise us all by embracing this objective. He may follow the example of Sean MacManus. I hope that he does, but I am sure that if and when he does that it will be when he has been firmly pointed in the right direction by Mr Blair. Remember, it was Mr Blair who told the world that the train was leaving the station and that it would wait for no one. It is now over to him to deliver on his promises and on the guarantees that he gave about substantive talks.

With today's carry-on out of the way, the two governments are now to table a procedural motion to move this process into substantive talks. They should have done that by the time you get to read this.

What will the Unionists do then?

It's Good to Talk

Movement towards substantive negotiations, with the Unionists involved at last.

When last my words graced this page, I asked what would the Unionists do when the two governments tabled the procedural motion to move the process into substantive talks. We got our answer a few days later when an agreed formula was put to a plenary session late last Wednesday night. The UUP supported the motion. There have been acres of print and hours of broadcasting analysis of what happened and why it happened. The answer is easy. Mr Trimble knew the two governments were going to have to put the procedural motion. I knew that. So did everyone else in the talks building. The governments had delayed... and delayed... and delayed as they tried to get a pre-cooked package. Every one of the parties in the talks was united behind the objective of getting the Unionists in. We and the two governments shared that common objective. By Wednesday evening all the parties felt we had dallied enough. It was up to the governments to move. Once that was clear, Mr Trimble's room to manoeuvre was limited.

He could have delayed a little longer, which in essence would have meant that the motion would have been tabled on Wednesday night but not discussed until the following Monday. That was not a good position for the UUP, given the divisions within that party. The procedural motion was all about bringing the Unionists in. Everyone knew that, and by five o'clock that day I reckoned David Trimble was coming in. Sure, there would be a bit of to-ing and fro-ing before he finally said yes, but as I listened to Ken Maginnis in a radio interview, I told our delegation, "They are in tonight."

Of course, there was no certainty about this. But Sinn Féin had been involved in all the machinations and perambulations to ease the UUP's entry. We had already agreed our positions with the two governments and informed some of the other parties of this. Our view was a pragmatic one. We would support the procedural motion but dissent from one section which the

29 September 1997

Unionist clearly intend to make a blockage further up the road. That section concerns – surprise, surprise – the issues of decommissioning and consent. Once we were satisfied that the UUP was on for the motion, we were freed up to take the pragmatic option.

We put down our marker and moved on. So did everyone else. It was a good night's work, and at the plenary session which concluded all our efforts, I commended everyone involved on behalf of our party. Of course, the UUP are still not talking to Sinn Féin, and they have yet to recommence talking to the Irish government, though that will probably come before they talk to us. In the meantime some of them return pleasantries when we bump into one another. Others ignore us. Ken Maginnis persists in calling Martin McGuinness "a murdering bastard". Fortunately for the peace process, he has got that one wrong also. But it does show you where Ken is coming from.

Our group is working on the assumption that all of this will settle down in due course. There is still a very long way to go, but at least progress is being made; and while I sometimes give a critical view of developments in these columns, I am genuinely delighted to see the UUP around the table with the rest of us. Hard work isn't easy, and every party has difficulties, but at least a start has been made.

It would be easy to get angry at the Unionists, but there is little point in that. I wish Ian Paisley was in the process also. And Bob McCartney as well. I detest it when English politicians look down their noses at the Unionists and sneer at their antics. The more extreme Unionists behave as they do because for a very long time indeed English politicians told them that they were special. They were so special that English politicians gave them their own little statelet. The rest of us didn't matter. We were inferior. So when some Unionists continue to treat us like that I cannot help thinking that it is despicable for English politicians to go on about tribal hatreds and sectarian bitterness as if Unionist extremism was nothing to do with them. A convenient cop-out!

For a long time now I have worked on the basis that people respond to the political conditions in which they live. Improve the conditions and you empower the people. Therein lies our future. Unionists cling to the old order because they think it protects them. They believe their advantage is rooted in our disadvantage. And so it has been. So is their loyalty to the Union. They are Unionists because that made them top dog. Change that and everything changes. For they are really no more loyal than I am. Equality will be a great equaliser. And that is over very much to Mr Blair. He, too, has a long way to travel; but he also, with the rest of us, has made a good start.

Today, Tuesday, when the Business Committee met, there was more progress. All the parties reported back on a good working meeting, and the two Sinn Féin representatives, Martin McGuinness and Bairbre de Brún, agreed that there was no messing about. The substantive negotiations are due to start next Tuesday.

"At last," sez you.
"Indeed," sez I.

13 October 1997

Mayo, God Help Us!

On 21 September, Kerry defeated Mayo in the All-Ireland Football Final by 0–13 to 1–7.

The hangover of the 1997 All-Ireland defeat is like a shroud over the county. Even now, weeks later, it slumps heavily over Mayo. It is there in the flags which still fly forlornly from townland telegraph poles. Its echo mocks us in the banners which bridge village streets.

Ballina welcomes Sam.
Céad Míle Fáilte, Sam.
Welcome Home, Sam.

The red and green flaps everywhere. It's like the morning after the night before when the party has gone askew and the hosts feel let down, so nobody can be bothered clearing away the decorations. Only a few weeks ago I sat in a sea of red and green. My heart was with Mayo. Third time lucky. But my head was with Kerry. So was Maurice Fitzgerald, languidly, lazily scoring point after point. And that's the only way to win. By scoring.

But the All-Ireland is more than a game of football or hurling or camogie. The pain, the joy, the pathos, the drama and the excitement of it all is about us. It's about a sense of place, of pride and prowess, of skill and courage. It is about us but it is uniquely universal. It is local but it is national. It is Gaeldom. It is a dream. In Mayo it is about shattered dreams.

I was there overnight in Gaoth Saile, a small village near Belmullet, for Sinn Féin's *Slógadh*. *Slógadh* is an Irish language conference which travels each year to a Gaeltacht area to discuss matters of the day and to enjoy local hospitality. *Craic, ceol agus ól*!

It is easy to see how Gaoth Saile – Salty Wind or Wind from the Shore – gets its name. I walked the road westwards towards the sea beyond which New York beckons. All around me was a wild, windswept, poor, rugged landscape. But it uplifted me. And, more importantly, the new houses along the road are a sign that others are uplifted also and that they are staying here in their own place.

An Irish Journal

It was not always so. At *Slógadh* a local historian told us of the Famine. I, like you and most Irish people, have read and come to know a lot about the Famine, especially in this 150th anniversary of Black '47. But when the *Gorta Mór* is explained in local terms and translated into the fields and byroads, the sand dunes and hillocks beside us, then it takes on a new immediacy. The people were forced from their homes by the landlords or their agents. They lived in sod houses or in ditches. In 1847 people were dying all around. Neighbours were afraid to bury the dead. They collapsed the sod houses in on top of the corpses. Ballina Union and Workhouse were overwhelmed. At that time there were well over a million people living in Connacht. Belmullet and its hinterland were not the deserted places that they are today. But this richness in people brought its own misery. A contemporary report describes Bangor Erris, a mile from us, as "the fag end of misery". Another report notes that Belmullet exported two cargoes of grain.

That's when it hurts. In your imagination. When you face into the wind and stand in a field of dying people looking at a field of golden grain. Or look from a field of golden grain at the stricken crop of dying Mayo children. A local writer could only lament, "It wasn't our own fault. We didn't deserve that." And I can only agree.

Then came emigration. Walking the roads it is easy to visualise the people fleeing, presumably the fittest, the youth, leaving the middle aged and the elderly. Emigration is always like that, even in less troubled times. And in Mayo emigration became a way of life.

But all is not lost. At another talk in *Slógadh* we learned that emigration has slackened off this last few years. We learned of the efforts to create and sustain local regeneration. From the despair of 1847 we heard of the hope of 1997. The spirit of Michael Davitt lives yet. Small business and cooperative schemes are generating local capital. A man back from the USA has developed grand new houses. Another is employing local people in a knitwear factory. A bright modern supermarket – only a month old – sits at a crossroads. The football pitch opposite is knee deep in the tide. No need for a final whistle there.

By now they will be thinking of next year's All-Ireland. By

13 October 1997

now the county panel may even be thinking of starting back to a bit of training. Or maybe they will leave it until after Christmas. Maybe Mayo will make it back to Croke Park next September. Who knows? One thing, however, is for sure. They won't be for giving up.

An Irish Journal

DOING BUSINESS

On 13 October, Gerry Adams and Martin McGuinness met British Prime Minister Tony Blair for the first time in Stormont's Castle Buildings.

I started Monday, 13 October, at a book launch in Conway Mill on the Falls Road. Fr Joe McVeigh had asked me to launch his *Crying Out for Justice,* a timely and perceptive collection of talks and writings; I was delighted to do so. Monday was a beautiful morning here, and our gathering was further uplifted by some wonderful fiddle playing from a young woman from Tempo in County Fermanagh. Sunshine, fine music, good company and the birth of a book is a great way to start a week.

I had a rake of engagements that day. These included important constituency business, some lobbying that I was conducting and other business, so I had arranged with Martin McGuinness that he would head up our delegation in the plenary session of the talks process that morning in Castle Buildings at Stormont. When we were told that British Prime Minister Tony Blair was coming to the North and that he wanted a meeting, there had to be some rescheduling. After contact between our offices, it was agreed that we would meet at three forty.

I left my last appointment that afternoon and travelled in bright autumn sunshine the short journey across Belfast to the talks venue. When I arrived, a muddle of media was laying siege to the building, and I ran the gauntlet of their questions before making my way indoors to our offices. Although I was looking forward to meeting Mr Blair, I was a bit bemused by all the media focus and the attention that was being given to the handshakes. I have only learned in recent times about the symbolism and sensitivities of handshakes. I first encountered this when I was an invited speaker at a debate in Trinity College Dublin: in the scrum of pre-debate formalities I was introduced to a welter of people; to my surprise, one of them refused to shake hands with me.

"There is blood on your hands," he declared.

"He used to write speeches for Garret Fitzgerald," someone

20 October 1997

informed us.

That explained it; or did it? It is a reality of the human condition that some people could be so antagonised by someone else that they would not want to be near them or to engage with them. But once you do decide to be near them, especially in a effort to engage them, to influence them, then a modicum of civility is required, unless like my speech-writing acquaintance, you are into gestures (or non-gestures). Because the symbolism of not shaking hands is that the victim of your refusal is not worthy of even this recognition of his or her humanity. They are beyond the pale. They are sub-human. Inferior.

I have no time for such nonsense. Treat everyone as equals. Or try to. If you cannot bear people then avoid them. If you cannot avoid them, and especially if you want to do business with them, swallow your prejudice. If the consequence of all this may be the difference between war or peace, then we have a duty to reach out. To make the difference.

The question of the meeting with Tony Blair was not about shaking hands. It was about doing business, and that is what we did.

The British government was represented by Tony Blair, Marjorie Mowlam, Paul Murphy, Jonathan Stephens and four officials. Sinn Féin was represented by myself, Martin McGuinness, Pat Doherty and Siobhán O'Hanlon. We were to meet in a ground-floor office in an administration room of the talks building. Our team arrived there a few minutes before the engagement, and we sat drinking juice and tea and nibbling biscuits while we waited for the visitors. After a short delay they were ushered in. I was at the tea and coffee table when Mr Blair led his entourage into the room. Our first encounter was entirely informal and friendly. He appeared to be genuinely glad to see us. For a few minutes there was a confusion of chatter as everyone met everyone else, as we found our seats and got tea or coffee and so on.

Then, as we all settled back in our chairs, the meeting proper opened with a short exchange of greetings. It was to be a friendly and cordial affair. I told Mr Blair: "You are very welcome to Ireland. *Céad míle fáilte.*"

He began by telling us that he was pleased that we were in the process. He went on to outline his views of the situation and his government's commitment to change. It would not be right for me to report all his comments, though I have a full record of our discussion, and his side have given their version of this. Suffice to say that he was very engaged and engaging, and our respective contributions were straightforward and frank.

I acknowledged that the new government in London had moved speedily to remove the obstacles to the talks process which the last government had erected. I stressed Sinn Féin's longtime commitment to our peace strategy.

"We have always said there had to be a level playing pitch. We want you to be the last British prime minister with jurisdiction in Ireland. This is part of Ireland. From our view the biggest cause of conflict is British government involvement. The British government have to be the engine for change. Try to understand what it is like to live in your own country without rights.

"There is a need for constitutional change. I heard you say you valued the Union, but for us and other people the Union is of no great value. With all of the goodwill in Ireland and Britain, there could be a new relationship between our countries. I think the equality agenda needs to be pursued with vigour. The previous Tory government signed up to an equality agenda but they did nothing. Even in the 1920s the Tory government signed up to an equality agenda. Yet we have Garvaghy Road, and other provocative Orange marches.

"There is a need to move on justice issues, on rights issue, especially demilitarisation. But the core issue, the central issue, is the constitutional one. This is the biggest issue. You can be the person who can make the difference as we move towards the millennium. There needs to be movement on prisoners. All these issues need to be dealt with."

Tony Blair responded to all these points. He told us that his instinctive belief was that this was a moment in history. "This is clear. I will do my bit to achieve it. It is pointless to go on in the old way."

We went on to discuss sectarianism. I pointed out that what underpins sectarianism here is what feeds racism or that type of extremism anywhere. There is a perception of privilege, and a reason to hate is created because there is a fear that the disadvantaged, the dispossessed, will take away the privilege, or what

20 October 1997

is sometimes a perception of privilege.

"The Unionists are my neighbours. We want to reach out and to be flexible, but we will not put up with what our grandparents put up with. Partition has failed. Your generation of English leaders may feel you have have no responsibility for the origins of the conflict in our country, but the reason the Unionist leaders feel like they do is because they were in a privileged position. A previous prime minister said he would not have a Catholic about the place. Unionists now realise there has to be change. John Major made a mess of things. The peace process could have been much more advanced by now if he had engaged properly. We all need to improve upon this new opportunity. We are trying to bring people with us, but the British army is still patrolling our streets. There is a slowness in dealing with prisoners. At times the process is not making progress. If there are not premeditated outcomes, if your government really does not have any selfish reasons for being here, then now you cannot sit on your hands. Your agenda has to be about moving forward. The security agenda has been running this place for thirty years. A way of getting rid of it is to embrace a political agenda and to create a sea change."

At this point Mr Blair asked: "Are you in a position to hold the ceasefire?"

I told him as far as I was concerned the last cessation was a good one. The quid pro quo for the first one was that there would be substantive talks. "We are going to physical-force people and saying that there is an alternative. Most of the people I know have been the victims of violence from the British side. The [IRA] people have stopped. We have to build on that. It is a big challenge. We have to bring people with us."

Martin McGuinness also spoke on this issue. "The most amazing statement made in relation to the last ceasefire was by Jim Molyneaux, the previous leader of the UUP. He said it was the most destabilising thing that had occurred here. You have to get behind the mind of someone who thinks like that. The objective of British intelligence is now to split the IRA. The British government need to recognise that this conflict is a political problem that needs to be resolved. Last year I listened to Cyril Ramaphosa and Roelf Meyer in Belfast. Roelf Meyer made a brilliant contribution. He said that for years they had looked at the conflict as a security problem until Nelson Mandela was released. I think John Major's stewardship through the ceasefire shows he was working to a military agenda, and the role you have taken shows it is a political problem. But there is much to be done. It is an imperfect process. Our problem is, we are sitting in a room with Unionist representatives who won't speak to us or John Hume, Seamus Mallon or the Alliance Party. The question is, who can bring those people along? The only person is you. It is only when you say, as you said, for example, on decommissioning, 'Let's get on with it,' that they were forced to think and get on with it. We have argued for peaceful negotiations. Why should another person lose their lives or go to prison? When the equality agenda is mentioned, people should know it is about more than jobs. It is about the constitutional issues. People have lived as second-class citizens. This has to end."

Martin also spelt out our attitude to Bloody Sunday. "I talked to relatives. There is speculation about an apology. Relatives are not interested in an apology. They want an international public inquiry. This is a massive issue which needs to be resolved by the British government."

After Martin had finished speaking, I gave notice that I intended raising the Brian Nelson affair and the entire issue of collusion and British involvement in killings here. Pat Doherty outlined our view on consent, and Siobhán O'Hanlon rounded off our meeting, which was by now running late, with a short contribution on the absolute need for the British government to adopt a policy which includes withdrawal from Ireland.

This account deals mainly with the Sinn Féin contribution to the meeting. It may give an unbalanced view of the discussion. This is not my intention. I do not detail the British contribution because it is not my business to do so. What I can say is that Tony Blair dealt with all these issues in a forthright way. He upheld the British government's position as we expected he would. But the task of democratic opinion in Ireland and Britain and further afield – and this includes the USA – is to get a change of British policy from upholding partition and the Union to a policy of ending partition and the Union in consultation with the people of this island. Our meeting was part of that

20 October 1997

effort.

The last time Sinn Féin and the British government got together was over seventy-five years ago. The British made a mess of it that time. As I said to Tony Blair, "I hope we all do better this time."

Negative Campaigning

When Gerry Adams said he would vote for Mary McAleese if he had a vote in the Irish presidential election, there was a strident reaction of outrage, leaks and dirty tricks.

By the time you get to reading this, the votes will have been counted and we will all know who the new president is to be. Then hopefully the begrudgers and naysayers will have got their comeuppance and the hurt and anger they caused will start to abate. Some silver linings are emerging, all the same, from the dirty dealing of the last few weeks. The negative campaigning which has marred the presidential election contest has sparked off a debate which is truly national and which I hope will continue beyond polling day. I also hope that this debate will be conducted in a more reasoned, inclusive and informative way than we have seen so far, and that those political leaders who have taken up positions of trenchant opposition to the views espoused by Sinn Féin will play a constructive role in informing this debate. For my part I will seek to do the same.

The debate is about how the people of Ireland see ourselves. Is this, no matter how positively it may be described, a narrow, partitionist and factionalised dysfunctional community which has never come to terms with our own history or our own potential to grow in an inclusive and equitable way? Or do we have an all-Ireland view which tries to embrace all the people of this island as equals? Have we a vision of an island people at peace with ourselves and our neighbours, developing our own society in a way which reflects our diversity as a nation? Or does "official" Ireland stop at the border? Are we two nations? What is our relationship with Britain? What should it be? What role has Unionism in all this? What role do Unionists want?

There are many other questions which need to be answered as part of this debate. They include core issues such as how we see the peace process and its objectives. What is Irish Nationalism? Or Unionism? What is our attitude to partition? To the Union? What is Republicanism? What effect does the political dimension of partition have on the social or economic well-being of the

27 October 1997

people of Ireland? What is Irishness? What is Irish culture? What is our vision for the future?

There are other issues about the conduct of politics – North and South – which need to be explored in a balanced way. These go to the very core of what politics should be about. I believe that politics should be about empowering people. Do they? Can they?

There have been many instances recently of the corruption and selfishness which drive some political ambitions. The leaking of sensitive confidential government documents is just as reprehensible. So, too, is the way in which these documents were seized upon to advance a narrow political agenda. The national interest was put to one side.

It is a matter of some concern and an insight into the mindsets of the politicians and commentators involved that my observations on the election were misrepresented negatively by them as being in some way more worthy of controversy than the leaking of these documents. It has also been said that my comments on the presidential candidates were a strategic intervention in the election as part of a plan on my part to "colonise" the presidency. This is patent nonsense. My comments on the election were a reasonable response to reasonable questions, and not part of any calculated intervention.

Sinn Féin has not endorsed any candidate, but we do have the right to express opinions, and I and other Sinn Féin spokespersons will continue to do so as part of our legitimate agenda of promoting a better understanding of our political views and of informing public debate on the issues of the day.

It is no accident that those who pursue a narrow partitionist agenda seek also to exclude or to misrepresent all other views. It is no accident that these are the people who criticised John Hume and myself when we started the peace process. They are the same people who condemned President Mary Robinson's visit to West Belfast in June 1993. Their agenda is a neo-Unionist and pro-Union agenda. In the past, censorship and revisionism made their task a relatively easy one. Negative campaigning, misrepresentation, disinformation and campaigns of McCarthyism are the easy option. Now much more is demanded of them. Are they up to the challenge? Are they capable of being part of a real debate on the real issues?

An Irish Journal

BinLids

A review of BinLids, *a play from DubbelJoint Productions, a professional company, and Justus Community Theatre.*

Imagine a play written by the people who act in it. No big deal? Imagine these people have no real experience of telling their story. In fact, their version of our recent history has rarely been heard. So, imagine a play which tells their story from their viewpoint and experience instead of from the viewpoint of the hundreds of others who have written whole libraries of books, screenplays and dramas which purport to tell this story. A good idea?

Imagine a play about the trauma, joy, fear, love, hate, cruelty, dignity, humour, resilience and survival of a Nationalist community, and especially the women of that community in Belfast. Would you like to see this play in New York? Or Boston? Or Philly?

Then maybe you will be able to help, or you might know somebody else who is able to help, or you might even know somebody who knows somebody who could help.

The play is called *BinLids*. A dramatic presentation of the lives of local people in West Belfast, set during the introduction of internment in 1971 and the turbulent seventeen years which followed, it is a story which has been told by many but rarely by those it is about. And never like this. Never in such an innovative and riveting way.

BinLids is also an important play because it represents a piece of the jigsaw which has been missing for some time. When I say that it has been missing, I mean that it has been kept until now to one side, out of sight and on the margins with the rest of us, struggling to be heard.

Now it has a voice, a creative voice testing its range and rhythm and trying to sing out for itself in explanation of its existence and celebration of its survival, telling its own tale.

It appears to me that part of the process of making peace includes and needs people reclaiming their own stories and telling their own tales. This has to be a fundamental part of any

10 November 1997

healing process. Getting others to listen is another part. The sum total of all of this, of all the parts and all the stories, and understanding it in its totality, is what peace and the making of peace will be all about.

Of course, if this was all there is to it then *BinLids* could be a collection of statements about the various events which it encompasses. But it is more than that. It is fine acting. It is imaginative writing, a brilliant set with superb lighting and sound effects and the coordination of a large troupe who move seamlessly from scene to scene with faultless timing.

It is partisan, but it is also history relived with all its memories remembered and its myths reborn in a way which makes some sense of it all. When I watched the entire play after seeing bits of it in rehearsal, I was riveted not only by some of the performances but by the audience's reaction. Here in West Belfast the play was about that audience, but it is not only that reason, important though it is, which makes the audience reaction part of the action.

It is because they are part of the action. *BinLids* is acted out on five stages with the action shifting back and forth from stage to stage and sometimes into the audience itself. It is inclusive and gripping theatre where the distinctions between the audience and the actors becomes blurred as they mesh together so that at times it is hard to tell if the person beside you is a spectator or a performer. In *BinLids* everyone can be a player.

And that includes you, dear reader, because the people behind *BinLids* are trying to bring their play to the USA and they are looking for your help. The people behind *BinLids* are the hugely successful and inventive DubbelJoint Productions, a professional company, and Justus Community Theatre. DubbelJoint and Justus' other production, *Just A Prisoner's Wife*, won the Belfast City Council Award for Best Arts Partnership.

Note: BinLids *arrived in New York on 2 October 1998. The play was put on in the Angel Orensanz Foundation, an old synagogue transformed into an arts venue in New York's lower east side. There they gave twenty-eight enthusiastic performances to over 10,000 people. One emigrant told the cast that watching the play was like "going home for the night".*

An Irish Journal

HAPPY BIRTHDAY TO US!

Gerry Adams takes time off to engage in some important matchmaking.

It is not easy being a columnist for the *Irish Voice*. At least, it isn't easy being this columnist. Others may be able to regurgitate an Irish-American version of their story of the day. Some may be able to indulge themselves in short story escapism – and do a fine job of it. Our publisher even manages to take up a Sunday job to pass his time and our editor writes an advice column. Me? I have to get exclusives! I'm the one who gets sent behind enemy lines to generate dispatches from the front. None of your old double jobbing here, swanning around Manhattan or the Bronx. I'm the guy who gets the call in the middle of whatever crisis we are in at the time; I'm the guy who gets told, "We need a front page. Any chance of you going to the ....?" (Fill in the dots as the fancy grabs you.)

That's how I started filling this space. I met Neil O'Dowd (he hates his name spelt like that) one time. Well, I met him many times, but this particular time I asked him about writing a piece for his very fine newspaper. When I am looking for something I can crawl as good as any of ye.

"How much are you prepared to pay?" he asked.

"Well," I said, rather taken aback by his query but not letting on in case he thought I was stupid, "I really can't pay you anything. I'm poor."

He was unimpressed. He gave me his tough newspaperman look for what seemed to be a very long time. Then he melted. "Look, kid," he said. He always calls me kid.

"Look," he said eventually, "we'll give you a trial run. Let's not worry about money for now."

That was about three years ago. To be more precise, it was two ceasefires, two British prime ministers and three *taoisigh* ago.

I think the first column I wrote was about my first trip to the USA, on a forty-eight hour visa. I met our editor on that visit, and I introduced her to our publisher. They actually knew each other before that, but as happens sometimes as part of the

24 November 1997

human condition, they probably were so caught up in the hectic business of newspaperism that they didn't really see how destiny was shaping their lives and bringing them closer and closer together. It took a matchmaker.

Me.

Well, I was not actually a matchmaker who matchmade for them directly. It was more a case of a ricochet from the matchmaking I was doing for Ciaran Staunton and Orla O'Dowd. I was also matchmaking for a man from North Leitrim, but he was a reprobate who was leading the woman on, and me as well, so I won't even mention his name. Anyway, as well as writing this column and trying to shake hands with as many people as possible just to satisfy the media's handshake fetish, I was also trying to make peace with the elusive Patrick Mayhew and his boss and all the other things which go along with that, and all the while I was slinging Cupid's arrows at Orla on Ciaran's behalf, and didn't one of them miss and hit Debbie, and didn't she look up and there was your man O'Dowd. Until then, she confessed to me later, she had always thought of him only as the man from Drogheda, which is a place between Belfast and Dublin.

From that day on they have never looked back. Neither did Ciaran and Orla, who got married, and they had the decency to do it in Ireland – in County Cavan actually – so a lot of us got to go, and I got to go rowing in Lough Sheelin near Connie, who is a decent man. The wedding was great, and I got to see Bill Flynn shawaddywaddying, which he and Mrs Flynn did with great style, and all of this got our editor and our publisher thinking – you could see if you were alert – about doing their own merger, which they did later, so that nowadays, thanks to the efforts of your trusty columnist, the *Irish Voice* is a family affair. Which is nice.

So are the people who work there. Well, the ones I've met are. The one and only time I got to get into the offices they gave me champagne and two different types of almost defrosted desserts. Chocolate fudge and banoffee. I think they were. And they gave me a nice framed photo of me trying to escape from a yellow cab without paying. That was another of the front pages I provided.

Yup, I really did enjoy that visit to our offices. I say "our" offices just 'cause it's a nice way to feel part of things, but if you must know, I've never been allowed back. It would be easier to get into 10 Downing Street. And to make matters worse, after my visit they got this phone system which means that when you phone – or perhaps it's only when I phone – you get talking to a computer who never connects me to anyone, except itself, who will talk to me. It's a bit like this phase of the peace process.

So you can see, dear reader, that this *Irish Voice* columnist's lot is not a happy one. But for all that I like it. It connects me to writing in the midst of all this madness. It gives me a connection into a section of humanity, Irish-America, which I love and which intrigues and uplifts me. And ten years on it lets me say well done to Niall and Debbie and all the other writers and contributors who make the *Irish Voice*.

Not that any of these fine words will get me to the tenth birthday bash. Nawh. I'll be the one who is sent off to get the inside story on why David Trimble isn't talking. . . to John Taylor.

If only I knew when my trial period was over. Happy birthday, *Irish Voice. Comhghairdeas.*

15 December 1997

10 Downing Street

On 11 December a historic landmark in the peace process was reached when a Sinn Féin delegation met the British government in Downing Street, London.

By the time our transport pulled up alongside the gates at Downing Street last Thursday I was banjaxed. Our delegation had arrived in London on Wednesday evening, and after checking into our hotel we gathered in my room for our final team talk. There was me and Lucillita Breathnach, Martin McGuinness and Martin *eile* from Kerry, Martin Ferris, along with Siobhán O'Hanlon and Michelle Gildernew. We were backed up by our intrepid press officer, the wonderfully unrufflable Richard McAuley.

We were, as Martin McGuinness put it, on the eve of our most important meeting for thirty years. Ours was a motley crew: a handful of Irish men and Irish women from the north, south, east and west of Ireland, former political prisoners and ex-internees representing the Irish Republican position, crowded into the small hotel room. Sprawling alongside and on top of our bags or perched on the edge of the bed, we sipped tea and guzzled soft drinks while rehearsing once again our game plan for the Downing Street engagement.

Then off to bed for an early night. I slept like a top. Our meeting was at two o'clock, but the media interviews were to begin at dawn. Richard and I slipped out of the hotel after a hearty breakfast and, minded by Eamonn McCaughley, we meandered our way around London and through a maze of media until we met again eventually with our comrades for a lunch of tuna sandwiches, coffee and bananas in the basement of BookMarks shop where I was doing a signing. Our numbers were increased by the arrival of Pat Doherty and Gerry Kelly, two of our leadership people who were finishing off a visit to Republican prisoners scattered throughout Britain. The talk was all about prison conditions and the morale of the prisoners as I left to gather myself and my thoughts.

By now it was one fifteen. Outside BookMarks curious passers-by watched as I detached myself from the media pack. A

An Irish Journal

London bobby held up the traffic for us as our vehicle made its way into the rush hour. A few people waved. Two black people raised clenched fist salutes as we passed. Minutes later we were in Covent Garden, journeying unhurriedly through pleasant narrow streets of theatres, bookstores and restaurants as we made our way to the Thames and the spot I had picked for a walk.

It was a beautiful day, sharp but dry, with little faint traces of blue in an otherwise grey sky. The river itself was cocoa coloured, swollen and fast flowing. There were lots of people about, presumably on lunch break parole from work, immersed in their own affairs. Our little group was invisible, as I planted myself on a high bench below a large wintering tree above the Thames. It was time to think. Time to pray. To contemplate the road we had travelled. To envisage the distance we had yet to go. To think of all the people who were depending on us.

Minutes later we were walking up Downing Street past the biggest media gathering I have ever seen. Mrs Restorick, the mother of the last British soldier to be killed in Ireland, was waiting for us. We had a few private words together. Then a few words from us to the media in Irish and English and the door of 10 Downing Street opened.

Quentin Thomas, a senior British official, greeted us, and everyone engaged in small talk while I found the men's room. British Secretary of State Mo Mowlam arrived late and dashed past us, presumably to confer with her boss. The walls of the ante-room were decorated with paintings. Three were of British prime ministers: Balfour, Gladstone and Lloyd George. In acknowledgement that the English perspective on these gentlemen is much different from the Irish one, I joked to Quentin Thomas that I thought it a strangely English custom that they should exhibit their failures in such a prominent place.

At 2pm on the dot we were ushered into the Cabinet Room by Tony Blair, who was accompanied by Dr Mowlam; Paul Murphy, one of her ministers; Alaister Campbell, Mr Blair's press officer; John Holmes, private secretary; Quentin Thomas; and Jonathan Powell. Mr Blair was in good form. He opened our meeting with words of welcome.

I opened for our side. I explained that we saw this engagement as being part of a process; that we wanted to build upon

15 December 1997

our first engagement and that we saw this meeting as being more than each side setting out our stock positions. We wanted him to take a leap of imagination and to try and see how the relationship between Ireland and Britain would look in five, ten or fifteen years' time. Ours was the smaller island. More people lived in London than in Ireland, and the centuries of British involvement in our affairs had been marked by suffering, grief, death and division. We wanted to see an end to all of that. We wanted to enter the endgame. We wanted him to be the British prime minister to make the difference. I made the point about the portraits of his predecessors: how they had sought to settle the issue on terms which stopped short of giving the people of Ireland our rights as a sovereign people.

Mr Blair did almost all of the talking for his side. All of our group spoke. Our conversation ranged through the prisoners, to an independent inquiry for Bloody Sunday and the equality agenda, but because we were raising all of these issues on a regular basis with other British ministers and with the Irish government, we focused mostly on a strategic engagement which sought to get the British government to think itself into a new mindset about Ireland. In other words, we were trying to get them to come away from the old agenda and to embrace a new one.

Why, I asked, should any British government be against Irish unity? Why could they not be facilitators, or encouragers, or persuaders or agents for change? I pointed out that the issue was bigger than any in that room or than any one individual. "Every one of us," I said, "in this room will be dead in fifty years. What legacy will we leave? This isn't about us; this is about our children."

We talked about the Unionists. Martin McGuinness spelt out our sense of their difficulties. He stressed the importance of Tony Blair's role in moving all obstacles and resisting the securocrats agenda. "There has to be an end to the Unionist veto."

By now it was coming to 3pm, longer than the time allotted. Tony Blair was clearly engaged. I summed up our position by identifying British policy towards Ireland and the Unionist veto as the crux issues which needed to be changed. Mr Blair concluded for his side.

During the goodbyes he and I had a few private words. Then we were off again. Out to the waiting media and an evening of interviews. Later, as we waited at Heathrow, a contingent of Unionist MPs, including the former leader, James Molyneaux, arrived into the departure lounge. They were clearly displeased to see us and ignored our greetings. Once they were on the aeroplane they refused to talk to anyone.

"If they had any real principles," Martin McGuinness said to me with a smile, "they would have got another plane. Isn't it funny what people will do when they have to?"

5 January 1998

"Acceptable" Killings

In 1997 there were many attacks on Catholics and Catholic-owned property, including churches and schools. December 1997 and January 1998 witnessed a range of killings and attempted mass killings, which saw eight Catholics killed by Loyalist groups, mainly the UDA. Among those killed by Loyalists was Terry Enright, who was married to Gerry Adams' niece, Deirdre. Two Loyalists, one of them LVF leader Billy Wright were killed by the INLA.

Over the Christmas break I watched a film on video, *Ghosts of Mississippi*, starring Whoopi Goldberg and Alec Baldwin. It told of the story of the killing of black civil rights leader Medgar Evers in 1963, and of how his killer beat two trials until twenty-five years later when he was brought to justice and found guilty. One of the qualities of this film, and there are many, is the way in which it explores how the prejudice, the fears, hatreds and cowardice of that time allowed the killer to boast openly of his crime in the knowledge that he would be applauded by sections of the local population and be untouched by the system. Yet in the climax of the film, when he is eventually found guilty, that judgment is applauded by the local populace.

In the opening scenes of the film there is graphic testimony of how it was acceptable to kill a "nigger". In the closing scenes all had changed. A lot of this reminded me of how here in the North of Ireland it is still unfortunately acceptable in some circles to kill a "Taig". Like the white supremacists of the southern states of the USA – and they included all sections of that society from the landed gentry, through the business class, to the poor whites – when they felt threatened by the demand for change and by the struggle for civil rights, some of them used the language of prejudice, some of them created the environment for discrimination and some of them killed.

Over Christmas there were two attempts at mass murder. This follows on a year in which there were numerous attacks on Catholic-owned property, including churches and schools, and in which a number of individual Catholics were killed. One of the mass-murder attempts failed because of the courage of a doorman, Seamus Dillon, who died protecting the hundreds of young teenage Nationalists at a disco in the Glengannon Hotel outside Dungannon. Another man died in an attempt to wipe out the customers in a small Catholic pub in North Belfast on New Year's Eve.

The fear on the streets of Belfast and throughout Tyrone is palpable, very much as it must have been in the sixties in the southern states of the USA. This latest round of killings comes following the shooting dead by the INLA of leading Loyalist Billy Wright in the H-Blocks of Long Kesh. While it was inevitable that such an action would lead to the targeting of Catholics, all of the killings have come in the vacuum within the peace process which has been created by the Ulster Unionist Party's refusal to engage positively in negotiations. It is this vacuum which has been filled by the bodies of dead Catholics.

As we go to print, the PUP have said they are not returning to the talks on Monday; and the other Loyalist group, the UDP, say it is unlikely that they will be there. Both parties blame what they call the bias towards Nationalism within the process. This claim was first articulated by the Ulster Unionist Party, which has been campaigning for the removal of British Secretary of State Mo Mowlam.

They all claim that all of the concessions of the process are going to Republicans. When asked what concessions, they are unable to name them. Because, of course, there have been no concessions to Republicans. There has been a recognition of our mandate in the meetings which have been held between Sinn Féin and the British and Irish governments, but so far there has been no real change in the political landscape. There has been no implementation of an equality agenda. There has been no substantive constitutional or political change. But the presence of Sinn Féin, the SDLP and the Irish government in the same room as some Unionist parties and the British government has been enough to incense the Unionist leaders. And unfortunately for them, and for us, all of the Unionists are engaging negatively and the competition between them is in negativism. In this climate it is hardly surprising that every Loyalist group, including

5 January 1998

those represented in the talks, has broken their cessation. When the Orange card is played in a climate where it is acceptable to kill "Taigs", it is hardly surprising that "Taigs" are being killed.

So, people need to get real. The Unionists are trying to bully both the British and the Irish governments into abandoning the peace process or into reducing the potential for change which is necessary if it is to lead to a real peace settlement. As I have said before, the Unionists are not testing Sinn Féin; they are testing London and Dublin. Nationalists are watching anxiously to see if the Unionist veto will prevail once again. I see the Unionist veto every day. I see it in the faces of the RUC men and the British soldiers who patrol our streets. I see it in the faces of some of the civil servants whom we engage with on civil rights issues and more mundane matters. I see it in the sullenness of some of the staff in government buildings. I see it in the refusal, even yet, of some church leaders to meet with Sinn Féin representatives.

The talks are due to begin again on Monday, 12 January. I don't know if the Loyalist or Unionist parties will be there. Neither does anyone else. Tonight their leaders are threatening a return to violence "worse than anything we have ever seen before". No one knows whether their bluff will be called, whether there will be more funerals, whether there will be more dead "Taigs". If they are in the talks, of course, it will be claimed as a great step forward, or at least a step back from the abyss. It may well be both of these things. There is only one thing which can be said for certain at this time and that is, if there is to be change of the kind that is needed to anchor a peace process, then both governments, but especially the British government, have to trump the Orange card, both inside the talks and outside.

It would still be judicially acceptable in the USA today to kill "niggers" if the environment and subsequently the hearts and minds of people had not been changed. That's what we need to do in Ireland. It will not be done by pandering to Unionism.

An Irish Journal

DANGEROUS TIMES

Following the involvement of the Ulster Freedom Fighters (UFF), a covername for the Ulster Defence Association (UDA), in the killing of Catholics, the Ulster Democratic Party (UDP), which is politically associated with the UFF and UDA, was expelled from the talks.

As regular readers of this column will have noticed, I have not written for you for some weeks now, since my nephew-in-law Terry Enright was killed. There has been plenty to write about, but getting the time is difficult. I am just back from Derry, from the Bloody Sunday march. According to RTÉ, 40,000 people turned up. That's more than were there the day the British tried to terrorise all of us by killing some of us. Today's turnout shows the futility of that policy. Ideas and ideals cannot be shot away.

There have been a lot of killings here this last month or so. As you will probably be aware, Catholics have been the main targets. Ordinary people – any Catholic will do. The media describes this campaign as tit-for-tat murders and retaliation killings. True, two Loyalists have been killed: LVF leader Billy Wright and a UDA leader, Jim Guiney. The pain and grief for their families is no different from the pain and grief of all the other bereaved families, and I have made it clear that Sinn Féin is against all the killings. But suggestions that the spate of attacks against uninvolved Catholics is anything other than a campaign of indiscriminate terror have caused deep offence not only to the bereaved families but to the wider community.

The first couple of killings triggered a wave of fear. This changed quickly into hurt and then anger. Many factors contributed to the mood, but most influential was the way the establishment fudged the issue. It was bad enough that all Catholics were targets and that they were being killed on a daily basis. It was almost as bad that the RUC were refusing to acknowledge that this was the case. Time and again RUC statements declared "we have an open mind" about the latest murder.

Before Christmas, in the midst of the UUP, UDP and PUP grandstanding, before the UDA prisoners publicly withdrew

2 February 1998

their support for the peace process and before her visit to the H-Blocks, I told the British secretary of state that the UDA had decided to end its cessation (all Loyalist factions have broken their cessations on numerous occasions). I told her that it was going to operate a "no claim, no blame" policy and that it was also using the LVF as a flag of convenience. She told me that if this was the case the UDP would be put out of the talks. Shortly after this I gave the same report to the Irish government.

After Christmas, as part of our strategy to put pressure on the Loyalists to get the killing ended, Sinn Féin called on the RUC to release the forensic history of the murder weapons. During the IRA campaign the RUC regularly released forensic information on the weapons used in IRA attacks. However, it refused to do so now. Despite repeated calls from bereaved families, community representatives, as well as Sinn Féin, and despite the fact that the world and her brother knew that this was the Orange card being played in traditional and brutal fashion, the RUC stuck by its story until, nine deaths later on 22 January, RUC boss Ronnie Flannigan eventually admitted that the UDA was involved. He also traced its involvement back to the killing of Edward Trainor in Belfast, three weeks earlier on New Year's Eve. This RUC statement provoked a speedy response from the UDA in which it admitted these killings. This in turn led to their representatives and the British government facing up to their responsibilities.

Why did Mr Flannigan take so long to come clean? When did he tell his political bosses? Why did the British secretary of state fudge the issue? These questions remain unanswered even after the expulsion of the UDP.

Sinn Féin's view is straightforward. The two governments had no choice but to expel the UDP; that it took so long for this to happen raised many other questions in the Catholic community. "How many dead Catholics constitute a ceasefire?" is how one man put it to me.

The British government drew up the rules on exclusion in order to wrong-foot Republicans and to keep Sinn Féin out of the talks for a very long time indeed. Sinn Féin wanted different talks: inclusive ones, without pre-conditions. We are still prepared to talk to the UDP, or the LVF for that matter; but we

An Irish Journal

are not prepared to collude with double standards. That is why we faced up to London and the Loyalists on that issue. That is why we faced up to the two governments on the Propositions of Heads of Agreement. That is why we focused so relentlessly on rectifying that situation.

Good work was done in Lancaster House. More of that another time. And good work was done on the issue of Bloody Sunday. All involved deserve warmest commendations. But the crisis is not over. More needs to be done. There are lots of positive elements to the current situation. I could just as easily have written about them. I did not plan to write a column like this, but that is a sign of the times we are in. Dangerous times. And this is the kind of column which came out of the word processor. And out of my head.

9 February 1998

LANCASTER HOUSE

On Monday, 26 January 1998, a session of the multi-party talks opened at Lancaster House in London. The British and Irish governments introduced a new discussion document on the proposed nature of cross-border bodies.

My last column did not have the space to bring you up to speed with all the twists and turns of the talks process which we experienced in Lancaster House. A lot has been written about the grandeur of the place, and it certainly is a grand old place. In fact, it was once the home of the grand old Duke of York: he who marched his 10,000 men up to the top of the hill before marching them down again. I suppose that may have been more humane than the fate usually suffered by the men of English dukes, or any other race of dukes for that matter, but as I don't know the finale of that particular nursery rhyme I will say no more, except to agree that this grand old duke had a grand house which is, probably like other grand houses of its time, built upon and decorated with treasures taken from other people's countries. Regular readers of this column will, I am sure, defend me against any charge of begrudgery which may be levelled against me by less learned folk who may be affronted by what they may presume to be my lack of respect for old historied buildings. On the contrary, I respect and admire them greatly. Everyone should have one.

Which reminds me that I once worked in a Belfast public house called the Duke of York. No relation, I think, but who knows? It, like Lancaster House, had great wee snugs and nooks and crannies well suited for quiet trysts. Much better than the diseased place they usually stick us into up at Stormont: rooms without natural light and with the heating on full blast at its hottest. It's little wonder the Unionists won't talk.

Not that Lancaster House chilled them out, but at least some useful work was done there. It is also adjacent to a very nice park which for its part is also opposite Buckingham Palace. I never got that far myself, unlike one closet royalist on our delegation, but I certainly enjoyed the ultra-brisk early morning walk from our hotel to the talks venue. That took us across the park. On the three frosty mornings we were in London, we tramped along pleasant pathways, flanked by huge trees reaching heavenward into an early spring sky. Occasionally during breaks in the sessions indoors, Martin McGuinness and I escaped to stretch our legs and to admire the trees and encourage the daffodils which were poking their shoots above ground beneath the trees. Invariably we were saluted by nice English people who wished us good luck.

The food in Lancaster House was also very good, and some people said that the food in the large media tent was much better than the grub indoors. The media facility, which was two million times superior to the one in Belfast, was managed by people who do the big rock concerts and that kind of thing. Nice people also.

Now Lancaster House seems a million years ago. I know this process may appear to spectators to be (and in reality it actually is) dreadfully slow, but for the participants, and certainly for Sinn Féin, it is all-consuming. This last week or so the media focus has shifted to the differences in Sinn Féin's and the SDLP's attitudes towards an assembly in the North. I will resist the temptation to elaborate on that at this time, but I must say that I am disappointed that elements in the SDLP have chosen this time to attack Republicans with such gusto. Maybe they think they have spied some weakness in our position? Maybe they see some advantage for themselves or they are defending a party position of their own? Or maybe they have just lost the run of themselves?

Whatever caused them to initiate this run against Sinn Féin – and leaving aside the details of the argument from either side – now is the time for the maximum focus from Nationalists of all persuasions to get the very best deal possible out of the present process. It is not the time to make a gift of an assembly to the Unionists. It is time to concentrate on negotiations which will bring about the basic and fundamental changes which a peace settlement requires.

23 February 1998

MANAGING CRISIS IN PURSUIT OF PEACE

On 20 February, Sinn Féin were expelled from talks following RUC claims that the IRA had been involved in the recent deaths of two men.

Efforts to manage the current critical situation and rescue the peace process so that the search for a lasting peace can succeed prohibit me from dwelling too much on the past few weeks. In other words, recriminations serve no useful purpose. We are where we are and we have to work forward, or attempt to work forward, from this reality.

At the same time, it is important to understand the cumulative effect of the Unionists' refusal to engage, of the lack of movement on the prisoners issue by the British government, and particularly the Unionist sabotage of an agreed agenda for the talks before Christmas. In the New Year, the Loyalist killing spree, the publication of the Propositions of Heads of Agreement document and, most critically, the expulsion of Sinn Féin have all eroded confidence in the talks process among Nationalists, and particularly within the Republican constituency.

Of course, positive things have occurred. This includes this British government's rejection of the Widgery Report and the move at Lancaster House by both governments to reassert previous commitments made in the Framework Document. If one takes a broad view, there is no doubt that despite the current difficulties this British government is, in theory at least, best placed to change the status quo. This Irish government is probably the most Nationalistic on offer at this time. And no informed observer could be really surprised at the Unionists' stance. It was never going to be easy to create the conditions for a just and lasting peace.

The current crisis began with the killings of two men, Brendan Campbell and Robert Dougan, in Belfast. That is clear. The difficulties in the process go back much further than that, but the current crisis started then, and it is important in all of the twists and turns of the situation to remember the real tragedy for the bereaved families. In my final submission in Dublin Castle, when I formally rebutted the British government indictment and the indictment from the Alliance Party, I repeated Sinn Féin's commitment to end all killings. This remains our priority. And we have kept every commitment made by us. Our party disavows all killings. We have worked for an end to all killings.

How then has the situation come to its current crisis? Whatever the specific reasons for this crisis, as opposed to the last one, or indeed the next one, a number of factors govern the twists and turns and ups and downs so far. The most important of these can be summed up as follows. Peace means justice. Justice requires change. Change or the suggestion of change causes fear. Fear creates opposition. This can be true in any human relationship. It is all the more so in a conflict situation. So change must be managed, and until all of the elements come to accept or to embrace the need for change, then the focus on managing the situation must be relentless and the process involved must be urgently pursued.

Part of the problem for all of us is twofold. One, some elements need least change. Indeed some who should know better limit their vision to notions of structures with no attention whatsoever to an equality agenda or to the type of fundamental constitutional or political movement that is required. They see the process as a fairly restricted political one. Where does demilitarisation feature? What part do prisoner releases play in their strategy? It is clear that the Unionists would have a negative attitude to all of these matters. It should be equally clear that others, and particularly the SDLP, must be most positive and progressive. If they are not, then the first part of the problem comes into focus because many Republicans and Nationalists will ask, as they are doing, where is the consensus?

The second part of the problem affects all progressive elements, and that is that a lot of this is a learning experience. So getting rivals to understand the politics of peacemaking means stretching ourselves beyond party political certainties into new and uncharted strategies. And that can be difficult because, of course, political parties exist to further their own political agendas.

However, the promotion of a peace process, especially in the Anglo-Irish situation, makes huge demands upon political leaderships. Before August 1994 all of these leaderships, except Sinn Féin, colluded in the lie that what was happening in the

23 February 1998

North was a criminal conspiracy. Before August 1994, the policy was to marginalise, to exclude, to demonise, to censor. That policy has not been changed voluntarily or as a result of a realisation that marginalisation strategies failed to end the conflict. The changes which have occurred, and they are welcome, came because Sinn Féin developed a peace strategy. They came when I went to John Hume. When he had the courage to stay with me. When the Irish government got involved. When Irish-America backed us. Then that led to the IRA cessations. And let me say on a day when a bomb has exploded in Portadown town centre, let me say that the IRA cessation remains intact.

What condemnations, denunciations and marginalisation could not achieve, we achieved by reaching out and dealing with people in a political way and in their own terms. It was part of putting an argument that there could be another way. And the IRA, in fairness to them, facilitated this. Which brings us all back to the current crisis, because if there is to be another way then it's up to political leaders to produce it. That is the big challenge, which ironically enough may demand the most from those who may have initially felt the situation required only the minimum of change.

Sinn Féin has been accused by the Unionists of having an exit strategy, that we want out of the process. Sinn Féin has no exit strategy. We have no more control of the current situation than any other political party. We are the one party which wants to see the most change, but we are wedded to that change being managed through negotiations and being pursued by democratic and peaceful methods. That is the challenge for the governments, for the church leaders, for editorial writers and the political leaders of all of the main parties.

An Irish Journal

ALLELUIA

On 15 March, a Sinn Féin delegation met President Clinton, his advisers and Secretary of State Madeline Albright in the White House.

On the Sunday before St Patrick's Day I went to morning service in a little Baptist church in Virginia, just across the state line from Washington. It was an uplifting and joyous occasion. There were only about a dozen white people in the congregation – all from Ireland. That Sunday was a very beautiful spring day, and our service matched the weather. Between the singing, the pauses for reflection, the inclusiveness and the sheer energy of it all, ours was a very bright, promising, prayerful morning indeed. I left full of the joys of life and appreciative of a lovely morning spent in good company. My thanks to Colleen, whose guests we were, and to all her friends.

The following evening our little group made its way to the White House for a meeting with President Clinton, his advisers and Secretary of State Madeline Albright. For us this was a very important engagement, and as with all our meetings we prepared our case with great care. Bill Clinton has played a highly commendable role in encouraging the search for a lasting peace in Ireland. This was the case with a reluctant British government led by John Major when the US president went against the system to nudge the process forward. Now that Mr Major is gone, and with him a lot of the minimalist style, Mr Clinton's good relationship with the new British prime minister puts him in a pivotal position to assist the peace effort once again.

Our meeting was in the Oval Office. President Clinton awaited us at the door and greeted each of our team warmly: Rita O'Hare, Martin McGuinness, Mairead Keane and me. The president was extremely relaxed, and as our discussions opened up I was very impressed by his detailed grasp of the overall situation in Ireland and of the positions of all the parties, including Sinn Féin.

Later someone said to me that we were in a unique position to see how Mr Clinton was bearing up to all his pressures. We did not discuss these, of course, but I did tell him that people in

23 March 1998

Ireland were concerned about him and that I was glad to see him looking so well. And he was. He looked both fit and well. He was not at all like the subject of a media feeding frenzy. He was presidential.

He is also famously committed to a lasting peace agreement in our country. Such a deal may be agonisingly close, but it is also agonisingly far away. Such a deal will require huge changes in the situation here. These changes will have to be driven. David Trimble should not be in the driving seat – as far as change is concerned Mr Trimble is a learner driver – so the governments must take the lead. As someone from outside the frame, President Clinton can show the way. We gave the presidential team a copy of our policy document, *A Bridge to the Future,* and during our fifty-minute engagement our delegation outlined how we think peace can be built: on a foundation of justice and freedom.

"We are not displaced persons or an ethnic minority," I said. "We are living without rights in our own country. I cannot be expected to think like an Englishman or an American. I'm Irish. We have the right to govern ourselves. In peace and on a basis of equality."

Later, when Martin McGuinness had concluded his remarks, I told the story of the first time I met the late Ron Brown. Ron, commerce secretary at the time of his death, and his close adviser Chuck Meisner, who was killed in the same tragic air crash, were hardworking allies of the peace process. Ron was an African-American, and he was the first political representative of the White House to meet me. Until then my contact was with Tony Lake and Nancy Soderberg. We met in Tony's office in the White House. After a detailed discussion of all the substantive issues, about which he asked all the hard questions, Ron Brown leaned towards me on the settee where we were sitting.

"What should I *not* ask you to do?" he smiled.

"Don't ask me to sit at the back of the bus," I replied.

Bill Clinton smiled exactly the same way as Ron Brown had when I told him of this engagement.

"That's why David Trimble won't talk to us. He has a back-of-the-bus mentality," I told him.

The president then told us of how the Palestinian leader and the Israeli premier had sat in that very same room. He recalled how they had fought each other for four decades. How they had yet to shake hands. But they talked. He told of one particular problem about a border crossing. He left them to it, and they settled the issue over coffee in a side room off the Oval Office.

"I don't see how people can solve problems if they don't talk," Mr Clinton told us. We agreed.

Later at the Speaker's lunch on St Patrick's Day he repeated that story. And again that night at the reception in the White House. He also pointedly quoted President Kennedy: "Civility is not a sign of weakness."

All in all it was a good St Patrick's week.

By the way, if you see Hilary Clinton in an Aran *geansaí* you know who brought her it. We did. And one of Kit de Fever's very fine Conamara prints for her husband. Our mammies would have been proud of us. They always said you should bring a wee present when you go to visit someone in their home.

That's also why there is a little Celtic Cross made of turf from Ireland in a wee Baptist church in Virginia just across the state line from Washington.

Alleluia !!!

Postscript. Sinn Féin went back to the talks at Stormont today. We were in the same room as David Trimble's party. All day! He has still to talk to us.

30 March 1998

THE ENDGAME?

On Thursday, 26 March, George Mitchell, independent chairman of the multi-party talks, set a deadline of 9 April for the finding of an agreement between the parties. Meanwhile, in the midst of negotiations, there can be welcome distractions.

There is a break in the discussions here at Stormont, so I have dashed from the negotiations room to the Sinn Féin suite at Castle Buildings to send you this dispatch. Despite what I think is a dreaded flu bug, and my present tenure in a building which thrives on such afflictions, I have to say that I am in good form. On such a beautiful day it would be impossible to be anything else. Opposite this building there is a line of trees. They are adjacent to the media swamp and, given that this is the first day of what has been described as the endgame here, there are more journalists and broadcasting people about than usual. All of that, the trees and the media, is behind me as I sit at this laptop with my back to the window. Behind the trees I am reliably told there are badger setts, but I won't write too much about that today in case you wonder how on earth I get to know about such things when I am up here to discuss much more serious matters.

Forgive me, because this is written during a break from such serious things. And as I turn my back to these less serious matters of trees and badger setts in the grounds of Stormont... Do the badger setts pre-date partition? Are they Unionist badgers or Nationalist ones? Could the presence of badger setts here constitute an underground movement right at the heart of what used to be the Unionist establishment? How did they survive the Special Powers Act? All these questions I will return to *arís*. For now it's back to work.

Yes, work! Making peace is work. Hard work! Today we were back to decommissioning. That was resurrected by the Unionists. Clearly UUP strategy remains one of trying to reach an agreement with the SDLP and to cut Sinn Féin out of the process.

In his submission to the Forum for Peace and Reconciliation in Dublin just before Christmas 1995, F.W. de Klerk offered the advice that it is crucial to the success of a peace process that the participants sit down around the table and treat each other as *human beings*. That hasn't happened yet with the Ulster Unionist Party, and it is clearly an impediment to progress. The two weeks before us are an extraordinary time, in which we must solve extraordinary problems.

Mr Trimble may think he is undermining Sinn Féin by not talking to us. On the contrary, he is undermining Unionism. Sinn Féin does not need to talk to the Unionists, but we want to. Mr Trimble may not want to talk to Sinn Féin, but he needs to.

Once he starts to think strategically this will become clear. At present Mr Trimble is thinking tactically. He may not want to do a deal at all at this time. But I would not be surprised if the UUP leader plays hardball on all fronts with a major hardline offensive starting today on the decommissioning issue as a prelude into an attempt to do a partial deal with the SDLP. In my view, Mr Trimble is prepared to move further than his public posture would suggest. Whether he does so now or at some other time will emerge in the next few weeks. The danger to the search for democracy from this UUP tactical approach is that if and when Mr Trimble moves to do a deal with the SDLP it will be hailed as a great breakthrough.

Whether it is or not will be a matter of opinion and the target of massive hype. I am satisfied that the SDLP leadership understand that a partial agreement will not work. They know that the real issue is whether such a deal will bring an end to conflict. In my opinion it will not, and Sinn Féin will not acquiesce in any arrangement which does not have this effect.

The two governments know this. So do all the other parties. Today Senator George Mitchell outlined the plans of the independent chairs to move the process forward through a series of bilaterials and other meetings while he tries to synthesise a paper which will hopefully allow all of us to get down to real negotiations on the substantive issues. Don't hold your breath on that happening this week. If we are lucky, maybe the parties will get it by Thursday or Friday. A weekend of consultation between all of us and the chairs and then into the real business next Monday. So there you are. Is it any wonder I have a *grá* for the badgers?

23 March 1998

And finally: the Brian Nelson affair jumped back into the headlines again this weekend. Regular readers will know that this columnist has campaigned for a very long time for an independent international inquiry into the circumstances whereby Nelson, a British army agent, was used by British military intelligence to kill, or to direct the killing by Loyalists, of Nationalists and Catholics. The *Sunday Telegraph*, of all papers, editorialised on this yesterday on the back of a big news story based on its journalists seeing British army briefings and other records of involvement with Nelson and with the Loyalist killing campaign.

An Irish Journal

DOWN TO THE WIRE

In Belfast's Castle Buildings an intensive round of meetings started on 30 March and went on for ten days and ten nights. On 6 April, George Mitchell, independent chairman of the multi-party talks, gave each of the parties his version of a possible draft Agreement based on the talks to that date. On 9 April, the deadline that had been set for the completion of the multi-party talks, negotiations continued through the last day and into the night, until on Good Friday, 10 April, all the parties taking part in the multi-party talks signed an Agreement.

As you can guess, this column is extremely busy, so I find it hard to get space to keep you abreast of all developments back home. However, with the indulgence of our delectable editor, I am submitting this edited diary of the last few weeks of the Belfast negotiations leading up to the Good Friday document. This is a shortened version of the report our chief negotiator Martin McGuinness gave to the Sinn Féin Ard-Fheis last Saturday.

It will be impossible, and it would take too long, to give you the detail of every single engagement we were involved in. This report deals only with a general sweep of our discussions, but I should tell you, as well as meeting with the governments and the independent chairs, Sinn Féin talked to and listened to the smaller parties.

During a five-hour engagement with senior Irish government officials on 25 March, Sinn Féin made detailed proposals across the entire range of issues. These formed the basis of Sinn Féin's negotiations in an intensive round of meetings that started on 30 March and went on and on for ten days and ten nights.

On Monday 30th and Tuesday 31st we met Senator Mitchell, the Irish government and the SDLP. We sought to positively influence the document that Senator Mitchel was preparing by lobbying the Irish government and trying to secure common positions with the SDLP.

On Wednesday, 1 April, I met Taoiseach Bertie Ahern ahead of his meeting in London with British Prime Minister Tony

20 April 1998

Blair. The taoiseach was fully briefed on the Sinn Féin position and what, in our view, Nationalists needed to achieve in this phase of negotiations. This was an opportunity for us to influence positions positively or at least to ensure that the Irish government was in no doubt about our position on these issues.

At Stormont intensive negotiations began in earnest. We gave Senator Mitchell an informal paper covering all relevant issues and including, for the first time, in writing and without prejudice to our opposition to an Assembly in the North, a detailed position on the safeguards required if such a body came into existence.

Sinn Féin and the SDLP were the only parties advocating a sufficient consensus position. The Unionists were vehemently opposed to this. The Irish government was given the same list of points, and they endorsed the sufficient consensus position. The same position was also given to the SDLP.

Thursday, 2 April: The Strand Two engagement between Tony Blair and Bertie Ahern on the Wednesday evening had been inconclusive. The Irish government was insisting that the All-Ireland Council have meaningful powers, effective implementation bodies and be legislatively based in Westminster and Leinster House.

We began to get a clearer sense of positions agreed between the Irish and British governments on issues of equality and demilitarisation, including policing, rights, justice and the Irish language. We continued to push hard for improved positions on this range of issues. We also pressed on the constitutional issues, arguing against specified changes in the Irish constitution and stressing the need for the maximum change in British constitutional legislation. We made concrete proposals for Northern representation in political institutions in the South.

Lobbied by us, the Irish government suggested giving Seanad seats to Northern parties, the setting up of a special committee from the North on the Seanad, and to positively consider giving people from the North votes in presidential elections and referenda. We told them that this was not an adequate degree of representation but welcomed the fact that they were giving consideration to this concept. We also pressed the British government to include a clause in their constitutional legislation which makes clear that all previous and existing constitutional legislation, which we wanted named, would be superceded by the new legislation resulting from these talks. We were told that the British presence will be left solely dependent on the wishes of the people in the Six Counties. We adopted a wait-and-see approach to this.

On Friday, 3 April, negotiations continued in tandem in London and Stormont. There were indications that Strand Two was near agreement in London. At Castle Buildings we continued to push the Irish government and the British on the equality agenda, the Irish language and on the demilitarisation and policing issues in advance of agreed papers being submitted by them to Senator Mitchell.

We suggested a trilateral meeting with the Irish government, the SDLP and Sinn Féin. This was arranged for Friday evening and lasted for over an hour. The Sinn Féin delegation outlined the key requirements for Nationalists. The meeting had the effect of ensuring that all three parties knew each other's positions and were clear that there was no room to move towards the Unionists on the key issues.

Although Strand One was not agreed, Senator Mitchell indicated that he would issue the synthesis paper with options to cover the areas which were still not agreed.

On Friday evening, despite pressure from Senator Mitchell to produce an agreed paper, the two governments pulled the Strand Two paper, and Senator Mitchell was forced to postpone the issuing of his synthesis paper. It later emerged that the Strand Two paper had been leaked to the Unionists, and they pressurised the British government to pull back.

On Saturday and Sunday, 4 and 5 April, we were given a briefing on the state of play between the two governments, and our team outlined our view on this. This work continued through Saturday and into Sunday afternoon. By this stage we had a fairly accurate read on what would emerge in relation to

- constitutional issues;
- Strand Two;
- Strand Three;
- equality and rights;
- policing;
- and prisoners.

20 April 1998

During the course of all these deliberations, our negotiating team was in constant session, continuously reviewing and updating our position. On Monday, 6 April, we held a major review of all the issues under negotiation. On the basis of this we decided to have a series of focused engagements with the two governments, urging them to improve their position on a number of matters, including the Irish language, prisoners, policing and the equality agenda. The Irish government took many of our points on board.

A briefing with British officials on their approach to prisoners precipitated a crisis. The British position on prisoners was totally unacceptable to us. I made two phone calls to Tony Blair on this issue and emphasised its importance to Republicans.

It also emerged that the Unionists were blocking the release of the paper because of their discomfort with Strand Two, their refusal to agree Strand One and a range of other issues. On Strand Two the Unionists were opposed to the establishment of the North-South Council and its implementation bodies by legislation in Westminster and Leinster House, and they also wanted it to begin to function after, rather than simultaneously with, a Northern Assembly.

Eventually, at 12.30am on Tuesday, with key areas still not agreed, the paper was issued to the parties.

On Tuesday, 7 April, we prepared a comprehensive response to the Mitchell paper. It took over twenty-four hours but it was the most detailed response submitted, containing seventy-six amendments. The principal purpose of this was to act as a bulwark against Unionist attempts to negotiate the paper down.

Tuesday was dominated by Unionist unease with the paper and their public rejection of it. There was increased speculation that Tony Blair was to travel to Belfast. Our engagements with the British continued, but our main focus remained on the Irish government and included a number of phonecalls from *mé féin* to Bertie Ahern. We continued to push for better positions on the prisoners, on policing, on justice, the equality agenda, on a wider remit for the North-South Council and its implementation bodies, and for effective safeguards in an Assembly. At the same time we pressed for maximum changes in the British constitutional position with minimum concessions from the Irish side.

An Irish Journal

British Prime Minister Tony Blair arrived that evening and met David Trimble at Hillsborough. Unionist unease with the Mitchell paper and the direction of the talks was undisguised and continued into Wednesday, 8 April. In the morning, Martin McGuinness and myself met Taoiseach Bertie Ahern and then Tony Blair. I also talked to the White House officials twice. There were a number of separate meeting with Bertie Ahern and Tony Blair. All of our engagements emphasised that we wanted to be part of an agreement but pointed out that we could not be on the basis of the positions on offer on constitutional issues, policing, prisoners and the equality agenda, including the Irish language. We emphasised that these were critical areas for us, touchstone issues as we described them.

John Hume informed us that the SDLP's meetings with the UUP had made no progress.

Our comprehensive response to the Mitchell paper was submitted to Senator Mitchell and to the Irish government.

The main focus remained on the Unionists' rejection of the Strand Two position and their failure to move in the Strand One areas. We stayed in close contact with the SDLP and the Irish government in the face of the Unionist hardballing.

In the early evening Tony Blair and Bertie Ahern met Trimble. This produced no clear movement, and in the early hours of Thursday morning the UUP and the Irish government met to discuss Strand Two. The meeting was reported to be acrimonious.

On Thursday, 9 April, I met the taoiseach again, and I was briefed on the UUP meeting. Bertie instructed the Irish government negotiators to raise all the issues contained in our response to the Mitchell paper with the British government and to take these issues as far as possible.

After another review by our team, we focused on trying to push the paper forward once again to counter the Unionists' attempts to dilute it and unpick the substantive issues. After a series of meetings with the Irish government, the Strand Two position eventually settled down somewhere between the position the UUP had demanded and the position we had put. We were satisfied that we had neutralised most of the concessions made to the UUP.

Meanwhile the Strand One element was still unresolved. The

20 April 1998

UUP had not yet moved at all on this, and we were concerned that the SDLP would feel under pressure to move towards the UUP position. However, we had already put our position on safeguards in an Assembly into the public domain.

We continued to work on the other issues, pushing the Brits and the Irish government on prisoners, the Irish language, rights and equality, policing and other demilitarisation issues. Two phone calls between myself and President Clinton underlined our need for movement on these issues.

In the early hours of the morning, the UUP conceded almost the entire Nationalist position on an Assembly. Sufficient consensus provided a counter to the Unionist veto, and, crucially, the Unionists did not get the procedural device around decommissioning which they had sought to disenfranchise the Sinn Féin electorate. While most of the final paper had now taken shape, the issues of prisoners and policing were still major concerns.

We took a firm line in a series of meetings which took place throughout the night involving Sinn Féin (mainly Martin and myself) with Tony Blair, Bertie Ahern and Mo Mowlam. There may have been up to a dozen engagements; at least three of these were joint meetings between Martin, myself, Tony Blair and Bertie Ahern.

Finally, in the early hours of the morning, the British government agreed to give a firm commitment in the Agreement that all prisoners would be released within a defined period of two years, and that this may happen sooner. We also negotiated separately with the Irish government on the question of prisoners in their jurisdiction, on constitutional matters and the rights of citizens in the North to be represented in Irish political institutions in the South.

By this stage the pressure from Senator Mitchell on the two governments was intense. The document was now almost agreed between the two governments, but we continued to negotiate beyond this. We asked for assurance that our issues of concern would be dealt with. We got a commitment from Tony Blair to meet Sinn Féin post-Easter, and that meeting would take place next Monday. In the second phone call to President Clinton at 9.45am, Friday, 10 April, I asked for his continued interest and support for movement on the entire range of issues.

At twelve noon the document was circulated to the parties with the intention of calling a plenary. We prepared a response to this paper and told Senator Mitchell we wanted to put our concerns on the record in the plenary. We submitted twenty points of concern.

When they received the paper the UUP went into crisis. They were eventually moved into the plenary, which was held at 5.30pm on Friday afternoon, and David Trimble voted in support of the document. The UUP had been moved much further than they had intended. They will have to keep moving, but at least a start has been made. At last weekend's Ard-Fheis I commended Mr Trimble. Next week I will give you the Sinn Féin view.

11 May 1998

Don't Stop Now

On Sunday, 10 May, at the party's Ard-Fheis in Dublin, Sinn Féin members voted to change their constitution to allow candidates to take their places in the proposed new Northern Assembly. The removal of the policy of abstentionism ended seventy-seven years of refusing to participate in institutions of government in the North.

I suppose you saw news coverage of Sunday's Sinn Féin Ard-Fheis on your television screens. It was a good Ard-Fheis. Historic? Yup! That overworked word certainly fits. So do "watershed", "unprecedented" and so on. Part of the problem is that there have been so many unprecedented and historic watersheds recently that we could get used to them. Part of the other problem with overworked clichés is that they are boring. Part of the danger of all this is that people outside of Ireland might think it is all over. That we have peace.

We don't!

Not yet.

But we are getting there. Slowly but surely. And last Sunday's Sinn Féin Ard-Fheis was a mighty step by Irish Republicans and an immeasurable contribution by us to the search for a real and durable peace settlement. The significance and pain which this caused to many activists needs to be fully appreciated.

The period between Good Friday and the first session of our Ard-Fheis on the weekend of 18 April and the reconvened session on 10 May saw the most intense debate within Republicanism in my lifetime. And as someone who knows how hard our people work, this column can assure you that the Sinn Féin leadership exhausted itself talking and listening to our grassroots. I personally lobbied hundreds of activists. So did Martin McGuinness and Mitchel McLoughlin and Joe Cahill and Rita O'Hare and Mairead Keane and Lucillita and Pat Doc and Martin Ferris and Caoimhín and Sean MacManus and all the rest of a great team of leaders.

And we delivered! The scale of this achievement and the way we stretched our own credibility, and the maturity of our activists cannot be overestimated.

But politics is never static, so none of this can be taken for granted. Others need to deliver also, especially the two governments. The British government's political will is central in all this. On the evening after the Ard-Fheis, Martin Mc Guinness, Bairbre de Brún and I journeyed up to Stormont to talk once again with the British secretary of state.

Understandably a lot of our focus was on the difficulties within Unionism, and although he might not thank me for it, this column is mindful of the problems facing David Trimble. It is my intention to do all I can to minimise these. As I said at the Ard-Fheis, in an effort to assure Unionists, "When Sinn Féin calls for the end of the British presence in Ireland, we do not mean our Unionist neighbours. You have as much right to a full and equal life on this island as any other section of our people... Let me try to assure you and your leaders that Sinn Féin comes to these latest developments and that we face the future seeking a good faith and a genuine engagement with you."

All of this presents great challenges for everyone, but it does not remove the need to make change. On the contrary, the mechanisms of change need to deliver *now*. One particularly important aspect of this – the crucial bit – is London standing up to hostility and resistance within its own system as well as from the Unionists. I could give copious example since Good Friday of how this resistance within the system, within the *permanent government,* has manifested itself on a whole range of issues which require urgent and deep-rooted change.

The attitude of the officials in the British government's Northern Ireland Office reflects the UUP agenda. This is about winning concessions for Unionism and diluting the equality agenda. With an eye to the referendum battle within Unionism, there is a real chance that British advisers will argue that such concessions are necessary to win the Yes vote for the UUP. This would be an unmitigated disaster.

So let all of us be alert to this. You, dear reader, have a particular role to play in this. You need to monitor the situation here. You have to ensure that your Congress members, your senators, your media keep their eyes on the situation here. Any

11 May 1998

judgment on the Good Friday document must be determined by whether it produces justice and how quickly it positively affects the day-to-day lives of citizens.

How quickly will the prisoners be released? When will the RUC be replaced by an acceptable policing service? When will the British army be taken off the streets? How quickly will the equality agenda take effect? How will the mechanisms of change be managed? How will the British government process the constitutional changes which they have agreed? Is this truly a rolling process? Will the British and Irish governments pro-actively pursue the establishment and development of all-Ireland bodies?

So there is work to be done. Lots of work. Crucial work. All of this needs to be monitored.

Irish-America has played a key role so far. You are now going to have to redouble your efforts. In many ways your work is only beginning. Everyone is in uncharted waters now. You have to help us to navigate through many stormy squalls towards the future. That is what Sinn Féin is trying to do. We are charting a course for the future.

That's what the Ard-Fheis was about. A big day. A big decision. Let's make sure it is built upon. Don't stop now.

An Irish Journal

The Beginning

On Friday, 22 May, a referendum was held throughout Ireland, in which the vast majority voted in favour of the Good Friday Agreement. The actual figures were Yes 85.46 per cent, No 14.54 per cent.

For all the acres of newsprint and the miles of TV coverage about the referendum result, there is no feeling of euphoria or great excitement amongst the populace here. There is a sense of expectation, of hope. A sense of qualified belief that things are changing – have changed – and that that change will continue. I am speaking, of course, of that huge section of our people who voted Yes last Friday, or at least that section with which I have most contact: the people of the Republican and Nationalist areas. They, with their Unionist neighbours who voted *Tá*, took a leap of faith. They voted for a future. A new future.

The big danger, of course, is that the British government will not be up to the challenge of delivering on the changes which this requires. The danger is that London will seek to pander to the No men of Unionism. Many of the No voters voted out of fear. Fear of change. The very change which the Yes vote endorsed. That fear was whipped up by the No men of Unionism. I have called upon the No voters to reflect on their position, to reconsider it. I was not surprised when the No men claimed victory. I will not be surprised when they try to block or prevent the work which has yet to be done, nor when they are joined in this by some of the leaders in the Unionist Yes camp.

That is why there is no widespread euphoria here, because the people in the Nationalist and Republican areas know that also. They have a quiet conviction that everything will eventually work out okay, but they know that this is only the beginning.

The biggest priority now is to put in place the mechanisms of change. So far the media agenda has been dominated by the issue of decommissioning. This is not the most important issue. It is one of a raft of issues which need to be resolved, and these issues deserve as much attention as the decommissioning one. In fact, if they are to attain the same prominence, they need much more attention. That's what people voted for: a raft of issues and an inclusive process. That is why there can be no cherry-picking. By anyone.

So let's put in place the mechanisms which will begin the process of change on all fronts. That means demilitarisation *now*. That means prisoners out *now*. For good. That means huge investment in deprived areas to reverse the generations of discrimination. It means equality *now*. It means all-Ireland structures established as soon as possible after next month's election. It means the disbandment of the RUC. It means a real policing service which the young people of the Republican and Nationalist areas can join. It means Garvaghy Road and other areas having a peaceful July. It means an end to division on this island. It means and needs all this and much more.

Last Friday was the beginning of sections of Unionism saying Yes. They need to keep saying Yes. They need to follow the logic of this through every aspect of life on this island. They and we need to shape and share our future. Then we will be making our own history, because then we will have justice and peace. Ourselves Alone. Then this column can relax.

Now we have a beginning. Let's build on it.

CHANGING TIMES?

In the elections held on Thursday, 25 June, Sinn Féin increased its vote. The UUP emerged as the largest party in the Assembly, with twenty-eight seats, followed by the SDLP with twenty-four, the DUP with twenty, and Sinn Féin with eighteen.

The Assembly election was a very good election for Sinn Féin. We achieved a record result, winning more seats and taking more votes than ever before. We are now very clearly the largest party in Belfast, and our combined vote in the Nationalist constituencies in Counties Fermanagh, Tyrone and Derry now makes Sinn Féin the largest Nationalist party in that area. In the Assembly we will have five women members, 50 per cent of the total number elected. None of this would have been possible, of course, without the hard work of the Sinn Féin candidates, activists and supporters, and those tens of thousands of voters who demonstrated a confidence in this party and in our policies and peace strategy by voting for our candidates. None of it would have been possible without the help and ongoing support of our friends in the USA. I thank you all.

Eighty per cent of those who voted in the Assembly election voted for those parties which backed the Good Friday Agreement. They voted for change, for a new start. Our collective task now must be to build on the progress which has been made. This will require a new partnership, an inclusive process. There is an enormous amount of work to be done. And it will not be easy.

Unfortunately, there are those within Unionism and within the system, still frightened by the prospect of change and of equality, who are determined either to wreck the Agreement or to minimise the change which it promises. The DUP, the UKUP and some independent Unionists elected to the Assembly are determined to thwart the spirit and the letter of the Agreement. This is regrettable and predictable. Of greater concern, however, is the fact that David Trimble, leader of the UUP, has also indicated his intention to delay progress on putting in place the institutional structures agreed on Good Friday, and on implementing much of the Agreement itself. This is not good enough. The No

29 June 1998

politicians and the Maybe politicians of Unionism cannot be allowed to subvert the opportunity to advance the goal of a permanent peace settlement.

There is a heavy onus on Mr Blair to ensure that the Agreement should not be undermined either by Unionists or by British government concessions to Unionism. I spoke to him today by telephone about this. On Tuesday I will meet with the taoiseach, Mr Ahern. Together everyone in leadership will have to focus on the tasks ahead.

The key words now must be delivery and equality.

People here want and need to see delivery on the institutions; delivery on the Executive, and on the All-Ireland Ministerial Council and bodies; delivery on the equality agenda; delivery on the release of prisoners; delivery on demilitarisation; delivery on the promised constitutional change; delivery on equality for the Irish language; delivery on a new policing service; and delivery on the other elements of the Good Friday Agreement. And all of this on the basis of equality. There can be no more second-class citizens.

For *Irish Voice* readers who are wondering about the time-frame for all this, the Good Friday Agreement clearly indicates that the shadow executive and the All-Ireland Council will come into being in the transitional period, and early enough for the completion of a work programme by 31 October.

The election results confirm that the UUP, the SDLP, Sinn Féin and the DUP will hold positions in the executive. Sinn Féin will have two places. So there you are: interesting times. And by the time you get to read this column, the Orange march to Drumcree will be upon us.

Mr Trimble is playing hardball on that issue once again. At the time of writing the Parades Commission has yet to make its determination known. That will happen on Monday. On Wednesday, Mr Trimble will almost certainly be elected as first minister at the first "shadow" meeting of the new Assembly. I say "almost certainly" because Ian Paisley is threatening to prevent that. Difficult times? And tonight Mr Trimble, the almost-certain first minister, is warning of dire consequences unless the Orangemen get down Garvaghy Road. Changed times? We'll see.

An Irish Journal

ONE OF THE GOOD GUYS

Paul O'Dwyer, New York human rights lawyer, died on 23 June.

Paul O'Dwyer was my friend. I'm delighted to be able to write that. He was a great and a decent human being, and like everyone else who knew him, I was blessed by that relationship. It is another blessing that he lived long enough to see and to be part of all the possibilities of this time. The last time I saw Paul was here in Ireland. We brought him and Pat up to the talks building at Stormont. We had a good day. The last time I spoke to him was by phone during my last visit to New York earlier this month.

I have no doubt that thousands of words of tribute will be said and written about Paul: about his integrity, his honesty, his courage, his radicalism, his commitment and decency. Paul O'Dwyer was one of my heroes. He was one of the good guys. My sincere condolences go to Pat and all the O'Dwyer family and to all Paul's many friends. *Go ndéana Dia trócaire air.*

He is being buried on Monday in his beloved Mayo. I won't be there and I'm really annoyed. It's quicker to get to New York than it is to get from Belfast to Bohola. But Paul will understand my absence. At twelve o'clock on Monday, the time of his funeral mass, all the newly elected Sinn Féin Assembly members are meeting to discuss our approach to upcoming events. My head will be in that meeting, but my heart will be with Paul and all his friends and family in Bohola. The last thing I said to him was the last thing I always said to him. Up Mayo! And he would laugh.

27 July 1998

Josie Donnelly

On the night before Bobby Sands was elected as the MP for Fermanagh/South Tyrone, I spent the night in Enniskillen. The election campaign was over. We were satisfied that Bobby was elected. In fact I said as much at a late night rally after the polls had closed. All the indications were that we had done it. The past few weeks of canvassing across the two counties, the statement writing, the endless meetings: everywhere the message was the same. But still... you could never be sure.

On the day of the count I drove across country. I was heading for Glenmore in County Louth. As the name implies, Glenmore is a big glen. It is wedged between two mountains, Sliabh Foy and Sliabh Na gCloch on the Cooley Peninsula. It is a very beautiful place. It is where Josie Donnelly lived. Colette and I were renting a house there belonging to the Berry family, and it was up the same lane and close to Josie Donnelly's house. That is how I got to meet Josie.

When we got the house it had been empty for some time. None of the Berry family remain in Ireland, though there are some of them, I am told, in the USA. Their house used to be the local smithy, and the remnants of the old forge survived the family's demise. It was, indeed it still is, a two-storey house on what was once a cobbled street with outhouses and the forge. The house was walled in and there were big double gates fronting the lane. With horses queued up for shoeing and the banter and talk of their owners, Berry's used to be a very busy place indeed, according to Josie.

When we moved in it was deserted. A little river which flowed from below Meabh's Gap high in the Carlingford hills to where we were formed one side of the garden and gurgled and grumbled its noisy passage past the house. That was the only noise, but it was easy to imagine how things used to be. And Josie was a master at conjuring up the sounds and the images of the past. He was a good neighbour.

He was also the first person I met on the day that Bobby Sands was elected. The news came to me on the car radio as I drove up Glenmore. Although we were confident that Bobby was going to get elected, when the newscaster intoned his confirmation of that historic ballot, I pounded the steering wheel and yelled at the top of my voice, as the car veered dangerously from side to side on the lonely road. Minutes later I was up our lane and there was Josie busy in one of his fields. I abandoned the car and yelled the good news to him as I scrambled up the little incline to where he was. Then like two dervishes the two of us danced a little joyous jig on the side of his mountain. I told Bobby about that later. And Bik. I knew they would enjoy the image. Josie and I certainly did.

We also enjoyed long summer evenings, taking in the hay, walking, looking at the countryside, discussing affairs of state and the international situation, examining local historical sites, spying on badgers, exploring the merits of *poitín*, dipping sheep, counting whin bushes and fuchsia. Fixing the water supply, peering at primroses, whitewashing stone walls, bird watching, drinking pints, playing tig with rabbits. Minding the mountain, eating huge dinners, following the *Táin*. Every spare minute I had was spent in Glenmore, and generations of young nephews and nieces joined Gearóid and Oisín and the rest of us for summer after summer. They, too, learned from Josie about foxes and tractors and trees and sucky calves, and ate rounds of his bread sprinkled with sugar.

We lost tenancy of the house after a decade of happy years, but Josie provided a plot of land just across from it for us. We planted a rather primitive caravan there and our relationship with Glenmore continued, though our sojourns became less and less frequent as time went by and an increasing workload did away with the notion of free weekends.

I was reminded of all this last week when I returned once again to Glenmore. I got word that Josie was ill and he wasn't expected to last too long, so big Eamon and I sped down from Belfast. It was some time since I was in Glenmore, although I kept in touch with Josie. He had been ill for ages and had moved from his bachelor abode in the family home to his sister Rose's house. Rose and Margaret have always looked after Josie. Even when their husbands, Jimmy and Dinny, God rest them, were alive, these two good women cleaned and cooked for Josie. They lived not far from him and from each other. He was spoilt.

I was very sad when I left Josie that day. He was in bad shape, propped up in bed chained to a breathing machine, unable to

27 July 1998

speak but telling me loudly with his eyes and a firm handshake that he was glad to see me. I wandered up to our lane afterwards, around Josie's, which has been lovingly restored by his niece Breda, and Berry's which is still empty.

And our dilapidated caravan. Years before it had become the target of local reactionaries. This was after the IRA executed a man named Tom Oliver, whom they accused of being an informer. Mr Oliver was the father of a large family of young children, and his killing caused understandable outrage. It was also exploited as part of an anti-Republican campaign by some unscrupulous elements who called for all Republicans to be ostracised. Our caravan, and consequently Josie Donnelly, became targets. Josie was told to get it moved. . . or else. I spoke to him at that time, volunteering to move the caravan which we had not used in some time anyway.

"No," said Josie. "That would make them think they were right. And they're not." The caravan stayed.

Josie died the day after Eamonn and I went to see him. We buried him last Saturday: Oisín, who did him proud, and his sisters Rose and Margaret and Bridgie (Mary couldn't attend because she is in a wheelchair this last ten years) and all his nieces and nephews. And the rest of us, including me and Colette and Gearóid. It was a fine funeral on a beautiful rain-free, warm summer day.

Arthur Morgan said a few fine, fitting words at the graveside. He spoke of Josie's gentleness, his love of nature, of the time he used to feed sweet milk to two young hares until after a time they would come into the kitchen. "The fattest hares in the land," Arthur said. That was Josie! Imagine it: two wild hares, eating in his kitchen.

Arthur also paid tribute to Josie's patriotism, his knowledge of world affairs, his desire to see Ireland free of British rule, his humour, his kindness. Arthur spoke wonderfully well. Josie would have been pleased. Afterwards a neighbour shook me by the hand.

"Josie Donnelly was a good man," he said. "I never heard him say a bad word against anyone. He was a gentle man."

And so he was.

Go ndéana Dia trócaire air.

An Irish Journal

DANCING AT LUGHNASA?

On 9 August 1971 internment was introduced. In four days twenty-two people were killed and scores were injured. Thousands of people were forced to leave their homes and refugees streamed across the border. Only Nationalists and civil rights activists were interned, and later it emerged that several of those who were picked up were subjected to a variety of forms of torture.

Almost thirty years ago, on 9 August 1971, here in the North of Ireland, internment was introduced once again by the old Unionist regime with the active support of the British government. Internment had been used in every decade until then against Nationalists. Some older political activists have spent up to a decade imprisoned without any possibility of charge or trial. In the early hours of 9 August, when the troops swooped on homes throughout the Six Counties, they met with fierce resistance from the local populace. Twenty-two people were killed and countless others were wounded.

From those first swoops, thousands, mostly men though some women were also interned, spent months or years in a prison ship or in the barbed wire compounds of Long Kesh prison camp. Most were subjected to "inhumane and degrading treatment" during brutal interrogations. I was interned twice. My father and most of my brothers were interned along with uncles and cousins. And our family was not unique.

The internment operation disrupted family and community life on a huge scale. Not surprisingly, the people fought back, and the Civil Rights Association, then in the midst of the civil rights struggle, sponsored an anti-internment campaign which lasted until the internees were released sometime in the mid-seventies. During this campaign there were special demonstrations around the anniversary of 9 August. These have continued ever since. The anniversaries invariably were used as occasions for violence by the state forces, and August rarely passed without street riots and wholesale disruption. Once again local communities suffered, and many people, especially young people, were injured or killed. At different times there were

3 August 1998

efforts by community leaders to organise events which harnessed the local anger and channelled it constructively. Such initiatives, for one reason or other, lacked continuity. Until now. Now Republican Belfast has a generally peaceful August. Yet internment and the resistance which it created is remembered and continued. How?

Through thousands of events embracing every aspect of community life and every section of the community. Because the largest community festivals in Europe are happening all week in North, South, East and West Belfast. From sporting events, hill walks, bus and other tours, to sing-songs, street parties, debates, poetry readings, drama, films, concerts, exhibitions, and so on and so on. Streets are festooned with buntings. A radio station, staffed by local youngsters and some not so young, is a huge success. All manner of *craic* and fun, loud music and louder discussions, the odd drink or two, will make this a Mardi Gras week in this city.

In West Belfast the People's Festival – *Féile an Phobail* – is the oldest of these events. Now in its eleventh year, *Féile* is hosting the world premier of *One Man's Hero* starring Tom Berringer, the story of the St Patrick's Battalion – the San Patricios – which fought on the Mexican side against the USA in 1846. At the end of the war, ninety of them were captured by the US army; fifty were hanged, the rest were flogged and branded.

Films, even of rediscovered history like this, are not the only dramatic presentations of the *Féile*. Two local theatrical groups, DubbelJoint and JustUs, which have had outstanding successes with other presentations, have been denied funding by the Arts Council for their new play *Forced Upon Us*, a story about the RUC, a force which is subject to a special commission into policing. I saw the play myself last Friday. It is a very powerful and dramatic presentation, the like of which should be encouraged and not censored as the Arts Council have done. When one considers that community theatre involving "ordinary" people, and mostly women, is filling theatres in working-class areas, then this surely is to everyone's benefit, enlightenment and entertainment. It is real art; whether one agrees with the storyline or the politics is immaterial.

North Belfast, not to be outdone, has a *Fleadh* (a festival of slightly sober music) to which huge crowds throng to join with some of the top Irish music bands in a huge celebration of life, jigs and reels, and happiness.

All of this is very reminiscent of the old Celtic celebration of *Lughnasa* which commemorated the coming of the harvest in an inclusive and hugely important way for our people of that time. This is one tradition which we don't need too much encouragement to continue today.

So there you are. This week Belfast is entertaining itself, but as well as that we will be joined by thousands of visitors. Maybe if you're around these quarters you'll drop in, or maybe you'll make a note in your diary to be here for the first *Féile* of the next century. You'll be very welcome.

17 August 1998

The Fifteenth of August

On Saturday, 15 August, a bomb planted by the self-styled "Real IRA" killed twenty-nine people in Omagh, County Tyrone.

Colette's appointment with the hairdresser was for two thirty. We were late, but not to worry. It was the fifth day of our holidays and the first one without rain, and we knew there would be no fuss over our lack of punctuality. Everybody was pleased at the summer sunshine. So were we. No phones, no meetings, faxes or overwrought schedules. And today, no rain!

At two forty I dropped Colette off.

"How long will you be?" I asked.

"Hold on," she said, "I'll find out."

She disappeared for a few seconds into the village hairdressers. Then with a smile and a wave she bade me *au revoir*. "I'll be forty minutes."

I drove off towards the beach. One of our dogs, Oscar, lay curled up in the back seat. Below her were a couple of hurling sticks. The beach was ten minutes' drive away. It stretched for miles, acres upon white acres of firm clean sand. There was a slight wind blowing; it whipped a frenzy of fine sand off the top layer. It also carried the *sliotar* further than usual when I pucked it away into the middle distance. Oscar darted in pursuit as I ambled in her wake breathing in the beauty of this heavenly place.

Across from us were Inisbofin and the other islands. Beyond them was Toraigh. Between us and them, the choppy waters shimmered in the bright sunshine. I was high on it all, the sight and the smell and the sound of north-west Donegal. I was cutting and driving the *sliotar* with such accuracy that I surprised myself. I'm sure Niall O'Dowd would have been jealous. Before I knew it, it was after three o'clock.

"I'll keep going until ten past three," I told myself. "A five-minute breather and then I'll make my way back again."

And so it was. Minutes later I planked myself on a low sand dune. Oscar sprawled panting at my feet, the *sliotar* between her paws. I checked my watch.

"Ten past three. . . twenty minutes back to the car. . . ten minutes' drive back. Colette should be finished by then."

I had a bottle of water in my bumbag. I sipped it slowly as I drank in the view. Seagulls dipped in and out of the waves. Apart from them and a few distant human figures, Oscar and I had the beach almost to ourselves. It was paradise.

At three twenty I took up the hurling stick again and struggled to my feet. Oscar sped away in front of me waiting expectantly and with great excitement for me to hit the *sliotar* for her to retrieve. In this fashion we made our way back to where the car was parked. En route I found a few beautiful stones and other little pieces of beach ware. By the time I got to the hairdressers Colette was gone.

"She's around the corner having a coffee," I was told.

Oscar and I dandered to the small café where Colette was sitting in a window seat, wondrous and wonderful in her new hair-do.

"I'll buy you a coffee," she greeted me.

"Get me a mineral water," I said. "I'll leave the dog in the car."

As I arrived back into the café the four o'clock radio news was beginning.

"There is a report of a bomb explosion in Omagh, County Tyrone. It is believed that a number of people have been killed. . ." the newscaster's even tones informed us.

"Jesus, Mary and Joseph," Colette exclaimed. "God help them."

We left the café and I went in search of a phone.

The sun was still shining. The day was still beautiful. But for the people of Omagh nothing would ever be the same again. For many of them 15 August was the day when their world ended, at ten minutes past three.

7 September 1998

A Good Week for the Peace Process

On Tuesday, 1 September, the longstanding Unionist refusal to talk to Sinn Féin finally ended when First Minister Designate David Trimble invited Gerry Adams to a round-table meeting. On 3 September, Bill Clinton, President of the United States of America, paid his second visit to the North of Ireland, delivering his keynote address at the Waterfront Hall in Belfast.

As this column confided to you last week, I was expecting David Trimble to meet with me this week. On Saturday he confirmed this. But just in case anyone thought otherwise, Mr Trimble told the media that he would not be shaking hands with me or participating in any of the normal civilities. Ach, well, nobody said it was going to be easy.

These meetings – one on Monday with all the party leaders, the other with David Trimble and myself – came as a result of the initiatives taken by Sinn Féin. While there has been an almost universal media welcome for both my statement of Tuesday last and for the appointment of Martin McGuinness as the Sinn Féin representative to meet with the decommissioning body, some sections of the media have suggested that these moves came as a result of pressure from the US and the Irish and British governments. Such assertions misunderstand the Republican peace strategy and our commitment to the search for a democratic settlement of the conflict in Ireland. Sinn Féin took the initiatives, not because we had to or because we were forced to, but because it was the right thing to do.

The Omagh bomb, the deaths of three young children in Ballymoney, the siege of Garvaghy Road and the other difficulties caused by the Orange marching season, including the evictions of hundreds of Catholic families – these were the imperative for urgent progress to be made to ensure the implementation of the Agreement. Our party leadership felt that we needed to send a very clear signal that there was an alternative to all this. That there is another option. We needed to give people hope; to take everyone forward out of the carnage and despair; to break the impasse which has been created by the Unionist refusal to talk to Sinn Féin.

The visit by President Clinton provided a perfect opportunity to accomplish all this. So it has been a good week for the peace process. And a good visit by the US president and Hilary Clinton. Like their last visit this one has helped to nudge the process forward. For that Americans and particularly Irish-Americans should be grateful to the president and the first lady.

Of course there will be many more difficulties ahead. Some of these were emerging even during the presidential visit. As you will guess by his posturing around the issue of handshakes, David Trimble moved reluctantly to respond to these initiatives. He is now seeking to renegotiate the Good Friday Agreement. He says there can be no executive role for Sinn Féin unless the IRA decommissions its arms. If Mr Trimble persists with this, he is clearly in breach of the Agreement he made on Good Friday. If anyone supports him in this, they also are in breach of the commitment they made.

The Good Friday Agreement is clear on the issue of decommissioning. It is part of the overall process of conflict resolution. Decommissioning is not a precondition. It is not a prerequisite to the establishment of the institutions nor to their full operation nor the implementation of other aspects of the deal. The Agreement must be implemented in full.

Sinn Féin will deal with the decommissioning body in good faith. We will be positive and constructive. We will do our best, and we are committed to carrying out the Agreement in all its parts. But to say, as Mr Trimble has, that there can be no Executive, no institutions, no structures unless we deliver decommissioning – that's not in the Agreement. If it had been we could not have agreed to it or supported it as we have, because we could not have delivered it. The Unionists know this. And everyone knows that neither we nor any other party to the Agreement, including the governments, have the ability to disarm the armed groups. That, as the British government has said, is a voluntary process. So, instead of seeking to undo what he did on Good Friday, Mr Trimble must now do his job. As first minister he must now deliver on his pledge to build a pluralist society and to implement the Agreement.

7 September 1998

The next steps are very clear. If you doubt me dig out your copy of the Agreement and look at it. I am bringing my copy to this week's meetings. The Agreement sets out the next phase in clear language: the establishment of the Executive, the policy and implementation bodies and the All-Ireland Ministerial Council. There is a time-frame for these structures and for the programmes of work for the implementation bodies. There are no preconditions blocking the speedy establishment of all elements or preventing participation by any mandated party.

So there you are. Lots of work yet to be done. Not just here in Ireland but in the USA as well. We all have a part to play and our focus at this stage is to get the Agreement implemented. Quickly.

An Irish Journal

STORMONT RULE IS OVER

On 10 September, David Trimble and Gerry Adams held their first face-to-face meeting at Stormont prior to the first meeting of the Northern Assembly.

Tonight as Offaly celebrate their victory over Kilkenny in today's mighty All-Ireland Hurling Final, the rain pitter-patters down on Belfast and I reflect on what I am going to say tomorrow at the Assembly. It is Sunday evening here in Ireland. The nights are shortening, there is a hint of frost in the air and the leaves are starting to change colour.

Tomorrow's Assembly meeting is the first at Stormont. The only other meeting was at the Castle Buildings, which is on the Stormont estate but not in the old parliament building. That is where we will be in the morning. That is where the "Protestant Parliament for a Protestant People" sat. It is the place from which Nationalists were excluded or from which they abstained. It was symbolic of monolithic Unionism.

Of course, it is too fine a building for this dysfunctional part of our partitioned island. But there can be no doubt that old Unionism had a grand notion of itself. That is clear from the way they put their parliament building together. It was designed by a Sir Arnold Thornley in Greek classical style. The bit that most people see, the exterior, is faced in Portland stone above a plinth of unpolished Mourne granite.

The building stands in a beautiful estate on an elevated position with striking views across rolling countryside. It is in East Belfast, close to the great burial mound of Dún Donald, but you can see it from the west of the city. From the hilly roads above Turf Lodge, Ballymurphy and Andytown, we can see Stormont looking across at us. A few weeks ago someone told me that when Ballymurphy, my home area, was being built in the late 1940s and fifties, the topsoil was shipped across town to improve the grounds of Stormont. I have not been able to check that out, but I must confess it does amuse me that I may be going back to my own turf.

The estate itself also has its own castle, built by a man called John Cleland, who was the Rector of Newtownards for twenty

14 September 1998

years from 1789 to 1809. As Cathal O'Byrne tells it, the Stormont demesne was formed when the Rev. Cleland "grabbed" all the land he could lay his hands on, including the public roads, and was not too particular as to the means he employed in so doing. Cleland was also a magistrate, who was described by Jimmy Hope, the '98 patriot, as Lord Castlereagh's spiritual guide and tutor. By all accounts he was a bit of a tyrant, running informers and agents and doing his bit against the United Irish movement. Little wonder his estate was originally called Stormount. Stormont is a recent spelling.

Stormont houses lots of bad vibes for Irish Nationalism. As can be seen from the above, our historical resentment of what it represents goes back further than partition. Most Catholics detest the place because of its history. And who can blame them? But it goes deeper than that. The very grandeur of the stately pile was an exercise in triumphalism. Stormont looked down its nose at the slums and deprived neighbourhoods of its disloyal, unwanted and unwilling citizens.

Things are different nowadays, of course. Republicans and Nationalists roam the corridors conversing in Irish. A US president comes to visit. There is no longer a prime minister of Northern Ireland. Instead, in the experimental and interdependent structure of institutions which is being established, a Nationalist and a Unionist share the office of first and deputy first minister, and a coalition executive of the rest of us has to be formed soon if the timetable of the Good Friday Agreement is to be kept to. Without this executive and the All-Ireland Council with its policy making and implementation bodies, there can be no Assembly.

These institutions, the equality agenda and our respective hopes for the future are some of the things David Trimble and I discussed when we met last week. That meeting was also at Stormont. It was a good meeting which lasted about forty minutes. As a first step in what I hope will become a history-making engagement between Irish Republicanism and Ulster Unionism, it was a positive beginning. In comments afterwards which were almost as important as the meeting itself, David Trimble was as positive as I was. Of course there are lots of difficulties ahead, but one thing is for sure: Stormont rule as we knew it is over. For ever.

Long Journey Home

I got back to Ireland on Sunday after a two-week-long journey along the eastern states of the USA and a brief hop into Canada. It was yet another good visit with lots of people coming out to greet and support us and to make their contribution to the peace process here and to Sinn Féin's democratic and Republican strategy.

I am continuously uplifted and intrigued by Irish-America, by the connection between the Irish in America and the cause of peace and justice back home. The first time I went there this was the case, and it has been the same every trip. This visit was no different. I suppose of all the places we were this time, Lawrence, Massachusetts, tells the story of every other place as well as its own history.

The Irish settled there in 1837, before the great famines, although the population was swollen by the terrible exodus which marked *an Gorta Mór*. Lawrence was a mill town, busy with textiles and the like. All that has ceased long since, but one thing has remained constant: the Irish in Lawrence have never lost the faith. They welcomed Parnell and bought Fenian guns; they came out behind Davitt when he visited; and they greeted Eamon de Valera during the Civil War. Of course, many other places did the same, and we visited them also on this trip, but where Lawrence makes the difference is that the Ancient Order of Hibernians (AOH) in that area has its own little museum with wonderful photographic and written records among other exhibits of its past.

This was Rita O'Hare's first tour as Sinn Féin representative in the USA. Her notion of all the places we visited was that each one has its own particular and special sense of its Irishness. So from New York to Philly, from Pittsburgh to Medina, from Albany to Fairfield and Boston and a few smaller but no less important places in between, we found this to be the case. Whether at community level or among the blue collar sector or increasingly among the white collar sector and in corporate America, there is a growing sense of confidence in all things Irish and a sense of their own influence on events back home.

That was certainly the message we brought with us. It was

26 October 1998

two-pronged: thanks for the work which has been done, and an appeal to keep working. Because if ever we need the support of our people in the USA it is now. This week should have seen the establishment of the shadow executive and the all-Ireland bodies, but the only institution established as a result of the Good Friday Agreement is the Assembly at Stormont. I am not surprised by this, nor deflated, but it is proof for those who need it that the Good Friday Agreement is the beginning of a process and not the end of it. Neither is the Agreement an end in itself. For all its promise it is meaningless if it does not deliver on the changes which were agreed and which are necessary if we are to have peace.

One of the lessons of Irish-America is that for as long as the Irish have been there they have supported the call for justice and freedom in Ireland. The museum at Lawrence has the evidence of that. But thus far freedom and justice have been denied us. Why? What have we not got right over the centuries? Are we getting it right now?

I think so. We have a lot to do – you in the States, we at home – but we are getting there. The Unionists may be in clear breach of the commitments David Trimble made on behalf of his party. They may have succeeded in breaking the deadline of 31 October, but they cannot stop the tide of history if there is a good Irish-American wind behind it. Those who are denying the people of this island the changes and benefits we voted for and which are due to us will only succeed if people in the USA give up the faith. All the evidence of my last two weeks there is that you have no intention of doing so.

An Irish Journal

A Unionist Go-slow

On Monday, 19 October, and Saturday, 24 October, David Trimble, leader of the Ulster Unionist Party, repeated his view that Sinn Féin members could not become part of an executive before decommissioning by the IRA. On Monday, 26 October, Taoiseach Bertie Ahern said that there was no chance of the North-South Ministerial Council being established before the 31 October deadline. David Trimble, first minister designate, said that 31 October was not an absolute deadline. Martin McGuinness accused Unionists of trying to rewrite the Good Friday Agreement.

Once when I was journeying through Dublin in a friend's car, she drove through a set of red lights. I was terrified. "Did you not see those lights?" I exclaimed as pedestrians leapt to safety and other motorists screeched their horns at us.

"Ach, *those* lights," she murmured sweetly, "they're just broad guidelines."

I was reminded of this incident when the Ulster Unionist Party explained why it is unconcerned at the passing of 31 October without the establishment of the institutions which were to be in place on that date.

"Deadline? What deadline?" Mr Trimble *et al.* murmur sweetly. "That's not a deadline. That was only a guideline."

So it is that we are into November and the beginning of the wind-down to Christmas. Beware the ides of October. It is now seven months since the Good Friday Agreement. So far the transitional administration in the North is represented only by Mr Trimble and his deputy, Seamus Mallon. The rest of us are cut out and, more importantly, those who vote for us are sidelined. Except for the Assembly, the interlocking and interdependent structures are nonexistent.

"So what's new?" ask the ghosts of generations of Taigs past. "Isn't that how Unionists have always behaved?"

Without doubt this is the case and without doubt it will remain the case. If anyone is waiting for any brand of Unionism

2 November 1998

to do a decent deal with any brand of Nationalism or Republicanism, then they will have a very long wait indeed. That is why it needed the intervention and the focused attention and presence of Mr Blair and Mr Ahern to get the Good Friday Agreement. That is why we have a Good Friday Agreement. Because the British prime minister and the taoiseach were involved, as well as President Clinton; it was he who made the late-night phone calls.

So if Unionism cannot be relied upon to make a decent deal of its own accord, we should not be surprised if it will not deliver on a decent deal of its own accord. That's the way it is. Only the workings out and the new age of enlightenment which will emerge from a genuinely new dispensation will change that. But in the meantime and in this period of transition, the UUP and its leaders continue to engage in what they clearly see as a grudge match.

So what is to be done?

Well, so far the two governments, for reasons which are understandable from their perspectives, concede privately that we are in a crisis, but publicly they insist that everything is hunky dory. So far Mr Trimble in his capacity as first minister designate has called only two rounds of consultation with the other parties. Inclusiveness how are ye?

Last week there were a few hours of discussion up at Stormont. These were very basic and routine discussions which should have been held some time ago; they also should have been brought to conclusion some time ago. The issues being discussed were the number of departments for a Northern administration and the all-Ireland policy-making and implementation bodies. The UUP refused to come to conclusion on the first matter and filibustered on the second. The following day Mr Trimble assured me that it will take ages to work these issues out.

It is now time for the two governments to step in. I will be contacting Mr Blair to tell him this. I remain in constant contact with Mr Ahern, and during my recent visit to the USA I briefed the White House fully on the current situation. It may be that Mr Blair will be reluctant to become personally involved at this point. His advisers may feel that he should not be inserted into this situation unless there is a pre-cooked solution to the problem.

That's politics for you. But it is also a failure of politics if one party to the Good Friday Agreement is allowed to exercise a veto.

Mr Blair is a party to the Agreement. He is also the prime minister whose government has jurisdiction over this place. Like the rest of us he has a responsibility to fulfil his commitment to the speedy implementation of all aspects of the Agreement. A Unionist go-slow should not be tolerated. Not if the British government is serious about its commitments to the peace process.

9 November 1998

ON REACHING FIFTY

I celebrated my fiftieth birthday around this time last month. On 6 October to be exact. I really enjoyed it. In fact, in the days before and for reasons totally beyond my control, I found myself looking forward to that date. When I tried to analyse my feelings, I could only conclude that my mood of quiet anticipation was caused by the thought that I was reaching half a century.

Three score and ten is what we are given. Three score and ten. Which leaves me with a score. If I'm lucky. Hardly time to squander. Yet I felt giddy.

For a full week before the sixth, from the moment I awoke I felt good. One morning, peering down over the duvet feetwards, I could not help but raise one almost-fifty-year-old leg towards the ceiling.

"Half a century old," I muttered admiringly.

I raised both limbs and completed a joyous little horizontal Riverdance jig.

"A century between the two of you. Well done."

Not that my legs are any great shakes, but they are the best I have. Apart from bony knees which can be uncomfortable if I sleep on my side, I have no complaints, because even the sharpness of my knees can be blunted by a strategically placed pillow or a well-positioned fold in the quilt. Not too bad after all this time. The rest of me is the same: nothing perfect but generally in working order. Most of the time.

I am even lucky enough to wear spectacles for a very long time. That way I escape the fate of many of my less lucky friends or associates who peer blindly and in panic at small print as they approach middle age. I was ahead of them in the shortsightedness stakes. Now they have to search for their newly acquired glasses or better lighting as they mutter about not being able to see a thing.

Many of my male friends are also going or have gone bald. I haven't.

Not yet.

Funnily enough, baldness is yet another thing over which none of us has any control and yet it is a great source of mirth among close friends. Or at least among my close friends, so I am fairly sure that wherever there is male bonding there are wisecracks about expanding foreheads or the intricate weaving of thinning curls which is required to cover up little bald spots. The male menopause is a very fine thing indeed.

Hair colour produces the same type of jibe. I am for ever surprised at the jealousy caused among my more colourless friends by the failure of my hair to lose its natural colour. Again this is something for which I can claim no credit, but grey begrudgers badger me with cutting remarks about Grecian 2000. All very childish. Especially for men of their age.

But it is not these things, uplifting though they may be, which have me happy. Even if I was as baldy as a coot, even if all my teeth fell out, if my middle age spread was elephantine, if I was dottering and dozy and even more absent-minded than at present (if that was possible), I would still be happy.

Why?

Because life is great. Twenty, thirty, forty, fifty? I am delighted to have survived it all. I have so much to do: forests to plant, hills to walk, skies to watch, beaches to comb. So many things to hear: babies laughing, people singing, music playing, winds whooshing, waves beating, silence sounding. So much to learn: about life, about nature, about history, about humanity, about God, about wine, about dancing, about myself.

And books to read. And write. And films to see. And hurling matches to argue about. And points to score. And friends to meet. And words to chew over.

All this and more.

As well as freeing Ireland.

So there is no time to waste.

Fifty? No problem. We need two lives. In case we don't get but one, I am making the most of this one, because thus far I have been blessed, and I thank God and all my many friends everywhere who have put up with me all this time. I am very very lucky indeed.

Regrets?

I've had a few, but then again too few to mention. I did what I had to do, and saw it through without exemption… I did it my way.

Happy birthday to me.

16 November 1998

MOTHER'S DAY

My mother died on 4 September 1992. She was sixty-seven years old. She died suddenly after a huge stroke. Her life was filled with stress and her health was never the best, but her going was so unexpected that even yet, at a certain emotional level, it is hard to come to terms with her non-presence.

I am her oldest child. I pause after the word *child* and I smile that I describe myself thus, but that is what I am. When all else is stripped away or set aside, that is what all of us are. Somebody's child. My mother had thirteen children. Three of us died at birth – three little boys. Our Sean's twin brother Brendan and two other brothers, twins also, Seamus and David. The rest of us survived. Five brothers and five sisters. My mother gave life to and for every one of us.

Her name was Annie. When I was born she was twenty-three. A child came every year after that. I don't know how she coped. We were poor. Not *Angela's Ashes* poor because we had the support of loving grandmothers and a wider family circle to sustain us, but we were poor nonetheless. So was everyone else. Or everyone we knew. That's probably why we children never noticed it at the time.

My mother carried our family. She was of that generation of Irish people in which the man of the house provided the wages if he was lucky enough to be in work, and the woman of the house did the rest. It wasn't fair. And then when the ten of us started to move out, the grandchildren started to move in and the cycle started again.

My Ma loved dancing. *Céilí* and old time were her favourites. She had a terrific sweet tooth. She read a lot, as did many of her generation, and she sang around the house all the time. Well, most of the time. All of these habits I have inherited from her, although my singing is not as good and I don't know one whole song right through.

I may have inherited other habits or traits. I hope so. Some day I must take time to find out. But one thing my mother gave to me without being conscious of it, and that is a deep appreciation of the unselfish, unconditional and undying nature of mother love. And of what mothers put up with. I told her that a few times over the years. Half joking, and serious as well. At set times or when I was in the mood. But when she died I wasn't with her.

She was rushed suddenly to the City Hospital in Belfast. All of our family gathered at her bedside, including our Sean who was released from prison, handcuffed to a prison officer. I was nervous about going. Not for myself because I could have gone and returned from the hospital quite quickly. If there was danger – and 1992 was a dangerous year – it would have been for those who were staying. So I didn't go. I don't regret that: it was the prudent thing to do. My Ma would have understood. But I am sorry I didn't get to tell Annie Adams how much I love her.

So thanks, Ma. *Tá mé buíoch duitse*. Happy Mother's Day.

23 November 1998

VIVA MEXICO

The San Patricio Battalion was made up mostly of Irish men who fought on the Mexican side in the Mexican-American War of 1846–48. In the USA these men were seen as deserters; in Mexico they are seen as heroes.

This column is in a permanent state of jet lag. I am in Ireland at the minute after spending two nights in Mexico. My flight for Irish freedom. We went and returned by the scenic route, going via Los Angeles and returning by way of San Francisco, which is one of my favourite cities in the USA. My thanks to everyone who helped with these visits or who attended the events. They were all very successful and well worth the air miles.

I was in Mexico to inaugurate "Hidden Truths", an exhibition about Bloody Sunday, that last Sunday in January 1972 when British troops killed fourteen Derry people who were demonstrating for civil rights. My consistent view, from that day, is that this was a premeditated and well planned attempt to suppress the movement for civil and democratic rights, with clearance at the very top of the British establishment. Perhaps they thought they were in Aden or Cyprus. Perhaps they forgot about the presence of cameras. Perhaps they didn't care either way.

Since then the families of the dead of Bloody Sunday have been trying to tell their story. They have persisted through lies and misrepresentation. After twenty-six years of campaigning by the families, British Prime Minister Tony Blair's decision to set aside the Widgery Report and to reopen an inquiry into the events of that day was a considerable breakthrough. But the families' campaign is not over; hence the exhibition. There is a book also by the same name, *Hidden Truths*. I found the exhibition overwhelming. It starts a US tour in January in San Francisco. You should make the effort of getting to see it when it reaches your area. I'll try to get you news of its schedule and of places where you can get the book.

Apart from all the obvious reasons for remembering Bloody Sunday, I am tremendously uplifted and humbled by the resilience of the relatives of those who died that day. Without their great dignity and endurance, there would be no chance of the wider world learning the story of Bloody Sunday. There would be no possibility of justice for those who died that day. In many ways the Bloody Sunday Justice Campaign is an inspiration and an example to the rest of us who struggle for justice. Despite the difficulties, including the current and not-inconsiderable ones, we must persevere and persist in our task.

But isn't Mexico a strange place for a Bloody Sunday exhibition? Why Mexico? you may ask. Because that's where the organiser, Trish Ziff, lives I could say, and that would be true, but Mexico is also an appropriate place for this event because of its links with Ireland. And not least because of the affection which the people of Mexico have for the Irish on account of the San Patricio Battalion.

The San Patricio Battalion was made up mostly of Irish men who fought on the Mexican side in the Mexican-American War of 1846–48. This war was a bloody competition between two colonisations, that of South America by the Spanish and that of North America by northern Europeans. It was a war which Abraham Lincoln described as an unjust one, and from the US side it aimed and succeeded in claiming large areas of Mexican-owned land, including Texas and California. About 24 per cent of the US army which was engaged in this war were Irish. A group of these, led by a Galway man, John Riley, left the US side, crossed the Rio Grande and joined the Mexican side. His second-in-command was Patrick Dalton from Mayo.

In the USA these men were seen as deserters. In Mexico they are seen as brave soldiers, as heroes who fought alongside the oppressed "against the oppressor". Given that these were the worst years of the Famine in Ireland, there can be little doubt about what motivated Riley and his comrades. Their battle standard made that clear: *Érin Go Bragh* (Ireland For Ever) it proclaimed. By July 1847 there were 200 soldiers in this unit, and it had established a reputation for bravery.

But the Mexicans were eventually outnumbered and heavily defeated. In the last battle involving the San Patricios at Churrubusco outside Mexico City, the San Patricios fought with particular valour. Thirty-five of them were killed; eighty-five were captured and later court-martialled by the US army;

23 November 1998

seventy were sentenced to death; and fifty were subsequently executed.

The San Patricios – and as a result the rest of us Irish – enjoy a great affection in popular Mexican culture, and the story of the St Patrick's Battalion is taught as part of the school curriculum. Little wonder then that so many citizens of that fine city turned out to view the Bloody Sunday "Hidden Truths" exhibition.

Viva Mexico, Viva Irelande!

An Irish Journal

Breaking the Impasse?

It was announced that British Prime Minister Tony Blair would travel to Belfast on Wednesday, 2 December, to try to assist the search for a deal on the issue of the setting up of departments and the North-South Ministerial Council. At the weekend of 28–29 November, George Mitchell, formerly chairman of the multi-party talks, held meetings with Northern Ireland political leaders in Belfast.

I have been arguing for some time now that the British and Irish governments need to take a concerted and concentrated initiative to break the current impasse in the peace process. That is how we got the Good Friday Agreement. Mr Blair and Mr Ahern, with the active support of President Clinton, focused in a very direct and personal way and worked with all the local parties against a deadline, until a deal was done. Readers of this column are well aware of all that and of the arguments I have put, in this space and elsewhere, in support of this proposition.

Tony Blair's latest visit to Ireland is further proof of the validity of this argument. In the immediate build-up to the visit the Unionists had to apply themselves to working their way through the negotiations on the policy-making and implementation bodies. They have been stalling on these for some time now in much the same way as they have prevented movement, as prescribed in the Good Friday Agreement, on the other institutions.

I would not be surprised therefore if there was agreement in the short time ahead on the policy and implementation bodies. If this happens the governments will sell this as a great breakthrough. That is understandable from their viewpoint as they are seeking to placate increasing public concerns about the state of the peace process. It will be progress, of course, but it will be far short of what constitutes a breakthrough because there will still not be an executive or a council of ministers or cross-border bodies even in shadow formation.

The focus therefore which the Blair visit provided needs to be continued beyond the time the British prime minister was here.

30 November 1998

It needs him and Bertie Ahern to stay focused in a very direct and personal way, and working with the local parties. It also needs President Clinton. I know he remains engaged in this process. I have been in regular contact with the White House myself. I have conveyed all of the above to Washington as well as to the taoiseach and the British prime minister. Senator George Mitchell is in Ireland this week; I am meeting him in the morning and I will be making the same case to him.

The senator played a critical role in delivering the Agreement in April. The Agreement has missed the deadline of 31 October. The institutions were to be established in shadow form by then. The Agreement is therefore at this time in default in three crucial areas:
- the establishment of the Executive;
- the establishment of the All-Ireland Ministerial Council;
- the agreement of the all-Ireland policy and implementation bodies.

As I said above, there might be agreement on this third point in the near future, but if there is not, then the legislative timetable required by the Irish and British parliaments starts to run into real trouble. There is a big possibility that the February deadline will be missed also. This is the deadline by which power was to be given to these institutions. Where will the peace process be then?

The senator knows all this, of course. He also knows that there is a "Validation, Implementation and Review" section of the Agreement. This provides for a review mechanism under independent chairmanship. It may be too soon to trigger this mechanism. Indeed, the Unionists may seize on such a development as an excuse to continue their efforts to delay progress. Senator Mitchell himself may not want to be involved at this time, but it is something which needs discussion.

The senator's visit comes just before all the party leaders, and that includes this column, depart for a visit to the USA where we will meet with President Clinton. So whether or not the "Validation, Implementation and Review" section of the Agreement is to be activated, Senator Mitchell's visit comes at an opportune time. It gives all the main players here the possibility of direct engagement with the USA; and in the week running into our direct engagement with the US president, it also gives the White House the possibility of starting the type of focused approach which is needed.

If this type of engagement does not start soon, one thing is certain. The Unionists will continue their go-slow. The media will be filled with the hype of peace prizes and Nobel awards. Christmas will be upon us. Another year will end. And then in the new year everybody and everything will start to go down to the wire. Lemmings, how are ye?

14 December 1998

A Real Christmas Present: Scrap Third World Debt

The current collective debt of developing countries stands at around $2 trillion, which represents a monthly transfer of over $16 billion from the Third World to the industrialised northern hemisphere.

This Christmas most of us will quite rightly enjoy the seasonal festivities. That's the way it is in most Christian cultures. Even in the North of Ireland where this year there are unseasonal and unwelcome Orange protests planned right up to the feast day, at least on Christmas Day thoughts should ascend to a more spiritual plane. At least I hope so. But in many parts of the world, including many Christian places, it will be a different story. Christmas will be the same as any other day, only this year things may even be a wee bit worse. Or a big bit worse. For example, in Latin America where the disastrous impact of Hurricane Mitch has exacerbated the awful situation in that region's poverty-stricken Third World countries.

All of us were moved by the devastation wrought by nature, but since the hurricane struck the death toll from diseases could double the death toll of 9,000 killed by Mitch. There are reports of cholera, malaria and other illnesses throughout Nicaragua, El Salvador, Honduras, Belize and Guatamala. From Honduras the government confirms 208,000 serious cases of diarrhoea, 30,000 of malaria and 20,000 cases of cholera.

Can we blame a hurricane for all this? It is no accident that the poorest countries suffer most from any natural disaster. The route taken by Hurricane Mitch was well charted and predictable. In more affluent parts of its path, emergency services were in ahead of the hurricane doing their best to lessen the damage, but who helped the poor? And how are these people so poor anyway?

The reasons for that lie in the history of colonisation or of domestic exploitation which most of these countries have in common, but it is also a result of the heavy burden of debt owed by underdeveloped nations to the banks of developed countries. That is, to us; to our countries. In my opinion the development of the Third World is only possible through the cancellation of all outstanding debts.

The International Monetary Fund and World Bank have considerable financial reserves to facilitate such a process. Also the developing countries, which represent 80 per cent of the world's population, must be given greater influence in the decision-making processes at work in the multinational lending institutions. This can only be achieved through a democratic restructuring of these bodies.

Since its emergence in the 1970s, the debt crisis has arguably been the greatest impediment to development in the Third World. Whilst commercial banks, national governments and financial institutions in the wealthy, industrialised countries claim that financial lending to countries in the southern hemisphere can facilitate economic growth and prosperity, the facts point to a very different reality. Developing countries pay four times as much in debt repayments as they receive in either bilateral or multilateral aid. The current collective debt of developing countries stands at around a colossal $2 trillion, which represents a monthly transfer of over $16 billion from the Third World to the industrialised northern hemisphere. These figures are almost beyond our comprehension, yet they bind millions of people to a life of poverty. And it has been so for decades.

The consequences of this mean that debt is being paid with the health, welfare, education, and in some cases, the lives of people in the developing world. As the United Nations Children Fund (UNICEF) puts it: "Hundreds of thousands of the developing world's children have given their lives to pay their countries' debts, and many millions more are still paying the interest with their malnourished minds and bodies."

Isn't Christmas about children?

At present, the majority of developing countries are locked in a vicious cycle of debt which denies them the opportunity to improve the quality of lives of those in greatest social need. For example, last year Nicaragua paid eleven times more in debt service than it spent in basic heath care. Nicaragua owes $6 billion to governments and institutions like the IMF. Honduras owes $4 million.

14 December 1998

In Ireland many people have a natural affinity with the Third World. We have a very special ancestral empathy with famine-stricken areas. The people of this small island are generous in our giving to our brothers and sisters in other parts of the world. This is entirely right and proper. It does not make us special. It probably reflects the fact that we may be more informed on these issues because of our history than other countries which have different historical experiences. But it should not be up to ordinary people alone. Governments must act.

If we are really a global family, then it is time the better-off family members helped to eradicate the scourge of famine, disease and poverty which our brothers and sisters in the Third World are labouring under.

Wouldn't that be a Christian thing to do this Christmas?

An Irish Journal

BLIAIN ÚR FAOI MHAISE DAOIBH

I have the flu. Big deal. But I have. And it's no laughing matter. It's just my luck. It started sometime in or around Christmas Eve and slowly messed up my nasal tubes. I resisted it manfully on Christmas morning and crept downstairs before anyone else to check out my stocking. I even managed to make the traditional breakfast fry and struggled out with the rest of our clann to early mass and our seasonal nip around some aged or special friends for a quick ho ho ho.

Later that day after dinner I retired to my *leaba*. Coughing and spluttering, with the phlegm tripping me, I tucked myself in very tightly indeed and hibernated for the festive season. I like Christmas. It is indeed the season to be jolly. But Christmas in bed is something else. If you are not too seriously ill or incapacitated it can be sheer luxury, especially if the rest of the country is awash with floods or swept with gale-force winds.

Which is exactly the way Ireland was from St Stephen's Day onwards. Tens of thousands of families were without electricity, and if you think that means no lights then you have another think coming. We are so dependent on electricity these days that when it goes down then so does the heating, the cooking facilities, the water as well as the lighting. All over the country people were marooned as their fridge freezers defrosted and their televisions stared blankly into cold dark sitting rooms.

Not much fun. And then, to make matters worse, down in Cork the rain came in and, ye boy ye, when it rains in Cork nothing floats. Especially when it rains the way it rains when it rains like this. None of which is very funny for the poor, demented, sodden, electricity-less citizens who have to put up with it all.

"Christmas, bah!" you would expect them to say. "Christmas, bah! Humbug."

But they don't. They give off about the electricity or the lack of it, which is fair enough and well deserved. Despite the misery of it all, most of the victims of our inclement and unfestive weather remain in the main philosophical about it all. Lying in my warm bed with good books, boxes of chocolates and copious

4 January 1999

helpings of hot ones, my heart goes out to them. And I get philosophical as well.

That's the way the flu gets you. The hot ones help. From where I lie tapping on this laptop I can see the Divis Mountain. That's usually where the rain starts if it comes from the west, so you can tell how long it will take to get this far. If, however, it comes up Belfast Lough, which is its usual route, then it gets to sneak up from behind. That's the way the electricity men were caught out. The weather sneaked up on them. Or so they say. But we say, "Bah, humbug!"

The skyscape in Ireland is wonderful at this time of the year, especially just before the dusk descends. Then the whole show lightens up. It's like a scene from the resurrection. Bars of cold winter light brighten our world and outshine the failed neon. In the summer the light warms us. In winter it is without heat, and yet it brings cheer. Funny how we need the light. How it cheers us up. How even a storm with its savage beauty can be put in context by pale, quiet, anaemic rays of watery winter sunshine.

As long as you're dry. That's the main thing: staying dry. There is nothing worse than cold wetness. Water is so insidious when it is being contrary. If Jesus had been born in a stable in Ireland, he would have been foundered, and St Joseph and the Virgin Mary would have been no better. Which is why God chose a warm place for them. Cork, how are ye? Nazareth is your only man!

Still, Ireland isn't the worse place in the world. Where is? God alone knows. We in Ireland face into 1999 with more hope than we had this time last year. The peace process survived another cruel year, a year of great contrasts and greater contradictions. And, of course, all the time people like me say that it could and should have been better. And it could and it should have been, and it will have to be yet if we are to get to where we want to go.

But like those citizens faced with a Christmas week without electricity, while the vast majority of citizens moan about the service, they seem reassured that things could have been worse. And they have this faith that somehow, some way, it will get fixed. Let's hope so!

An Irish Journal

Old Ho Chi Minh had a word for it. "Without the cold and desolation of winter," he wrote in his prison poems, "there could not be the warmth and splendour of spring."

It's time I had another hot one. A Happy New Year to ye all. Here's to the warmth and splendour of spring. And to the cold and desolation of winter as well. *Sláinte. Bliain Úr faoi mhaise daoibh.*

18 January 1999

The State of Play

On 18 December six new North-South administrative bodies and an increase from six to ten ministries in the North were agreed after eighteen hours of negotiations between the parties. However, one month on, delays, obstructions and exclusions still frustrate progress.

As regular Ireland-watchers know and as readers of this column are aware, this week was to see a special meeting of the Assembly at Stormont to consider a report and proposals from First Minister David Trimble and Deputy First Minister Seamus Mallon about the departments and other matters agreed at 4am on 18 December. However, that is not the report which we received, and the reason why this is so is because the first minister refused to follow through on the logic of what he agreed to on Friday, 18 December, and he refused to recommend that agreement to the Assembly.

The Sinn Féin leadership has very reluctantly, and after considerable discussion, had to accept that the UUP has been able, once again, to buy time. In many ways this has become the character of this process, and it is disappointing, not least because the report on the "matters referred to the Assembly by the British Secretary of State" was first dealt with on 1 July 1998. At that time it was resolved that proposals be brought forward on the following matters:

- agreement on the number of ministerial posts and the distribution of executive responsibilities between those posts;
- preparations for establishing the North-South Ministerial Council and associated matters for cooperation and implementation;
- preparations for the establishment of the British-Irish Council; and
- the establishment of the consultative Civic Forum.

It is very clear that it was Seamus Mallon's intention was to have a proper report. It is equally clear that this is what First Minister Trimble refused to do. I am not convinced that this hesitancy is a result of DUP or UKUP bluster or a pandering to dissidents within the UUP itself. On the contrary, it is my view that the differences between the main Unionist parties are tactical. This should not be the case, of course. There should be a clear strategic, as well as tactical difference between pro-Agreement Unionists and anti-Agreement Unionists. But because of the way in which the Ulster Unionist Party has managed the process, there has yet to emerge a clear Unionist political formation which is prepared to bring in the type of changes involved in the Good Friday Agreement.

So Mr Trimble delays once again, perhaps in the futile hope that he can get the two governments to acquiesce to his game plan and to exclude Sinn Féin on the pretext of a spurious precondition. But, of course, the Agreement has clear timetables and a chronology for the establishment of the various institutions, without preconditions; so this week's report may delay but it cannot prevent the inevitable. Therefore I welcome that section which promises a final report, with associated procedural motions, to be submitted to the Assembly for 15 February in order to facilitate the transfer of power by London and Dublin by 10 March.

In my remarks to the Assembly on Monday, I dealt with the substance of the 18 December deal. Our party has made it clear for some time now that we believed that the UUP would have to agree to ten ministries, and this indeed was the case, and it is a good development. For the first time ever there is numerical equality in the exercise of political power between Nationalists and Unionists in the North. However, the rejection of a powerful ministry, not just by the UUP, but by the SDLP also, to tackle the core issue of equality, is a major sop to Unionism and in my view a major mistake.

The recent negotiations were also to establish dynamic and powerful all-Ireland structures as envisaged in the Good Friday Agreement. We now have six all-Ireland policy and implementation bodies, some of which are significant, but Sinn Féin retains considerable reservations about the outcome of these negotiations, especially the exclusion of inward investment from the all-Ireland business and trade body, and the way that tourism was dealt with.

Sinn Féin entered into these recent negotiations in good faith. For us the priority was strategic and political. We wanted to

18 January 1999

ensure that the legislative timetable required by the two governments was kept to; we wanted to ensure that the UUP did not succeed in its short-term aim of limiting the potential of the all-Ireland aspects of the agreement; and we wanted to clear away the undergrowth and to move towards the actual formation of the Executive with Unionist, SDLP and Sinn Féin membership.

With this in mind, our party held a series of bilaterals with the Irish government over the summer, and then trilaterals involving the Irish government, ourselves and the SDLP. We also held meetings with the British government and the first minister and deputy first minister. It has also been our consistent view that the two governments, and particularly the British government, have a special responsibility to make sure that the Good Friday Agreement is implemented.

We called, therefore, on a number of occasions for the British prime minister to be directly involved. He presided over a series of meetings at Stormont on the evening of 2 December, when a deal was done and then reneged on by the UUP with, in the memorable words of John Taylor, everyone being advised to take a holiday while David Trimble jetted off to the USA to do just that.

I also have considerable reservations about some other aspects of how these negotiations were conducted. I have put these very firmly on the record with everyone involved. In the thirty-six hours or so of negotiations leading to the 18 December, the UUP refused to engage in trilaterals with ourselves and the SDLP, even though under the terms of the Good Friday Agreement our three parties and the DUP are entitled to be involved in such discussions. So the negotiations became quite convoluted, but because of our priorities which I have outlined above, Sinn Féin remained engaged despite all the difficulties.

However, in the early hours of Friday, 18 December, we were cut out of the engagement, and Martin McGuinness, myself, and our team of senior negotiators were left sitting in our office while David Trimble and the SDLP's Eddie McGrady clinched a deal and announced it to the media.

The parties who are entitled to ministerial positions by virtue of their electoral mandates should have been fully involved in this negotiation and in its final agreement. This did not occur. I wrote to the first and deputy first ministers before Christmas, expressing this view, pointing particularly to the way the process of negotiations excluded many parties and most critically did not fully involve those parties entitled to ministerial office. I requested that they reflect this view, expressed on behalf of Sinn Féin, in their report. They failed to do so.

So, in summary, Sinn Féin would have preferred that this week's report would have moved this process into the establishment, in shadow form, of the Executive and other institutions. We welcome the commitment to do this in the final report. While underpinning our reservations about some of the matters involved, we welcome the progress which has been made.

One thing is for certain. Unless the Unionists can get the two governments to abandon the Good Friday Agreement – and this appears to me to be most unlikely – then very belatedly the next steps in the implementation of the Good Friday Agreement are clearly visible. The Executive must be established, and the All-Ireland Ministerial Council must be set up. The other institutions must be put in place.

David Trimble has now given a commitment to bring forward a final report and associated procedural motions for 15 February in order to facilitate the transfer of power by London and Dublin for 10 March.

Will he do it? Watch this space.

1 February 1999

BLOODY SUNDAY

On 31 January 1972, the British army opened fire on unarmed civil rights demonstrators in Derry, killing fourteen people and injuring many more. The subsequent tribunal of enquiry under Britain's Lord Widgery was a travesty, and for years the relatives of those killed in Derry campaigned for an independent international enquiry, which was finally established in 1998.

I was in Derry on Sunday for the Bloody Sunday Commemoration. So were tens of thousands of other people. You would not have noticed if you were watching or listening to the broadcasting media here. In fact, there was no mention of the rally or the huge attendance on any of the local evening news programmes. As far as BBC, UTV or RTÉ were concerned, nothing happened in Derry on Sunday. At least nothing worth reporting. Neither did they mention that Sunday was the anniversary of the Bloody Sunday massacre of twenty-seven years ago.

Tony Doherty, whose father was killed by the British troops, spelt out the families' attitude to the Saville Enquiry which has been established in the last year. This is the first time I have heard the families' considered view of that enquiry, and I thought they made a a lucid and well-argued case for a more open and transparent process. It is a pity that it was not reported, even as a matter of historical record, as well as from a sense of balance in the news.

The theme for this years rally was victims of state violence. There was a speaker from the victims and survivors of the Dublin and Monaghan bombings, atrocities widely believed to have been sponsored by British dirty tricks agents and which caused the largest fatalities and casualties of any day during the conflict. Thirty-three people were killed and several hundreds were wounded. Many people on the march carried photographs of loved ones killed by the British forces. In fact, the British have been directly involved in the killing of 400 people and through collusion with the Loyalists indirectly involved with the killings of many hundreds more.

Councillor Breandan Mac Cionnaith of the Garvaghy Road Residents' Association also spoke. He outlined the plight of the people of that beleaguered area. Since July there have been 150 (including many illegal) Orange parades, and the people there are under a daily sectarian siege. Garvaghy Road is a Nationalist suburb of Portadown. Since the siege commenced, Garvaghy Road people have considerable trouble shopping in the town. Now many of them are bussed to neighbouring towns to do their shopping, and local youngsters identifiable as Catholics by their school uniforms are subjected to beatings and sectarian abuse. None of this was reported either.

Why?

Well maybe, and this may not be the fault of individual journalists, but maybe there is an ethos in the broadcasting media here which has yet to catch on to the fact that we are living in a new era. You see, according to the old agenda the only victims here are victims of the IRA. Under the old rules nobody else counted. It was fairly straightforward. The IRA were always the baddies. Occasionally the Loyalists were the baddies also, but mostly they were a slightly suspect terrorising-the-terrorists wing of the establishment. And of course the British forces were always right even when they were wrong. There could be no equivalence between them and the IRA.

What of the victims of state or state-sponsored terrorism? Under the old rules they don't exist. They are not real people, real families grieving for loved ones. No side here or no section of our people have any monopoly on suffering. All the victims' families deserve the right to grieve. For most victims of British violence that requires an acknowledgement that they exist and that their pain is real. They have a story to tell, and the peace process will never be complete until they get telling that story. They also need to know the truth about the deaths of their loved ones. Out of that will come a healing process and a real foundation for a process of national reconciliation.

That is why, amongst all the other reasons, the broadcasting media here should have reported what the campaigning groups were saying at the Bloody Sunday rally. That is their role in the peace process: to dump the old agenda and to factor equality into the broadcasting ethos. Because, of course, if those who

1 February 1999

have suffered most during the conflict cannot feel the benefits of the peace process, then for them there is no peace process. And the usually loud and finger-pointing broadcasting élites can hardly blame the politicians for that if it is they who are silencing the voices of one section of victims.

Kathleen

Lily's husband always tried to look after me. Sometimes he got me into more trouble than I could handle, sometimes he confused me, but sometimes he delivered big time. When he introduced me to Kathleen's house, he delivered big time.

That was in 1972. I knew Kathleen long before that, of course. Not on personal terms, but as a singer. So did most music lovers in Belfast, because Kathleen McCready was one of our city's foremost ballad singers; she sang all over the country and could have enjoyed a lucrative music career if she had kept to "conventional" music. Indeed, during a sojourn in the USA she sang in Carnegie Hall. But Kathleen was first and foremost a Republican, and when she joined up with Eamonn Largey and they came together with some fine Belfast musicians as The Flying Column, their rendering of patriotic and street ballads electrified audiences throughout Ireland. That was in the late 1960s, and in 1970 and 1971 The Flying Column's recordings *Folk Time in Ireland* and *Four Green Fields* were best-sellers.

So in 1972 when Lily's husband directed me to the small kitchen house which he promised contained a bed for me, I was delighted when Kathleen opened the door. Her smile and warm welcome settled me immediately. Life on the run in Belfast was a dangerous and lonely existence, not just for the person involved but especially for their families. Kathleen understood this instinctively. Almost the first question she asked me was if I was married. I was, I told her.

"Well, get your wife to come here to see you," she told me. "Eamonn and I are away this weekend. The two of you can stay here. No one will bother you."

That became our routine for as long as we stayed with Kate. By this time Kathleen and Eamonn were married and they had one small daughter, Áine. She and I became buddies. Kathleen was pregnant with her second daughter, Maire. Colette was expecting our Gearóid, so a close bond quickly grew between all of us, and when Maire came along we became buddies also.

Eamonn Largey was a character. He was extrovert, eccentric,

8 February 1999

extremely hyper and happy-go-lucky. And very funny. He was also extremely goodhearted and generous. He was very, very good to Colette. Tragically, Eamonn was killed in a car accident in July 1973. Áine was about eighteen months old; Maire was six weeks. I watched Eamonn's funeral from a side street as it made its sad, slow way up the Falls Road. The British army watched from another corner. Eamonn would have been delighted.

Colette and I have numerous fond memories of his escapades. One story which Eamonn himself enjoyed telling was about the day that a priest stepped into Largey's butcher's shop just as a British army patrol was passing. Eamonn was busy behind the counter, serving and bantering with the customers. It was a minute or two before he saw the priest.

"Father," he exclaimed with a laugh, "you want to watch yourself about here. Jesus, Mary and Joseph, sorry Father, but Jesus, you are the image of Seán Mac Stiofain."

The priest reddened in embarrassment as Eamonn drew the attention of the other customers to him.

"Missus," he went on, full of *craic* and devilment, "isn't he the spit of Seán Mac? Don't go out there till them boys pass." He gestured to the passing patrol. "You'll end up in the Kesh."

Of course he didn't, but that was Eamonn's way. He slagged the priest relentlessly until he made his purchase and left. Then, as Eamonn tells it, an hour or so later a car drew up outside the butcher's. A number of large men in trench coats got out and took up positions outside the shop. One of them came in. He had one hand inside his trench coat (obviously carrying according to Eamonn). He towered over Eamonn.

"Sir," he said quietly in a soft Kerry accent, "sir, the next time you see Seán Mac Stiofain, we would appreciate it if you kept it to yourself. The boys don't like blabbermouths."

"What did you do?" I asked Eamonn.

"I became one of the wise monkeys," he said. "But I know now how Gypo Nolan felt."

Not long after Eamonn died I was arrested. Colette and Kathleen were by now close friends. They continued to stay together frequently. Sisters and soulmates together, they shared each other's heartbreak and happiness the way that only women can.

Our Gearóid was born a few months after I took up residence in Long Kesh. Kathleen was his godmother. A firm ally of Green Cross, by now she was heavily involved with Republican Prisoners' Welfare. Famously, after Long Kesh was burned down, she emptied the contents of a friend's clothes shop and transported them up to the jail, so that within days of the place being reduced to ashes, out of the ashes arose a crowd of bogging dirty internees kitted out in the latest and most fashionable flairs and shawaddywaddy gear.

Her home continued to be a resting place for Republican waifs and fugitives. That's how wee Harry came into the picture. He started to work for the prisoners, and he and Kathleen became very close. It was during this time that Kathleen was diagnosed with cancer, and when she and Harry were married in June 1976 she had already undergone surgery. She refused to acquiesce to her illness and continued with a hectic schedule of prisoners' welfare work.

By now the protests in Armagh Women's Prison and the H-Blocks had commenced. Kathleen visited both prisons frequently. She and wee Harry were a great team. By now I was out of prison again and on the road most of the time reorganising Sinn Féin and working with the Relatives' Action Committees and the fledging H-Block/Armagh campaign. I still saw Kathleen regularly, and Colette and she remained in constant contact, so that when secondary cancer set in Colette went to live with Kate. Áine, Maire and Gearóid, always close, were now to be reared together.

Until this time Kathleen was singing regularly for the Republican cause; this had been her life-long contribution to the struggle. She had a special and long-standing affection for the work of the National Graves Association and a long involvement, since the time of her old friend Jimmy Steele, with the Belfast Graves. A member of Cumann na mBan, something I was unaware of until after her death, Kathleen kept very close to the women prisoners in Armagh, and I am sure that Eileen and all the rest of them have as many stories as I have of Kate's generosity.

Confined more and more to the house and frequently in hospital, her inability to continue this work was the cause of almost constant frustration. Once, not long before her death, Colette

8 February 1999

found Kathleen in tears. Someone had sent her a new song about the H-Blocks and she was trying to record a demo tape on her tape recorder, but her once strong, beautiful singing voice was victim also of her illness which was now in her lungs. Kathleen just couldn't get enough breath. Her records were still selling well during this period, and not long before her death she released *The Price of Justice*. By now Kathleen was in her final struggle with the disease which killed her, and on the "Kerry" track, if you listen carefully, you will hear how she had to battle valiantly to control her breathing.

Visits to the hospital were more and more frequent, and everyone's routine was now built around that. It was a particularly harrowing time for wee Harry. By February 1979, Kate was confined for a particularly long time. I visited her, and on my last visit days before she died, because she was so much like her old self, I fooled myself into thinking she was going to recover. Áine's seventh birthday was on 8 February. There was a little party for her, and Colette visited Kate that evening. Harry was on a constant bedside vigil along with Kate's family. As Colette left, Kathleen hugged her.

"Take me home," she whispered.

But it was impossible. She was too ill. The next day she died. I was out of town, but I knew the awful truth as I drove up the street and saw the cars outside the house. Far from getting better, as I stupidly thought to myself, it is now my belief that Kate kept herself alive for Áine's birthday. That is what her last struggle was about. She deeply loved her two daughters, and it is to wee Harry's eternal credit that he, aided and abetted by "Auntie" Colette, raised the two girls as Kathleen wanted and that they are now two fine young women. Their mammy would be very proud of them. And of Harry. And Colette. I know I am.

I consider my friendship with Kathleen to have been one of the constants of my life. I know she shared her life and and love and talents with many people and that they have their own stories to tell, but Colette and I and our Gearóid were privileged to enjoy a special relationship with Kathleen, and our lives have been intertwined in many, many ways right up to the present day.

Next Sunday marks the twentieth anniversary of Kathleen's death. It is entirely fitting that her friends are organising a little commemoration in Belfast. Later in the year there are plans to relaunch some of her recordings. That also is a good thing. Kate would enjoy all of us getting together. She would be pleased that we can still hear her singing.

8 February 1999

"THE BRITISH WATERGATE"

Brian Nelson was a British agent working for the British army's Force Research Unit, who became the UDA's director of intelligence, responsible for selecting targets for assassination. He also smuggled hundreds of weapons, grenades and rocket launchers from South Africa into Ireland in January 1988.

In every war there are spies, agents and double agents, secret plots and dirty tricks specialists. The war in Ireland is no different, and even though the main focus of political activity here for some time now has been about building the peace process, there are some issues which will not go away. These include British covert operations and British military involvement, directly or indirectly, in the killings of Irish citizens.

The British Crown forces have killed almost 400 people here. That is, British soldiers or members of the Royal Ulster Constabulary have been directly involved in these killings. But members of these forces, through collusion with or management of Loyalist groups, have also been indirectly involved in the killings of an unknown number of other people. According to Malcolm Sutton's book, *An Index of Deaths from the Conflict in Ireland*, up until 1994 – the year this book was published – the Loyalists had killed 911 people. Elements of the British military and Intelligence services were involved in some of these killings. How many? No one knows. One thing is for sure: the body count is numbered in hundreds. The truth may never be known, because those responsible – the securocrats – remain in powerful positions. But in many cases the families of their victims refuse to stop searching for the truth. They want to tell their stories, and they understand better than most that successful peace processes involve healing and healing demands removing the causes of their pain. For many the cause of their pain is not just the loss of loved ones; it is also the cover-ups, the deceit and the lies about the circumstances of these killings.

Last week on the tenth anniversary of the killing of Belfast civil rights lawyer Pat Finucane, advertisements appeared in newspapers in Ireland, Britain and the USA calling for an independent judicial inquiry into Pat's death. The adverts contained the names of over 1,000 prominent lawyers supporting this call. On the same day, 12 February, Pat Finucane's wife Geraldine and other family members gave copies of a new report to British Secretary of State Dr Mo Mowlam and to an Irish government minister. According to the Finucane family, this report contains new evidence about the circumstances of Pat's death.

A well-known and successful lawyer, Pat Finucane was shot dead in his home in February 1988. His wife Geraldine was also wounded in the attack. The weapon used was a Browning 9mm semi-automatic pistol. It was the property of the British Ministry of Defence, which claimed that it had been stolen. But there were other elements of the British military community involved. Chief among these was a British agent called Brian Nelson. Nelson had been placed by his superiors into one of the main Loyalist organisations, the Ulster Defence Association (UDA). He worked for the FRU (Force Research Unit) of the British army and became the UDA's director of intelligence, responsible for selecting targets for assassination. These included Pat Finucane.

He also, with the direct involvement of British Intelligence, smuggled hundreds of weapons, grenades and rocket launchers into Ireland in January 1988. These weapons, obtained from apartheid South Africa, were used in many killing operations, including some which received world-wide coverage like the attack on the bookmaker's shop on the Ormeau Road in Belfast and the attack on mourners at Milltown Cemetery. One of the grenades was thrown at my family home. From the time of the arms shipment until March 1994, Loyalists killed over 200 people. One hundred and seventy-eight of these were innocent Catholics. Research has shown that the majority were killed with the South African weapons.

All of the above information and much, much more is in the public domain. Brian Nelson was actually tried in 1992 for some offences after the controversy over collusion between elements of the British forces and the Loyalists was subject to investigation, but a deal was done at Nelson's trial. He was charged with less serious matters and was imprisoned for less than five years.

8 February 1999

All of this has been written about in much more detail that this column can cope with. Television programmes have explored these issues. Yet the British government has refused to authorise an independent investigation. I have talked to Tony Blair about these matters myself. I have talked to Dr Mowlam. And I have written to them both and furnished a file of information for their attention. To no avail.

I can understand why this is so. In 1992 two prominent journalists quoted a "senior security source" who described the Nelson case as "the [British] Army's Watergate". But if a peace settlement is to be built here, it has to have justice as its foundation. That is why the Finucane family's appeal for an independent judicial inquiry should be supported.

Holy Wells and Peace Processes

It is raining very heavily here and I have been soaked a few times. I am well used to being soaked: it goes with being Irish. But today I discovered that my shoes are letting in. That means wet feet. Aside from corns and bunions, which thank God I don't have, the worst kind of feet are wet ones, unless you are swimming, or in the bath, or the jacuzzi, or even in the shower. But not in your shoes. And especially not in your socks in your shoes. And specifically not on a lonely hillside with the rain coming at you horizontally. That's the worst of all wetnesses. I know. I was that soldier. Or pilgrim.

I was on the hillside because of a whim. At the bottom of the hill there is a signpost which proclaims the way to a holy well. For years I have passed this hillside and for years I have meant to go and investigate the holy well, but for years I have resisted the call of curiosity. Until today. Today I decide to check it out.

Holy wells in Ireland are wondrous establishments. They can be small springs of water gushing out from a ditch at the side of the road. Or they can be grander affairs with placid pools of aqua sheltering in quiet little nooks. But they almost all have one thing in common. Somewhere adjacent they have a bush or bushes covered in ribbons and other small accoutrements: bandages, crucifixes, handkerchiefs, cigarette lighters, all kinds of things, swaying or rattling gently in the breeze. There is something primitive and occult about it; something surreal. Voodoo, how are ye?

But these are truly holy places. Visited, when we had our fill of both saints and scholars, by holy men or women, the waters from a holy well have healing powers. Some say the wells go back to the time of Christ. I think they go beyond that time. Back maybe to another millennium? When the druids were the holiest of priests. So apart from beliefs or myths or superstitions, the holy wells are spiritual places, not least because people have been gathering at them since the pharaoh was a wee boy.

Today the people had more sense, except me. But I was impressed by the well, so much so that I filled a lemonade bottle with its water; and then I saw another signpost. This one pointed the way to a mass rock. Students of Irish history will know that

15 February 1999

mass rocks were where masses were celebrated during the penal days when Catholicism was outlawed. So off I went again.

About half a mile beyond the signpost I discovered my shoes were porous. By then I had trudged my way up a sheep track, across two gullies and over three horizons. I almost turned back a dozen times, but the thought or the hope that the mass rock was only around the next whin bush spurred me on with evangelical zeal. Across from me I had a glimpse of a grey sliver of lake away off in the distance, and beyond that darker hills soaked up the rain. By now I was sodden. Then suddenly, through a copse of beech trees and mountain ash and down into a dip, a fold in the hillside, and there was a cathedral of rock and bracken and whin and whitethorn bushes. And in the centre of it was the mass rock. I almost forgot my drowning toes: it was well worth the walk and the wetness.

I believe in trees. Once during our recent visit to Australia I escaped to sit for ten minutes alone in the bush. Though I was only metres from a busy highway and although my companions were within earshot, I was lost in the noise and the majesty of trees and insects and wild birds. It was godlike in its spirituality. And dry. And warm.

Today was almost as uplifting. On a good day it would have been magic. But every day is a good day for someone. So I stood wet into the wind and thought of all the people who had stood where I was standing. I thought of them praying for their families, and I prayed for mine. And for Ireland. And for peace processes here and in Yugoslavia and everywhere where there is conflict. Then I climbed back the way I had come. Like thousands before me for thousands of years.

Then I went off to get wet on the inside as well as everywhere else.

The Prison Ship *Maidstone*

When internment without trial was introduced for suspected Republicans, a rusty, barnacled ship was used as a prison. Gerry Adams was one of those detained on board.

I was on a prison ship once. It wasn't much fun. This was away back in 1972. The prison ship was called the *Maidstone*, and it was anchored in Belfast Lough, berthed at the quayside which was itself subjected to the usual barbed-wire ramifications, watch towers, sandbagged gunposts and other security accoutrements so beloved by gaolers, especially gaolers of the military kind.

The families of the prisoners aboard this floating, rusty, barnacled, tin Sing Sing had to find their way from homes throughout the North of Ireland to the quayside, and then a visiting permit secured their passage through the barbed-wire fences via several search areas and into a makeshift row of wooden huts. There they would be granted visits with their loved ones, who were taken from the ship and through a similar gauntlet of searches.

Apart from this brief stroll along the few metres of quayside when I first arrived on the *Maidstone,* there was no exercise and no fresh air. For our sins, all the prisoners were kept below decks all the time. And below decks was stinking. Not only was the place overcrowded, but the limited, primitive and inadequate sewers were overcrowded as well. And because we were afloat, and stationary as well, when the sewers discharged their sewage, the sewage stayed where it was. We used to have a wee word game about it. Among other things we tried to say quickly, "The ship sits in the shit." Try it. No, quicker than that.

When we were finished enthralling each other with these juvenile verbal tongue-twisters, we protested about our conditions or we tried to escape. In fact, some prisoners succeeded in escaping not long before I joined the *Maidstone*'s motley crew. They slipped overboard and swam a very long way indeed across Belfast Lough to freedom. There were no escapes after that, but there were plenty of protests.

22 February 1999

They were all protests of non-cooperation, like, for example, refusing to leave the canteen area. In the beginning the regime reacted very sharply to this impertinence. They sent the British army, who were guarding us, in to subdue us or to clear the canteen or whatever was required. They would come charging down below decks, all dressed up in full riot gear, wielding riot shields and batons and backed up with a platoon or two of heavily armed combat troops. It was all a bit silly. Especially as there was hardly room to swing a cat below decks.

So, after a while better sense prevailed and the regime became less heavy handed in its approach, but not until some of our crew suffered a broken limb or two. Apart from the lack of exercise, the absence of fresh air and the omnipresent smell of shit, the overcrowding was. . . well, overpowering.

There were lots of us, you see. About 140, if my memory serves me right. Apart from the canteen area, which we had to use in shifts because it was so small, there were the toilets, which were frequently flooded, and there was our sleeping area. It consisted of fold-away iron bunks, three high and arranged in tight rows, with little pokey lockers for storing personal effects. We lived here in semi-darkness, our surroundings lit with flickering neon lights or in daylight hours by whatever brightness penetrated the ship's portholes.

After a week or so of protest over the lack of exercise facilities, we were granted "the privilege of exercise, weather permitting and at the governor's discretion" above decks. Again because of the tininess of the exercise area we walked there in shifts, a dozen or so at a time. Because of the height of the security fences around this small area, the only distance we could see was skywards. Nothing else was visible. The security fences were our horizon.

Food on the *Maidstone* was something else. We eventually got the place closed down by engaging in a mass strike when all of us refused the prison food, or any other food for that matter. It was less than a hunger strike but it was an effective spur for mobilisations outside. The British government was going through a sensitive period, and it was moved by dint of these protests to close the ship and to transfer us to another interesting place – the prison camp at Long Kesh out the other side of Belfast.

An Irish Journal

The funny thing about it all is that none of us were ever charged with any offence. We were all imprisoned without charge or trial on the *Maidstone* and in the internment camp. We were also survivors of the notorious interrogation centre at the British army base at Palace Barracks. That's one of the places where the British government torture practices led to it being indicted for "inhumane and degrading treatment" of internees at the European Court of Human Rights. But that, like the food on the *Maidstone*, is another story.

22 February 1999

DOGS I HAVE KNOWN

There are lots of interesting theories about the relationship between humanity and dogkind. I have read many of them. I am an unashamed and unrepentant doggie person. My own relationship with our canine friends goes back almost as long as I do, back to infancy. So dogs and I get on well. We have been about each other a long time, and there has not been a time when I can recall being dogless.

Even in the mid-1970s when I was imprisoned (interned without trial if you must know, but that is another story), me and a few similarly doggie-minded comrades managed to steal a black and white collie pup from the British army squaddies who kept the pup's mother as a pet. When the litter of wee ones arrived it was relatively easy to knock one off. It was harder to hide it in the high security section of the prison camp in which we were domiciled, so "our" pup didn't last long before it was returned by our inquisitive guards to its anxious mother; but it was worth the risk. I retell this story only to give you some sense of the calibre of doggie person you are dealing with: a real Steve McQueen hard-chaw, hard-core, irredeemable, never-say-die doggie man. Yes, sir.

I got my first dog when my Uncle Sean emigrated to Canada. His dog was called Darkie. Darkie wasn't allowed to leave so I inherited him. I was about five; Darkie wasn't much older, but he was bigger. In fact he was almost German Shepherd size. Which was useful, especially when the boys of our street clashed with those from the neighbouring streets in mock and sometimes, as we got older, not-so-mock battles. Many a fight was won when Darkie arrived on the scene to scatter our foes. He used to follow me to school, and once he ran alongside the bus when me and my granny journeyed from our neighbourhood to visit relatives in the suburbs. Darkie was a wonderful dog, the first of a long line of worthy mutts whom I have been honoured to know over the years.

When Darkie died, Rory came along. Rory was a small mongrel, a cross between a fox and a bull terrier. He was all white except for a brown patch over his left ear and eye. By this time we were living in Ballymurphy, a new but badly designed and even more badly built public housing estate on the lower slopes of the Belfast hills in the west of the city. Rory and I and our friends spent all our free time in those hills, on the Divis and Black Mountains. When Rory disappeared never to return again, I cried for weeks and frantically searched everywhere in vain for my friend. Even now I have to confess to a certain lump in my throat as I write these lines.

There was an epidemic of dogs in Ballymurphy at that time, and many of the men bred lurchers. They are a cross between a greyhound and anything calculated to increase speed or stamina. The lurchers were used for hunting, and they weren't really street dogs at all. Every other dog was. Canines of all shapes and sizes, all colours and pedigrees, they roamed the place at will, usually with a gang of small boys somewhere in tow. They weren't really considered to be pets. They were much too equal for that status. They were part of the family. In fact, every dog had its full title by right to the family name.

So we had Rory Adams, Spot Grogan, Lassie Magee, Snowy Gillen, Randy O'Toole and so on. Once my brother's wee girl came into the house in tears with her terrier in her arms,

"Mammy," she sobbed, "isn't our Tiny called Tiny Adams?"

"Yes," her mother replied.

"Well, will you come out and tell these wee boys. They say she is Jack Russell."

Incidentally, Tiny was a bit of a monster. Jack Russells are like that: yappy wee dogs. I've never had one myself, but I have been herded by them a few times. Once I got a Jack Russell pup for a women who needed a little company because she lived on her own; the dog lived till it was fifteen years of age.

Our cocker lived almost as long. She was knocked down. Once we had three dogs. That wasn't so so long ago either. Two dogs and a bitch. We had to send one of the dogs away to the country because he and the other dog fought all the time. A dog will rarely fight with a bitch, but two bitches or two dogs can be quite quarrelsome. Now we have a dog and a bitch. The dog is a rottweiler. Cara, which is the Irish word for friend, is his name. He is a decent sort. The other one is nice also. She is nearly all King Charles and she is very handsome. She is a lap dog. Her name is Oscar.

Some other time I will tell you how Oscar got her name and about other dogs I have known.

1 March 1999

Faraway in Australia

Gerry Adams visited Sydney, Melbourne, Brisbane and Perth with a Sinn Féin delegation in February 1999.

If you ever get the chance to go to Australia – go. It's a wonderful place. The publisher of this newspaper described it to me as having all the best aspects of the USA and Europe, and he was right. It has all that and more. I was there last month for a week as part of Sinn Féin's effort to build our international support and to consolidate global support for the peace process. Our delegation visited Sydney, Melbourne, Brisbane and Perth in a hectic round of speaking engagements, press interviews, political meetings and television broadcasts.

I was there because of a successful effort by the Australian-Irish to get a visa ban on me removed. The Australian government until now has refused to let me visit. When pressed to explain why, the government spokespersons said that it was because I was not of good character, which is exactly the reason given when the Irish were transported there 200 years ago when Australia was an English penal colony. It is a funny old world. Indeed, and it is, and Australia is the oldest part of it, or at least the earth's crust there is the oldest. That is maybe why it is so primitive and harsh a place in terms of terrain and animal life. But it is also a relaxed and tolerant place. Or at least as far as I could see that's the way it is.

We met the aboriginal people wherever we went. Indeed, at my first press conference in Sydney, I introduced myself as an aboriginal person from Ireland. The Aborigines are a very spiritual people. In many ways their culture is similar to the traditional culture and customs of Ireland. They, like us, have an affinity with the land, and they like us have been cruelly treated by the colonisers.

Hibernophiles will be pleased to learn that the Irish in Australia get on well with the native people. This is not a recent development. Among the aboriginal people we met, there was a man called Mike Dobson and a woman by the name of Lowitja O'Donoghue. Their grandfathers came from Monaghan and Cork. Irish names are not uncommon among the Aborigines, and one of their foremost leaders, we were told, was named McGuinness. Every Irish event we attended included aboriginal people.

In Australia one in every three people traces their antecedents to Ireland. The links are old and enduring, beginning most notably following the suppression of the United Irish movement, with the transportations from 1791 onwards. By 1861, an analysis of the inhabitants of British colonies from as far afield as Tobago showed that the highest percentage of Irish in the Empire abroad was to be found in Australia. Yet the Irish in Australia do not seem to be as powerful as they are in the States. In this regard Australia could be the USA a hundred years ago. The Irish are represented in political life at leadership level, and in the labour movements – which are generally more militant than unions elsewhere. Maybe that is why they exist, unlike unions elsewhere? In corporate Australia the Irish are well represented also. And in the media.

We are also prominent in the literary world. Among the early poets of Australia, names such as O'Dowd and Fitzgerald stand out. In the genre of the novel, Colleen McCullough of *Thornbirds* fame and Thomas Kenneally, renowned for *Schindler's Ark* and *The Great Shame*, are among the world's best known writers.

The Australians are rightly proud of their "convict" history. The stories are legion, especially stories of political exiles. One with a USA connection is about the rescue of six Irish Republican or Fenian exiles in 1876. This rescue effort, like many other unsuccessful ones, was financed and planned by other Fenians from North America. The exciting and dramatic adventure aboard the whaler *Catalpa*, on which the escapees voyaged to America, galvanised the Irish worldwide.

So why today are the Australian-Irish less influential than the American-Irish? Distance from Ireland is a factor. The emergence of the USA, unlike Australia, as a world power is another. And, unlike the USA, Australia has no president, much less one who traces his lineage to Ireland. The English queen is, at this time anyway, the Australian head of state. And therein lies one of the reasons for the difference in influence between the Irish in Australia and the Irish in the USA. The USA is an independent republic. It has a good relationship with the British but it is

1 March 1999

not a dominion of theirs. This very issue is a big one in Australia at this time.

It is a real debate filled with passion. As one prominent Irish-Australian said to me, "I won't take Australian nationality until they become a nation." But without a charismatic figure leading the Republican argument, the prime minister, Mr Howard, a noted royalist, may succeed in confusing the referendum issues so that the future relationship with Britain may contain considerably more ambiguity than most patriotic Australians desire. While that remains the case, the huge goodwill in that vast and wonderful land for the cause of Ireland will find it difficult to attain the same influence as that other part of the diaspora in the USA.

I was asked at my last press conference in Perth to describe in one sentence how I felt about Australia.

"I want to come back," I said. And I do.

G'day! G'day!

Happy St Patrick's Day to you all.

An Irish Journal

Beware the Ides of March

At the end of February, David Trimble warned that he intended to press for the transfer of powers to a new Executive, even without Sinn Féin participation. On 3 March, British Secretary of State Mo Mowlam signalled her willingness to delay the triggering of devolution, while Deputy First Minister Designate Seamus Mallon called on the IRA to make a statement indicating that its campaign of violence was over.

There is a fallacy abroad that the only outstanding part of the Good Friday Agreement is the failure thus far of the IRA to decommission its weapons. The truth is that there are many aspects of the Agreement which have yet to be implemented. Some of these are matters like policing, which is the business of a commission that has some time yet to deliver its recommendations. Other aspects, like the institutions which should have been formed last year, are still outstanding because the Agreement has been breached by the Unionists. The issue of decommissioning is one of the few issues which is being dealt with in the terms of the Agreement, both in the spirit and the letter. The British government knows this. So does the Irish government. And the UUP leader Mr Trimble.

Yet Mr Trimble is pushing the entire process to the cliff edge. There must be, he insists, a verifiable and credible beginning of the process of decommissioning by the IRA before he will take part in the Executive or the other institutions which he signed up to on Good Friday. Mr Trimble is rewriting the Agreement. He knows this. So do the two governments and all the other participants. Decommissioning is not a precondition, but it is an objective which all of us need to strive to achieve. That is what Sinn Féin is doing, earnestly and seriously, both in the letter and the spirit of the Agreement.

Yet Mr Trimble is being supported or at least not being challenged by the governments. Why? Because he is threatening to walk out of the process unless he has his way. That is the essence of the pending crisis. Mr Trimble does deserve and he has been given credit for saying yes to the Agreement. The hesitant way

8 March 1999

that he did so, the half-a-step-forward/two-steps-back nature of his engagement, and the minimalism and at times downright rudeness of his approach since Good Friday, has been forgiven because of the essential need to have mainstream Unionist involvement in the process.

The hope that Mr Trimble may yet become a Mr de Klerk has insulated many of us against the frustrating negativity of his largely tactical attitude to the process. Patience and perseverance has got the process to this point, and the recent three quarters majority vote in the Belfast Assembly cleared the way for the British government to activate the mechanism to establish the Executive and the other institutions. Sinn Féin was assured by the British government that this would be done early in March so that power could be transferred from London and Dublin by 10 March. This was also the British government's public position. It now appears that London is going to break that commitment. If this is the case, then a British government will have acquiesced to the Unionist veto, perhaps only temporarily, once again.

And let us be clear about one thing: the Unionist game plan is not only about renegotiating the Good Friday Agreement and minimising, diluting and delaying the changes upon which it is predicated. The game plan also envisages the expulsion of Sinn Féin from the political process and the collapse of the peace process. Those who subscribe to this scenario, including elements within the British establishment though not the political leadership of Tony Blair and Mo Mowlam, hold to the old failed policies which seek the defeat of Republicanism and Nationalism, and particularly the defeat of the IRA. They are trying to force the IRA back to war in the misguided belief that a military victory over that group is still possible.

For those who believe this, the peace process is war by another means. They seek to slow it down so that the process of change is thwarted. They are prepared to slow it down for long enough, if they are permitted, in order to force the Republicans out, mop up the IRA and cast Sinn Féin into darkness. Then they hope to bring together what they consider to be more compliant elements of Nationalism with mainstream Unionism, and the Union is saved once again.

I have no doubt that David Trimble has contemplated these matters, but I am willing to give him the benefit of the doubt at this time. He is certainly not a willing exponent of the Good Friday Agreement, but he has come a long way. He knows he is wrong on the decommissioning issue, yet he persists in pushing it as a precondition. Will he push it to the point of collapsing the Agreement?

Yes. If the two governments let him. And given the failure to keep to commitments on the formation of the Executive and the other institutions, which I believe will become clear this week, London and Dublin will have to exert themselves in the weeks ahead with a greater focus than hitherto if the Agreement is to be saved. That is the reality. Mr Trimble is threatening to crash the process over guns which have been silent. He is ignoring the rights and entitlements of all those people who voted for the Agreement. He is ignoring the democratic mandates of the parties in the Belfast Assembly. He is also ignoring the Good Friday Agreement.

Many Republicans are justifiably frustrated at the slow pace of the peace process, but they should not be blinded by this. Indeed, there is an onus on all Republicans to understand the Unionists' game plan and to resist the short-sighted, destructive provocations which it contains. There is equally an enormous responsibility on all of us who have argued that politics can work, that politics can deliver real change, to prove that this is the case. The responsibility of the two governments cannot be underestimated. They should establish all of the institutions without delay. If they do not uphold and implement all aspects of the Agreement, then who will?

Sinn Féin have made it clear that we are totally and absolutely committed to democratic and peaceful means. All parties with entitlement to ministerial office will take a pledge. Those who hold office should use only democratic, non-violent means, and those who do not should be excluded or removed from office. If Mr Trimble needs any guarantees, then they lie within this clause of the Agreement and not in any kamikaze demand from the unreconstructed regions of Unionism.

15 March 1999

LIVING TO 110!

During the previous week, newspapers reported the the RUC had warned Gerry Adams of a possible assassination attempt.

There is a possibility that someday someone will kill me. He could be from the British secret services or acting by proxy at the behest of the British secret services. He could be an element from the British Crown forces disgruntled by the changes that will have to occur if a truly lasting and just settlement is to be the outcome of the peace process. He could be part of the myriad of Loyalist groups, some currently on ceasefire, some still hyperactive on killing missions at this time. Or he could be from some Republican microgroup.

All of that is possible.

That is why I was not surprised to be told last week that the Royal Ulster Constabulary had information that my life was in danger. My surprise is that the RUC contacted me at all. At other times, I have heard of plots to kill me through the media, from evidence in court cases or from other sources. Never once until last week had the RUC given me information that would help me take security precautions.

On the contrary, the RUC continues to deny me access to the basic security services available to other elected member of parliament. This is despite the fact that my home and offices have been bombed and that three people have been killed in my constituency office.

They were killed by an RUC officer who was later found dead of gunshot wounds allegedly inflicted by himself.

I, too, have been shot. It happened after I left a Belfast court building where I had a appeared on a "disorderly" charge that was later dismissed by the magistrate. The charge was brought by the RUC. In the shooting, I sustained five wounds. Three of my companions were also wounded, some more seriously than I.

My attorney had great difficulty getting the RUC to admit that I had been shot when he processed my claim for criminal injuries. Incidentally, I lost the case. The RUC has also refused to give me permission to carry a firearm for my own protection.

An Irish Journal

So you can see that they and I are old adversaries. Indeed, I have taken a civil action against the RUC for illegally detaining me last year at a roadblock in Belfast and preventing me from going about my business as a public representative. The judgment is expected at any time now. I will not be surprised if I lose that case also.

Truly, it is an indication of how much the peace process has brought the RUC under scrutiny that it contacted me at all about this most recent death plot.

The view of all Irish Nationalists and Republicans is that a new, proper policing service is required so that people can have confidence in the police, as opposed to the existing, justifiable distrust of the RUC. The future of that force is currently the business of a policing commission that was established as part of the Good Friday Agreement. That commission, headed up by the former British governor of Hong Kong, Chris Patten, is to deliver its findings this summer. For obvious reasons, the whole issue of policing is a touchstone for the peace process.

And for me, too. As a citizen, taxpayer and public representative, I ought to have been informed by the RUC of any threat to myself or my family. By not doing so, it has denied us our rights. Could you imagine such a thing happening to an elected official in any other jurisdiction?

The killing this week of human rights lawyer Rosemary Nelson is a terrible reminder of the risks taken and the price paid by those who struggle for justice in Ireland. Rosemary was a champion of the oppressed. She was the mother of three young children. She was also under constant threat from the RUC.

So, I take the threat to my life seriously. I have to. That is one of the reasons why I am still alive. But I cannot let these threats deflect me from my responsibilities to our people and to the peace process. Besides that, I have every intention to live to a ripe old age in a free and independent Ireland. If God spares me, my wish is to die at about 110, jogging to the local library or walking back from the local pub.

29 March 1999

HILLSBOROUGH

On 24 March it emerged that Taoiseach Bertie Ahern and British Prime Minister Tony Blair were likely to travel to Hillsborough Castle for talks on the political crisis.

As we go to press the peace process has moved into an acutely focused phase as a result of the rapidly approaching deadline of Good Friday and the presence in Belfast of Taoiseach Bertie Ahern and Prime Minister Tony Blair. The venue of the main negotiations has shifted away from Stormont to Hillsborough, where the larger parties and the two governments have been meeting.

Hillsborough is a beautiful old house set in idyllic parkland with its own lake. Usually the venue for British royal garden parties or stopovers for the English queen or her *clann*, last evening it was the place where Martin McGuinness and I took a leisurely stroll after a hectic round of meetings. Outside the walls, a small, slightly inebriated group of Loyalists sang Orange songs. Inside the walls the rest of us do our best to speed up the search for peace and justice as we try to unthread the Unionist knot tying up the process.

Elsewhere others were busy also. Loyalists broke the window of Sinn Féin Councillor James McCarry's home and threw a bomb inside. James was at a council meeting. The attackers must have known that. The only occupants were Valerie McCarry and the four McCarry children. The attackers must have known that also. Thankfully no one was hurt.

There were other developments. The IRA issued a statement saying that they had located the graves of a number of people executed by them, that they wanted these remains returned to their families and that the IRA was sorry for the distress caused to these families. In my opinion this is a welcome move. For some time now I have made clear my view, publicly and privately, that irrespective of the circumstances involved, these families have a right to properly mourn and grieve. Several years ago I was contacted by a number of my constituents in West Belfast who were concerned about relatives who had been missing since the early seventies and were presumed to have been killed by the IRA. I gave a commitment to do all I could to have this issue thoroughly investigated. It was my view that this was a human rights issue. If families were denied the right to burial, then this was an injustice. And if this injustice was caused by Republicans, then Republicans had to address the issues involved in an honest and forthright way. Whatever the reason given for the killings, the hurt inflicted on the families involved was compounded by their inability to have a burial, to fully engage in a grieving process or to have a grave to visit.

The first breakthrough came eighteen months ago when the IRA announced that it was going to conduct a thorough investigation into the claims that it had executed and buried a number of people in the early 1970s. A senior figure was appointed to conduct the investigation, and the IRA promised to do everything possible to alleviate the plight of the families affected. The IRA also made it clear that this practice had been discontinued at that time. The second breakthrough came this week with Monday's IRA statement. Like the peace process itself, the entire issue of the missing bodies has yet to be brought to a just conclusion, but progress has been made.

There must have been many difficulties involved in trying to get to the truth. The IRA clearly could not be responsible for everyone who has gone missing in the last thirty years. The loved ones of the families who had approached me were missing for over twenty years, and in one case twenty-seven years, so getting someone credible who could investigate these matters must have been difficult enough. The task they faced was mammoth. In the last twenty-seven years many of those who would have been involved in the IRA at the time have left, died or been killed, and of course people who might know what happened would be reluctant to talk. Yet people persevered, especially the families.

There is a lesson there for the rest of us. I don't know if we will be successful this week in our endeavours to advance the peace process, but one thing is for certain. We cannot give up. And Sinn Féin will not give up. All the parties to the Good Friday Agreement know what we have to do. Hopefully by the time you get to read this we will have done just that.

12 April 1999

A State of Chassis

As NATO continues its blitz of Belgrade, Gerry Adams calls for a halt to the bombing; while in Ireland the Unionists continue to refuse to contemplate involvement in new institutions unless the IRA disarms its silent weapons.

Last week's column came to you from the grand opulence of Hillsborough Castle, the official residence in the North of Ireland of the British secretary of state. This week's column comes from a windswept, wet hillside retreat in the wet, windswept west of Ireland. From here it is possible to see the world from a distance. And, as Joxer said, "The world is in a state of chassis."

In former Yugoslavia terrible things are being done by the Serbs, and the televisual images of bewildered people forced to make a slow painful exodus from their homeland makes its own painful commentary on the state we are in. The NATO operations are in turn inflicting their own terrible hurt, and as the flood of refugees intensifies and the blitz of Belgrade blunders on, the situation threatens to get out of control. Given that the search for peace in Ireland is so dependent on USA and British support, I suppose the most politically diplomatic course for me is silence.

But silence provides no refuge from the duty imposed on all of us by the humanitarian demands of this situation. Decency demands an end to all military operations in the Balkan region. The people have suffered enough. For most of this decade there has been conflict, in Croatia and Bosnia at first, now in Kosovo. And now conflict threatens the entire region. Undoubtedly Slobodan Milošević is mainly responsible for the disintegration of Yugoslavia. The ethnic cleansing of the people of Kosovo is unpardonable; the suffering of these refugees is heartbreaking; but the bombing of Belgrade is now affecting the civilian infrastructure, with heating and water supplies being cut off. Who will that hurt? The aged, the infirm and the very young. So on both sides the ordinary people are suffering. It is the same in all wars. A halt must be called to it all. Negotiations are the only way to end conflicts, and the UN has a role to play in brokering a deal to restore sanity.

During the Second World War, 305,000 partisans in this region died fighting alongside Britain, the USA and the other Allied forces. Hundreds of thousands of civilians were killed in that conflagration. Here in our own country elements of our history are being revisited. Attempts to find a way out of the impasse in our peace process before the Good Friday deadline of last week were adjourned until next week. There were some positive developments during these discussions, but the main issue – the blockage created by the Unionists' refusal to contemplate involvement in the institutions agreed over a year ago unless the IRA disarms – remains intact. It will take a mighty effort to break this logjam.

The Unionist demand is clearly outside the Good Friday Agreement, but despite this it has blocked progress. Only through implementating the Agreement will it be possible to find a way forward. The two governments did propose a way forward which they publicised in a draft working paper in the form of a declaration from Taoiseach Bertie Ahern and Prime Minister Tony Blair. But it was impossible to get agreement on this, and it will be totally counterproductive if this declaration is pursued by the governments as an alternative to the Good Friday Agreement. That would be an abandonment of the Agreement and a failure of politics.

The real way forward is through upholding and asserting politics and the imperative of the deal done on these issues. That is a shared responsibility for all the parties involved but particularly for the two governments. Aside from the needs of our own people and the demands of our peace process, there is a bigger issue involved. If they cannot build peace in Ireland, how on earth can they do so in Yugoslavia?

19 April 1999

GOOD FRIDAY AGREEMENT IN FREE FALL

On Thursday, 1 April, the multi-party talks at Hillsborough came to an end and a "Hillsborough Declaration" was agreed by Tony Blair and Bertie Ahern; this set out a framework for progress towards establishing the Executive while making concessions to the Unionist insistence that there should be decommissioning of arms by the IRA before Sinn Féin could sit on an Executive. Efforts to break the deadlock over decommissioning continued, but by 14 April the minister of state for foreign affairs, Liz O'Donnell, acknowledged that the Hillsborough Declaration would not be the basis for resolving the decommissioning impasse. On 15 April, Tony Blair and Bertie Ahern announced a series of bilateral talks in London for 19 April aimed at breaking the deadlock.

The Good Friday Agreement, which is now in its second year, is the political basis of this phase of the Irish peace process. By now if the Agreement had been implemented a structure involving an Executive in the North of Ireland, interlocked with and interdependent on all-Ireland structures including a Council of Ministers, would be in place. For the first time ever Unionists, Republicans and Nationalists would be in a coalition government. Our respective constituencies would by now have a stake in the political process. The rejectionists would be isolated. The transition from conflict into politics would be well advanced, and all of us who are committed to a democratic peace settlement here would be strengthened in our efforts to meet the other challenges of the Agreement.

Instead the Good Friday Agreement is in free fall. The Unionist tactic of using the issue of decommissioning of weapons as a brake on progress has paid off. The entire process is reduced more or less to that issue, and both governments are caught in this trap. Until the recent negotiations at Hillsborough, it was possible to argue that the contention that the implementation of the Agreement was dependent on the IRA doing something on weapons was entirely a Unionist position. It was also outside the Agreement. But at Hillsborough when the two governments published a working draft paper in the form of a joint declaration, they moved on to that ground. They also moved outside of the Agreement and away from the common ground on which the Agreement is based.

Since then the governments, and especially the Irish government, have backed away from this Hillsborough Declaration. But the damage is done and the Hillsborough negotiations can be seen as an important physiological moment in the peace process. Even now and even though we are told that the Hillsborough Declaration is dead, the governments have not moved back to the Good Friday Agreement.

I have no confidence that they will, at least not in the short term. For example, I have no confidence that the British government is going to establish the institutions which are the core of the institutional section of the Agreement. I am also concerned that London has yet to publish a demilitarisation strategy as it is obliged to and as it promised us it would as long ago as last November.

There are other issues of concern. The Orange marching season is approaching. That will bring its own difficulties, and those difficulties are already obvious. Almost 120 Catholic homes have been bombed in the last twelve months. Six people have died in these attacks. On Garvaghy Road the siege of that beleaguered community continues, and there are plans to resume a picket on mass-goers at a Catholic church at Harryville, in Ian Paisley's constituency. So the bigots are at their work and busy in the knowledge that they thrive in a vacuum.

There is considerable and justifiable anger within Republican grassroots at all of this. There is also even more anger at the British government's refusal to establish proper independent and international investigations and enquiries into the killings of human rights lawyers Pat Finucane and Rosemary Nelson. Pat Finucane's family have been campaigning now for ten years. Rosemary Nelson was killed last month. Will the Nelson family have to wait this long?

In both these cases there is widespread international interest. Only last week all of this was given a renewed focus by the support for the families' position from United Nations rapporteur Param Cumaraswamy, by the US International Relations

19 April 1999

Committee and by the European Union, which have all called for independent enquiries. This focus has also highlighted the unacceptability of the RUC: the allegations of collusion between it and the Loyalist death squads and RUC harassment of Catholics, all of which is, of course, contrary to the Agreement, which promises that citizens will be free from sectarian harassment.

So the backcloth for the next phase of negotiations is a gloomy one. It is all the more so because of the positive things which have been achieved and the frustration at how much time has been wasted and the knowledge of how much more should have been done. The governments have a lot to do. If they continue with their present stance, then one thing is certain: the Good Friday Agreement is as good as dead.

An Irish Journal

GUNS AND ROSES

As bombs rain down on the Balkans, in Ireland the IRA's guns are silent. Yet still it is the silent guns that are seen as the problem in some quarters.

The world news this weekend is dominated by guns: guns in Denver, Colorado, and the madness which consumed Columbine High School there. My heart goes out to the families of all the dead and injured, and I hope parents and survivors can make some sense of the futility of it all and that they can get some sense into their lives now in the aftermath of that terrible tragedy. Our young people, wherever they are, deserve roses, not guns.

There is also wall-to-wall news of guns and bombs in the Balkans and the craziness of the conflict there. And here in Ireland, while it does not make the world news at this time, not least because of the above, the issue of guns continue to be used as a brake on the peace process. Here, thank God, the guns are mostly silenced. It is, therefore, all the more amazing how tons of bombs dropped in Serbia are morally and politically acceptable to the British government and a jingoistic section of the media, while the silent guns of the IRA, we are told, are a threat to peace.

It was on this weekend six years ago that John Hume, the SDLP leader and recently appointed Nobel Peace Prize recipient, and I publicised our proposals to secure a permanent end to conflict and a democratic peace settlement. A lot of progress has been made in the time since then. Indeed, in many ways, the situation has changed utterly, but so far only on the surface because we have yet to achieve a permanent end to conflict. A variety of Loyalist death squads have carried out over 120 bomb attacks on individual Catholic homes, and the British Crown forces continue to conduct operations on an ongoing basis. There is understandable anger and frustration among Nationalists and Republicans that while we are prepared to work the Good Friday Agreement the Agreement has been effectively sidelined. The causes of conflict have yet to be tackled, and the fundamentals remain unchanged.

26 April 1999

So we have lots of work to do. Talks this week will once again attempt to break the logjam caused by the Unionists' success in linking retrospectively the establishment of governmental structures to the surrender of IRA weapons. This approach ignores the entire logic and direction of the peace process – a process of persuasion and confidence building in the efficacy of politics. Preconditions, vetoes and absolutist demands are no part of the Good Friday Agreement. In fact, they are totally counter-productive, and because of this the Agreement, as I have written here before, is in free fall. Those who seek to minimise, dilute and renegotiate every aspect of the Agreement have effectively closed down a process which represents the only possible prospect of creating the political conditions in which the gun can actually be removed from Irish politics.

The awful reality of the phase we are going through is that I have no confidence that the British government is going to spell out to the Unionists exactly how this process should work. Worse still, it appears to me that London will not implement the Agreement at this time. David Trimble has threatened to resign if Tony Blair does this, and Mr Blair so far has refused to assert the primacy of the Agreement and the deal done over a year ago. So while I will be approaching the latest phase of talks in a constructive mode, I cannot help thinking that if they make such a mess of our situation, how can they hope to resolve other more complex situations elsewhere?

Which brings us to the Balkan situation. Slobodan Milošević is undoubtedly a violator of human rights, but NATO bombing is not the solution to the complex political crisis in that region. All previous experience shows that this type of military intervention by foreign powers only deepens the national and social divisions in the Balkans and postpones the prospect of a peaceful long-term solution. The bombings should stop now and determined efforts for a peaceful negotiated settlement, under the auspices of the United Nations, should be redoubled. Negotiations are the only just way to end conflict. They should begin now.

An Irish Journal

TEN MEN DEAD

Bobby Sands was twenty-seven years old and sixty-six days on hunger strike when he died on 5 May 1981 in the H-Blocks of Long Kesh. During his hunger strike he was elected to the British parliament as MP for Fermanagh/South Tyrone. By August 1981 ten prisoners had died. The hunger strike was aimed primarily at rejecting the British government's attempts to criminalise the struggle for Irish freedom by changing the status of Sands and his fellow cellmates from political to criminal.

Bobby Sands was a very remarkable man. He died at 1.17am on Tuesday, 5 May 1981, after sixty-six days on hunger strike. Bobby was followed soon afterwards by Francis Hughes, who died on 12 May after fifty-nine days on hunger strike. They were the first of ten hunger strikers who were to die in the awful summer of that year. Patsy O'Hara and Raymond McCreesh both died on 21 May after sixty-one days on hunger strike. Joe McDonnell died on 8 July after sixty-one days on hunger strike. Martin Hurson died on 13 July after forty-six days on hunger strike. Kevin Lynch died on 1 August after seventy-one days on hunger strike. Kieran Doherty died on 2 August after sixty-five days on hunger strike. Tom McElwee died on 8 August after sixty-five days on hunger strike. Micky Devine died on 20 August after sixty-six days on hunger strike.

On Sunday last in Belfast there was, as there is every year, a rally in memory of the hunger strikers. Sunday was a beautiful day here. It was unseasonably summery, and those attending the rally sprawled about Dunville Park on the Falls Road, listening to ballads and traditional music before the main speeches. Many of the people there had been active in support of the hunger strikers. Some were former prisoners, but the majority of people were too young to have been part of all that. Many were children. Indeed a young boy and a girl recited poetry, and three Irish dancers, each no more than five or six years old, enchanted us with their baby *Riverdance*.

The state police – the RUC – patrolled the outskirts of the rally, but even their presence could not intrude on the sense of

3 May 1999

celebration as people remembered the huge sacrifice of the hunger strikers and their families. It's hard to believe that all of this happened eighteen years ago. On a sunny day all these years later it all remains so clear, yet at the same time it is impossible to recapture the sense of anguish and near-frenzied emotion which gripped Irish Nationalists at that time.

The hunger strikes of 1981 were the accumulation of five years of the most dreadful phase in our penal history. During this time, up to 600 Irish men and women were held in bestial conditions in the H-Blocks of Long Kesh and in Armagh Women's Prison. All of them were victims of a conveyor belt of British justice: of interrogation centres, no-jury courts, special rules of evidence and draconian laws. Eighty-five per cent of the prisoners were imprisoned on the basis of forced confessions. No corroborative evidence was required.

None of this was new, of course. Other episodes of penal abuse ranging through the history of English involvement in Ireland have been well chronicled. The H-Blocks and Armagh episode came directly out of an effort by the British government to criminalise the prisoners as part of an overall strategy to present the struggle for freedom and justice in Ireland and against British rule as a criminal conspiracy. Prisoners who had been accorded political status up until 1 March 1976 were no longer accorded those rights. The result was that hundreds of prisoners were confined, naked, without the right to exercise, or any of the normal human dignities. They had no reading material, radios or other "privileges".

As the criminalisation strategy intensified and the protest within the prison continued, all cell furniture was removed and the right to the use of the toilet and wash-up facilities was withdrawn. The plight of the prisoners was dire. They were subjected to frequent beatings. Unable to dispose of their waste, they smeared excrement on the walls of their cells. And when the late Cardinal Ó Fiaich visited the H-Blocks in August 1978, he described the conditions as comparable to the "spectacle of hundreds of homeless people living in the sewer pipes of the slums of Calcutta".

It was in these circumstances that the first hunger strike began in the women's prison and the H-Blocks in the winter of

1980. It ended at Christmas of that year with a deal to resolve these matters. All of this had developed against the background of campaigning on the behalf of the prisoners and escalating protests outside the prisons, not least in the USA. With the hunger strike over, everyone waited for the British government to implement their side of the deal. As we all now know, the British government reneged.

Bobby Sands, who was the leader of the prisoners at that time, was the first of this new wave of hungers strikers. I knew him fairly well. Before he was a H-Block prisoner, he and I spent some time in another part of the prison, in another era with political status. Bobby Sands was a very ordinary young man. Space prevents me from retelling his story, but that too has been chronicled elsewhere, not least through his own writings.

If you met Bobby Sands there would be nothing about his demeanour or his appearance that set him apart from the rest of us. Yet this very ordinary young man did a very extraordinary thing. He challenged the British government with the only weapon he had – his own life – and he did so on behalf of other prisoners and on behalf of those for whom he struggled on this island. He resisted all of the tricks and deceits and distractions so that the focus which began with the prisoners shifted to the bigger question of British involvement in Irish affairs and of the right of people to be free.

In the course of this, Bobby Sands became an MP. Two other prisoners, Paddy Agnew and another hunger striker, Kieran Doherty, were elected to the Irish parliament. A British government which tried to criminalise Irish prisoners was criminalised itself while ten men died on hunger strike. Weeks later, the British government gave the protesting prisoners their demands. The hunger strikers defeated their gaolers.

That is why it was appropriate that children recited poetry on a sunny Sunday eighteen years later. That is why it is fitting that children danced in their memory. Bobby Sands would have liked that; so would the other hunger strikers.

10 May 1999

Anger, Frustration and a Job of Work

On Saturday and Sunday, 8–9 May, Sinn Féin held its Ard-Fheis. Gerry Adams once again committed the party to implementing the Good Friday Agreement.

Last weekend the Sinn Féin Ard-Fheis was held in Dublin. Delegates from all over Ireland debated a range of matters of social, economic, cultural and political importance, and joined with visitors from Britain, the USA, Palestine, South Africa and other parts of the world to discuss the course of the peace process since this time last year. I think it would be true to say that all of us believe that the most important political developments in the past fourteen months, and probably in recent modern Irish history, were the Good Friday Agreement and its endorsement in referendum by all of the people of this island. All of the citizens of this island have a stake in the Agreement. Clearly, the vast majority of people who voted Yes did so because they wanted to see a transformation of the situation in the North.

Sinn Féin decided in an historic Ard-Fheis last year to advocate a Yes vote in the referenda. This decision caused difficulties for many of us, and it was taken after weeks of intense debate which saw Republicans accept that the Good Friday document is not an end in itself, but is a transition towards a full national democracy in Ireland. For Irish Republicans, the struggle for full independence and sovereignty is not over. The struggle continues. The mood of the Ard-Fheis and the quality of the debate provided ample evidence that Sinn Féin is neither weary in our stance nor limited in our horizon.

Irish Republicans made substantial concessions in committing ourselves to the Agreement. We did so in the context of our overall objectives and our commitment to the peace process, and because we believed that this would advance the peace process and move us towards those objectives. It is worth noting that the concessions made by us have been largely ignored by those who repeat the propaganda line that Republicans have given nothing.

In my presidential address I committed us once again to

implementing the Agreement. We have participated in the process on that basis and in good faith, and we will continue to do so. This party has honoured all our commitments. The Unionist political leadership and the British government have not. The Good Friday Agreement is now in its second year. The Executive, the All-Ireland Ministerial Council and the other all-Ireland bodies should now be functioning with full power. Instead only one institution, the Assembly, is in partial shadow formation. This is the one institution most desired by Unionists and least desired by Nationalists and Republicans.

Other aspects of the Agreement are in abeyance also. The most obvious of these is the right to "freedom from sectarian harassment" and the "right to freely chose one's place of residence". This is most sharply felt by the people of Garvaghy Road. Portadown is still the Alabama of these islands, and the killing of Rosemary Nelson is the most savage and recent evidence of that. In the wider context, hundreds of people have been forced to flee their homes because of intimidation and violence.

There is a need, as the Orange marching season looms, for the siege of Garvaghy Road to be lifted. Sinn Féin is participating positively and in support of the residents' efforts to achieve this. The Irish government also has a responsibility to defend the people of the Garvaghy Road. Since last July the people there have experienced over ten months of living under siege. Racism and sectarianism have been the daily diet of the men, women and children who have had to endure over 160 Loyalist marches in and around that district. The situation for these people has got worse since the Good Friday Agreement. Their plight is proof of how far we have to go before there is justice.

There are many, many other parts of the Agreement on which there has been little or no progress; for example, the British government is obliged to publish an "overall strategy" on demilitarisation. This was promised last November. We are still waiting. The recent killing of human rights lawyer Rosemary Nelson, the Robert Hamill case and the release of Lee Clegg all demonstrate the corrupt nature of the British judicial system in the North and the unacceptability of the RUC. There is also the killing ten years ago of another human rights lawyer,

10 May 1999

Pat Finucane.

So, it is little wonder that there is a lot of justifiable anger and frustration among Republicans especially, and Nationalists generally, and that some of this was expressed at the Ard-Fheis. In fact, I have been challenged and confronted many times in the last year in private meetings and one-to-one conversations in which Sinn Féin activists have made it clear where they stand. Notwithstanding the justification for this anger, we have a job of work to do, and I told the Ard-Fheis that. I told them we should not be mesmerised by the tactical manoeuvrings of the moment. We need to have a longer-term view – a strategic view. This week the Sinn Féin negotiating team will be in Downing Street at least once. We have urged the two governments to focus on the need to rescue the Agreement. We have also urged them to set a time-frame for the talks. The current negotiations cannot go on indefinitely; they have to move beyond talking.

We have also put a number of ideas, set firmly within the terms of the Good Friday Agreement, which we feel could break the present deadlock. I told the Ard-Fheis this also. It is now up to Tony Blair to create a new context in which he can liberate David Trimble to honour his commitments under the Good Friday Agreement. The next few weeks will show if Mr Blair can rise to that challenge. He made a good start to the process when he came into power. He now has to deliver. The hand of history rests upon his shoulder.

An Irish Journal

RADIOHEADS

Extreme censorship measures were employed for many years by both the British and Irish governments to suppress the voice of Republicanism.

The BBC has a local broadcasting station here in the North of Ireland called Radio Ulster. I am an avid radio fan: while travelling in the car or working at speeches or columns like this, the wireless is good company, and Radio Ulster has some good programmes. I also listen to what we used to call Radio Éireann. That is, RTÉ, the public broadcasting television and radio station in the South of Ireland. It is interesting and educational to flick back and forth between the two stations to listen to the news or current affairs programmes, especially about foreign affairs, and to get the sometimes different spins from the two "official" broadcasting outlets. Of course, there are a lot of commercial stations nowadays, and it is changed times since the days when BBC and RTÉ had a monopoly on broadcasting.

Both these establishments had censorship for many, many years. RTÉ was governed by Section 31 of the Broadcasting Act which forbade interviews with Sinn Féin. These restrictions lasted for almost thirty years, from the early seventies until recent times. This led to some amusing and even bizarre episodes. Indeed, not long after the act was introduced, the Dublin government sacked the entire RTÉ authority. They only had to do this once; the broadcasters got the point.

A programme about mushroom growing went off the rails when it was revealed that one of the mushroom growers featured in interviews was a Sinn Féiner. The same thing happened when the only witness to a dramatic hotel fire in a seaside town was a local Sinn Féin councillor. His account of the inferno was scrapped. At another time, advertisements for a book of mine, *The Street*, were deemed to be unsuitable for broadcasting. A celebrated court case was to involve the reading of passages of the book to the court. My publisher lost the case.

In the North and in Britain, censorship over most of this period was much more subtle. Formal censorship was not

24 May 1999

introduced until 1988. Up to this point the British government relied on the old boys' network to hide the truth of what it was up to in Ireland. Despite this, there were some very good investigative programmes into various aspects of British rule or into miscarriages of justice, and there were more examples of such programmes from British than there were from Irish broadcasters. These, however, were the exceptions.

From 1988 Margaret Thatcher decreed that interviews with Sinn Féin spokespersons could not be broadcast, or at least the voices of Sinn Féin persons could not be broadcast. This led to some broadcasters using actors' voices dubbed into interviews. While there was a certain novelty about this type of approach, it could only work with prerecorded programmes. Live news or breaking stories could not have actors on standby to mouth Sinn Féin words. So the truth lost out (though I have heard it said that my voice was considerably improved by this practice).

In my opinion the direct formal censorship of the British broadcast media was dropped because of US influence. When President Clinton granted me a visa to visit the USA, broadcasters there were amazed to learn that my voice could not be broadcast back home. They were so incredulous about this and they ridiculed it so much that the British became embarrassed. The Irish government had dropped its censorship laws a short while before this, and the Brits soon followed.

Over here nowadays interviews with Sinn Féiners are a dime a dozen, but the old values still prevail. A leaked internal BBC memo declared that all Sinn Féin spokespersons had to be treated as hostile witnesses. So our voices are heard, but only through interruptions and sometimes downright bad-mannered interrogations. Such is democracy. Or at least that genetically modified version of it which survives in this part of Ireland.

But I still love the radio. For music and *craic*, for drama and conversation, it beats most TV programmes any day. Besides, you can do a half a dozen other things while you are listening to the wireless. Even Maggie Thatcher couldn't interfere with that.

An Irish Journal

WE NEED A HEALING PROCESS

This week the news in Ireland is dominated by the search for the bodies of nine people killed by the IRA in the 1970s. These killings happened at the height of the war, and according to the IRA leadership the people killed were informers or agents working for the British government.

Some of the families involved have been campaigning for the return of the remains of their loved ones, and some time ago the IRA leadership committed itself to fulfilling the families' request. This, the IRA pointed out, would be a difficult undertaking. These "executions," it said, "had happened a long time ago. Many of those involved are themselves dead or no longer involved in the IRA." Nonetheless, a senior IRA officer was to be appointed to establish as much detail as possible. As soon as it could, the IRA pledged to reveal the outcome of its inquiries.

While the IRA was conducting its own investigation, the British and Irish governments were also busy. They passed legislation that established a special commission to deal with this sensitive issue. They also gave immunity to anyone involved. This week, that commission was established. Within hours, the IRA acted. A coffin bearing the remains of one of the missing people, Eamon Malloy, was left at Faughart graveyard close to the border in County Louth and passed to the commission. Since then, the media here, understandably, have been in overdrive.

All of those killed and buried in this way were young people. One, Jean McConville, was the mother of nine children. The IRA say she was working for the British army. The rest were young men, mainly IRA volunteers who had become agents of the British. In their statement accepting responsibility for the killings and for the way that the bodies were buried, the IRA pointed out that this practice was stopped at that time. The IRA also apologised to the families.

My response to all of this has been one of mixed emotions. I am glad that this long period of uncertainty and distress is, hopefully, coming to an end for the families involved. I say hopefully because, God knows, there may be further difficulties in retrieving the remains. I hope that this is not the case and that all the remains are returned as quickly as possible. But I pre-

7 June 1999

sume that there could be changes in the terrain and other conditions in the areas where the remains are buried – twenty-five years is a long time – which may even yet cause the closure of this sad chapter to be delayed. The evening news included a statement from the *gardaí* that because all the remains are in the South, this could be a "marathon search".

But perhaps this will not be the case. I can only imagine the trauma and distress the families are going through. I know some of them. Some are Republican families who have given a lot for the cause of Irish freedom in this phase of the struggle. These families have said very little about recent developments.

Others have campaigned justifiably to have their cases heard. I met some of them some years ago and gave Sinn Féin's support to their cause. Whatever the rights or wrongs of the killings of their loved ones, the inability of families to know the truth, to know what happened, was a human rights issue, and if the IRA killed these missing people, then the right of the families to a proper grieving process, to a proper funeral and to a grave to visit was a just demand. The dead could not be brought back to life, but at least the remains could be returned to their families.

It has taken a considerable amount of effort to get this entire issue to the point where it is now. Republicans can expect no praise or thanks for disclosing the locations of these burial spots, and indeed, I do not believe that they expect any. But the IRA did the right thing. It could have ignored the families' requests. It certainly could have survived the campaign. But while that may have been expedient, it would not have been right. Not for an organisation that professes to struggle for justice.

So, too, for Sinn Féin. We are in the midst of an election campaign, and no matter how much we protest that we are not the IRA, the grisly nature of the deluge of media reports is bound to rub off on us. Indeed, some of our opponents and some sections of the media are doing their best to ensure this. No matter. This issue is bigger than party politics. It certainly could not have been brought to this point without the peace process. And that also is, or should be, bigger than party politics.

So my hope is that the families of those killed and buried by the IRA can now conclude their grieving process. Many other families bereaved in this conflict also deserve and desire the truth. Most of them are victims of British actions. But how could I rail against their injustice if I were silent about injustice perpetrated by Republicans?

This phase of our history needs to enter into a healing process. It is difficult to see how this is possible given the failure so far of some of the parties to the Good Friday Agreement to honour the commitment they made, never mind the failure of the peace process to right all the wrongs done in Ireland during the conflict. But that has to be our objective. And in journeying toward that objective, we need to right as many wrongs as we can along the way.

14 June 1999

THE GIFT OF NELSON MANDELA

This is the month that Nelson Mandela stands down as president of South Africa. His retirement marks the end of a unique, exciting and uplifting period in the history of his own country and, in my opinion, in the history of the world this century. In fact, I consider the destruction of apartheid one of the most important and positive development of our time.

The very notion of apartheid is obscene. But it worked in South Africa for a very long time. And it was only overthrown by virtue of very hard work, heroic sacrifices and decades of struggle by the men and women of the African National Congress and their supporters throughout the world. I am pleased to say that Ireland played its own little part in that struggle – certainly no more than we were obligated to do and very little when compared to what people in apartheid South Africa contributed.

Foremost among those is Nelson Mandela. The stories of this man are legend, and it is little wonder that his release from prison was a world event that caught the imagination of freedom-loving people everywhere. In a century that has been plunged into darkness again and again by the horrors of human conflict, the spirit of Nelson Mandela and of the people of South Africa lit a beacon that brightened all our lives.

Mandela was in prison from 1964 to 1990. And he did hard time. The prison regime was cruel and harsh. Yet when he emerged from the shadow of that regime into the brightness of a new day, his magnanimity towered over the pettiness of his jailers and those who oppressed his people.

His release was the beginning of the end of the old ways. The ANC knew that. The apartheid regime did not. It hoped that Mandela's release would end the worldwide campaign for an end to its rule. It also hoped that Mandela himself would fade into retirement and that the ANC would split. In that context, the regime figured that a few reforms of the apartheid system would be enough to satisfy the demands of that time and bring an end to sanctions.

But it made one huge mistake: it believed its own propaganda about the ANC. It believed that black South Africans could not negotiate and that they could not develop and implement strategies. That was the apartheid regime's biggest mistake. It believed that its members were superior and that the black people in South Africa were inferior.

I was in South Africa in 1995 at the invitation of Nelson Mandela. I write that with considerable satisfaction, as it was one of the best experiences in my life. By then, democracy had been restored in the country. I met with President Mandela and with Thabo Mbeki, Cyril Ramaphosa and all their comrades. Walter Sisulu hosted an ANC Executive lunch for our group at the head office in Shell House and regaled us with tales of life in Robben Island prison. Later, I paid a poignant visit to the graveside of ANC leader Joe Slovo. Joe Slovo, a white South Africa progressive and a giant freedom fighter, is buried in a black township cemetery in Soweto – a fitting resting place for a great man.

Later, our group travelled from Durban to Johannesburg and from Capetown to Pretoria. Everywhere, our delegation was greeted with open arms. And everywhere, South Africans of all creeds and classes – all colours – were proud to be South Africans. That was Nelson Mandela's gift to them. That was the example he set. That is the result of his long contribution to the quest for equality and freedom for his own people and for humanity. His interest in the peace process in Ireland has been marked by a series of initiatives over the years. Only a few months ago, at Easter, he phoned me to wish us well in the negotiations at that time.

So it is fitting that Mandela has lived so long and has time now to retire. This week's elections, only the second democratic elections in the history of South Africa, reinforced the ANC's popularity. Thabo Mbeki is a fitting successor to President Mandela. I wish him well. I wish Nelson Mandela well.

Nkosi Sikelel' Afrika.
God Bless Africa.

21 June 1999

BUILDING SUPPORT

Recent elections highlighted the emergence of Sinn Féin as a political alternative party on both sides of the border.

There were three elections and a referendum in Ireland last week. The counts finished up at the beginning of this week. Two separate elections were to the European Parliament – one for each state on this island. There was also a local government election and a referendum about local government in the South.

Sinn Féin contested all of these elections. We were the only party in Ireland to do so. That was an achievement in itself. Sinn Féin is still a relatively small party. There are two different political realities in the two parts of partitioned Ireland. Of course, there are a lot of characteristics common to each state. In a country as small as this, it could not be otherwise. But two different political realities demand two different sets of policy documents and two different sets of research material and all the related analysis and information. That needs resources. It needs infrastructure. It needs skilled people. Election campaigns need candidates, campaign managers and publicity managers – more skilled people, more resources.

Sinn Féin is a party in transition. We are building our structures, developing our skills, and training and equipping our activists. Our successes in the North last year in the elections to the Assembly opened up gaps in the party that we are still filling. Many of our middle leadership moved into Assembly positions or into support roles for the newly elected members. And because of the demands of the peace process and the multilateral negotiations involved, most of our national leadership cannot pay the kind of attention to party building that is required at this time.

For all these reasons, Sinn Féin could not hope to realise its potential in these latest elections. I said that at the beginning of the campaigns. Nonetheless, we were able to mount a credible campaign. We had Mitchel McLaughlin, our national chairperson and an outstanding candidate, in the North. Here, our strategy was to target the third seat, as Ian Paisley and John

Hume were obviously going to win the first and second seats. Ours was an uphill battle because the gerrymandered nature of the statelet guarantees the Unionists two seats. Yet Mitchel ran the Ulster Unionist Party candidate to a third count, doubling our European vote in the process and coming within less than 2,000 votes of outpolling the UUP man.

We trebled our Euro vote in the South. We outpolled the Labour Party on first preferences votes in Connaught-Ulster and Munster, and we beat the outgoing Labour member of the European Parliament in Dublin. This was despite the almost singular focus of our organisation on the local elections. Republicans, North and South, have never been well motivated by the European Union contest. This was even more true this time in the South because the local activists had some sense that we could make a breakthrough this time around.

And we did! Indeed, the Sinn Féin performance was the main feature of this contest. We went from seven county council seats to twenty-one. We got thirty-one urban district council seats and ten town commissioners – sicxty-two seats in all, not a lot in the scheme of things but a very good beginning with our party moving into position as the fourth largest party in the state. So far.

But almost as important as the size of the vote was the spread of the vote. Not only did we break through in the border counties of Louth and Cavan and receive a huge consolidation of our support in Monaghan and advances in Sligo, but we did well in Cork, too. And in the capital, where the Dubs elected no fewer than six. Right across sixteen out of twenty-six counties, there are Sinn Féin elected representatives.

This was indeed mighty work. We now have the emergence of Sinn Féin as an alternative to the other parties and uniquely the only one transcending partition because we are organised nationwide. From Buncrana to Ballymurphy, from Bantry to Ballycastle, from Wexford to Waterford and various places in between, a vibrant, relevant and focused political community is emerging.

It's now time to organise for the next elections – building support for a bigger and better contest. It's hard work. But it's worth it.

21 June 1999

A LONG HOT SUMMER?

The Protestant sectarian organisation, the Orange Order, organises some 3,000 marches every summer. A few of these, which the organisers insist on pushing through Nationalist areas, where they are not welcome, cause enormous problems. For the fifth year in a row, attention is focused on the Orange parade at Drumcree, Portadown, County Armagh, which constantly seeks to march down the mainly Catholic Garvaghy Road. This year an extra march is being organised: the "Long March", which is due to travel through more than a hundred miles of the North of Ireland.

For those of you who have to endure the awful furnace temperature of New York or Los Angeles, or all the other hot spots in between, Ireland would be a great change. At this time of the year the place is luscious, wickedly so, with that lush greenness which Johnny Cash made famous. All forty shades of it have seduced me on my travels throughout the countryside this last few weeks. All that greenness compensates for the rain which nourishes it, and this month has had its fair share of sunshine so that you really can see the grass grow. There is nothing like it.

I like the sun, of course, but not that baked variety that the USA and other deserts contend with at this time. I like little warm breezes and soft days. Unless of course I have nothing to do, but even then lying in the sun was never my type of holiday. A few days of that is fair enough, or a few hours a day would not be too bad, but dropping down dead or frying is not my idea of fun. Especially if I have things to do, which true to tell and unfortunately most of the time is how I am. Doing things, that is. And I definitely don't know how I could do anything if it was too hot.

That is why Ireland in June suits me. There is only one problem: July comes after June. And in Ireland July means "the mad month". July means Orange marches. Three thousand of them over the summer. This year an extra march is being organised: the "Long March" is due to travel throughout a hundred and odd miles stretch of the North of Ireland.

An Irish Journal

I have already made it clear that provided it does not seek to go through Nationalist areas, Nationalists should ignore this march. Our main concern, and that of all democrats, should be to defend and uphold the rights of beleaguered communities like the Garvaghy Road area of Portadown, which is now under siege for almost a year. The "Long March" is about telling the people there who is in charge. It is about triumphalism, domination and sectarian supremacy. It is about forcing a march down Garvaghy Road. The people of that area have made it clear that they do not want an Orange march on Garvaghy Road, and nothing should deflect from that legitimate position.

There is no overriding right to march. That right has to be set against the right of individuals and communities to live free from fear and sectarian harassment. The Nationalist people of Portadown have lived in fear for a very long time. Their situation has worsened significantly since the Good Friday Agreement was signed. The shadow of sectarian hatred hangs over Portadown, and Nationalists view this "Long March" as provocative.

The Orangemen have quoted Martin Luther King in defence of their demand to march wherever they choose. This has angered and annoyed many people. If those Unionists who are using Martin Luther King to defend their position are serious and genuinely converted to this position and are embracing the spirit of Martin Luther King, that means accepting King's view that: "White America must recognise that justice for black people cannot be achieved without radical changes in the structure of our society." In the context of the North of Ireland, the logic of this position is that Unionists must recognise that justice for Nationalists cannot be achieved without radical changes in the structure of our society.

Unfortunately, the Unionist leaderships have not accepted that. Not yet anyhow. Change is traumatic for everyone, particularly those who perceive change to be to their disadvantage. But no one should be afraid of equality or of dealing with others on the basis of equality. That is the real test for the march organisers. They are threatening all of us with a long hot summer if they do not have their way. This is the background against which the latest round of negotiations about the peace

21 June 1999

process are to begin. This is no coincidence. The "mad month" has its own agenda. It is not peculiar to July, but it is one reason, despite the beauty of this season in Ireland, why some people here hate the summer.

An Irish Journal

GROUNDHOG DAY

On Tuesday, 15 June, Taoiseach Bertie Ahern said that the Irish and British governments would "set aside" the Good Friday Agreement and seek alternative means of political progress if a breakthrough was not made by 30 June. British Prime Minister Tony Blair said that the governments would "have to look for another way forward" if the devolution deadline were missed. On Tuesday, 22 June, Bertie Ahern said the Executive must be established before paramilitary weapons were decommissioned. Ahern said it would be possible to persuade paramilitaries to disarm only "in the context of a confidence in functioning democratic institutions".

Regular readers will have some sense of the difficulties which beset this column as we try to rise to the challenges of peacemaking. Everyone, I am sure, is fatigued by now with the endless circular arguments by which all the various factions, including the two governments, seek to defend or advance their own positions. At times it is as if we never had an agreement on these matters; it is all very frustrating, annoying and downright stupid and counter-productive.

But now there is a change. The two governments have said that there has to be a return to the Good Friday Agreement. That is a welcome, if long overdue, acknowledgement of where we should have been all along. It doesn't make the difficulties facing the peace process any less, it doesn't make the challenges any easier, but at least now we have a blueprint to guide us. The fact that that blueprint has been there since Easter 1998 and that it has been largely ignored is something which could cause any sane person to break down and cry. But while that may be the politically correct and, more importantly, the emotionally correct response, it would also be beside the point. Or at least it is a point that wouldn't be worth making. It is better to be thankful for small mercies, because having taken the scenic route, guided by those who said they knew the way, and having got lost, we are now hopefully back at the starting point with some chance of actually making it this time to our destination. That is,

28 June 1999

if we really are back to the Agreement and if the two governments don't let those who want to go somewhere else hijack the process once again.

British Prime Minister Tony Blair has made it clear that he isn't going to hang around for ever waiting for the Agreement to be implemented. On 1 July the British government is devolving power to Scotland and Wales. The same thing was to happen here, with both the Irish and British governments devolving power, but they have to have something to devolve powers to. And there's the rub.

Under the terms of the Good Friday Agreement, by now – in fact, by last November – a range of all-Ireland institutions should have been in place in shadow formation with a programme of government agreed. But the Unionists' refusal to do the business and to abide by the Good Friday Agreement means that none of this has happened. Neither has the British government delivered on all its commitments. For example, the long-promised publication of a strategy of demilitarisation has yet to be seen. In many areas, particularly South Armagh, instead of demilitarisation there has been remilitarisation. So, too, with the equality agenda. There has been little or no progress so far.

There is a lot to be done. This is especially so on the issue of Orange marches. As I have written here before, the Orangemen have the right to march. This means over 3,000 Orange marches. But there is no absolute right to march, especially into areas where the Orangemen are unwelcome, so there should be no Orange march on Garvaghy Road. The residents' refusal to acquiesce to a march is entirely reasonable and should be upheld by the two governments and the Parades Commission.

By the time you get to reading this, the next phase – and, we are told, the last phase – of this process of negotiations will probably be over. I will be in these negotiations to make them work. There is no alternative. No one should be contemplating failure. I have spoken to Mr Blair within the last few minutes. In fact, I interrupted this column to speak to him by phone. I spoke to the taoiseach earlier today. I told them both that it is my opinion that despite all of the difficulties, we can see all the institutions established and all the other outstanding and delayed aspects of the Good Friday Agreement implemented. That will require political will, determination and a large dose of common sense. It will also require a very focused understanding by all concerned that the only terms which can bridge the impasse are those which were agreed on Good Friday 1998.

5 July 1999

THE WAY FORWARD?

On Friday, 2 July, after a week of negotiations, including five days of discussions between the British and Irish governments at Stormont, the two governments issued a document called "The Way Forward" outlining a way forward to establish an inclusive executive, and to decommission arms.

A week is a long time in politics, especially here. The week of negotiations which concluded on Friday, 2 July, was an exhausting seven days, especially for your columnist. It was a week which saw Sinn Féin putting proposals to the Unionists. Twice. It was a week when the Unionists rejected our proposals. Twice!

The Sinn Féin approach to this latest phase of the peace process was first developed at the end of April and explained to the British and Irish governments at that time. Chief negotiator Martin McGuinness outlined these ideas to responsive US officials in Washington on 5 May, and they were further developed in discussions with the taoiseach and British prime minister in London on 6 May.

At the core of the Sinn Féin approach was a clear statement:
- that the two governments were returning to the Good Friday Agreement;
- that the impasse could be removed only within the terms of the Agreement;
- that there were no pre-conditions;
- that a deadline be set for the establishment of the political institutions which have been delayed until now;
- acknowledging that all parties to the Agreement have an obligation to help to bring about decommissioning.

Throughout all our engagements, the Sinn Féin team made it clear that it is only through the full implementation of all elements of the Good Friday Agreement, and all the parties and the two governments discharging our collective responsibility in regards to its terms, that the issue of arms under the aegis of the de Chastelain commission, as set out in the Agreement, can be finally and satisfactorily settled. This is the best guarantee that guns will never again have a role in the politics of this island. In all of this, the Sinn Féin focus and strategy was to keep the negotiations faithful to these requirements. Space restrictions and diplomatic imperatives prevent your columnist from disclosing the twists and turns, ups and downs, advances and retires, the jigs and reels which this required; suffice to say that it was heavy going.

Eventually the two governments issued their "Way Forward" propositions, and the negotiations concluded. Or so everyone thought. But now Mr Trimble is insisting on an exclusion clause in the legislation promised by the British government to underpin the fail-safe clause of last week's joint statement by the Irish and British governments. He wants to see the exclusion of Sinn Féin, but under the terms of the Good Friday Agreement this is not possible. There is no question of the British government introducing legislation to expel Sinn Féin; Mr Blair knows this would be a breach of the Good Friday Agreement. He also knows that there can be no renegotiating of the Agreement or of the propositions put forward by the two governments on Friday last. The Good Friday Agreement review section is crystal clear. There is no requirement for legislation at all beyond that already in place, and any British legislation has to be based on this review section. Mr Trimble knows this also. He also knows that Sinn Féin is serious when we say that we want this process to succeed. He can no longer delay the attainment of full rights and entitlements for that section of our people who have been denied these rights and entitlements for so long; not if he is really committed to the Good Friday Agreement.

The two governments, and in particular the British government, have a major responsibility in securing a satisfactory outcome to the issue of arms. Historically, the British government has been a hugely negative factor in the development of the conditions of conflict in Ireland. The conflict arises from the British government's involvement in Irish affairs. It was the British government which brought the gun into Irish politics. They must now play a central role in the creation of a future on this island in which the gun has no place. This is the challenge which all of us in positions of political leadership face. I firmly believe that it is a challenge we can meet.

5 July 1999

For my part, I reiterate my total commitment to doing everything in my power to maintain the peace process and to removing the gun for ever from the politics of our country and, through the out-working all of the new institutions, to creating a society in which there is total respect for Catholic, Protestant and Dissenter.

The initiative in the process to establish the new institutions rests with the British government. Mr Blair has said the d'Hondt procedure to nominate ministers will be run on 15 July. The transfer of power will take effect on 18 July. This is not the first time that the British government has set a deadline, but this time the deadline must be kept. The Unionists cannot for ever delay and prevaricate. The institutions must be established. The choice for the British government and the UUP is simple. The Unionist veto continues or the Good Friday Agreement is implemented.

The Challenge for Prime Minister Blair

On 15 July, the attempt to form the Assembly Executive collapsed when David Trimble, first minister designate, and other UUP Assembly members failed to turn up at the Assembly.

Last week was a watershed in the Irish peace process. Instead of a new government for the North, we had the sight of empty chairs and ticking clocks in the Assembly chamber in Belfast. For those watching the live coverage on their television screens, the absence of the Ulster Unionist Party must have been bizarre and unreal.

But as people have a chance to absorb the enormity of what occurred, I believe they will come to realise in hindsight that last Thursday was one of those pivotal days in the peace process.

How did we get here? David Trimble must have known that he could not dodge his responsibilities for ever. The house was bound to come crashing down around him because of his refusal to behave as a first minister designate. He got away with it for so long because the two governments gave him enormous latitude. How long did he think this would go on?

For example, before Thursday, the British government had set deadlines five times and then had moved off those deadlines as a result of Unionist manoeuvring. How long did Trimble think he could keep moving those deadlines? Both British Prime Minister Tony Blair and Taoiseach Bertie Ahern had engaged in crisis negotiations at various venues throughout the North and in London, all to no avail. How long did Trimble think he could continue to threat his own prime minister and the Irish taoiseach in that way?

The big question now is – where do we go from here? In seeking to figure that out, we need to examine the causes of the problems that have beset this island. One is the Unionist veto and the other is British policy. What has been happening in recent days is not really a battle between Irish Republicanism (or Irish Nationalism) and Unionism, but a battle between the Unionists and the British government. It is between the Unionist veto and British policy.

The securocrats in the British military and intelligence establishment (who have never been happy with the peace process) and those who make up the "permanent government" (who shape so much of British policy) appear to have moved this British government away from the inclusive ethos that underpinned the Good Friday Agreement. They are back to the failed notions of exclusion, marginalisation, and security options. This is the road to failure, and the British government needs to get off it quickly.

Understanding and recognising this makes it possible for us to chart a course through our current difficulties to the future. It means persuading this British government that Unionism is not only opposed to change, but also, quite clearly after recent events, opposed to sharing power with Nationalists and Republicans. And for some Unionists, that means refusing to share power with Catholics.

The two governments, especially the British government, must make clear to Unionism that the status quo is unacceptable; inequality, discrimination and injustice will not be tolerated; and that Unionists must come to terms with the reality of change.

That means immediate, urgent implementation of the other aspects of the Good Friday Agreement which are outstanding. If the Unionist leaderships think they are going to prevent the implementation of an equality agenda, the governments must prove them wrong. If they think they can prevent the establishment of a human rights regime, or of all the other necessary changes in social, economic, political and cultural affairs here, the governments must prove them wrong. If they think they can hold on to their armed wing, the Royal Ulster Constabulary, and prevent the establishment of a real policing service, then once again, the two governments must show them that they are wrong.

The governments, but particularly Tony Blair, must demonstrate the primacy of politics; he must insist that change will happen. The Republicans could have walked away from the process at any time in the last number of years. But we didn't — because we believe in the future. The credo of our philosophy is based upon the view that the people of this island can shape our future together within a new dispensation of peace and equality, between Orange and Green. We believe in the people of this island – all the people, Unionists and Nationalists alike.

Sinn Féin wants to work with Unionism. This process can succeed, but only if all political leaders face up to our responsibilities. Equality has to be the order of the day. Nothing else will do; Trimble needs to understand that.

But of course, the biggest challenge is to Tony Blair. He knows as well as I do that the progressive changes in British policy that he has brought about need to be implemented. Because either British policy will prevail, and the Good Friday Agreement will be implemented, or the Unionist veto will prevail. Only one of these roads leads to the future.

Sinn Féin knows which road we want to take. Despite all of the difficulties and the bad faith, our immediate goal is to work with others in breathing new life into the Good Friday Agreement. We are totally committed to this, and we are asking others to demonstrate that same commitment and work with us.

That is the only reliable guarantee for our future, but it will not succeed unless Tony Blair faces up to the challenge facing him.

2 August 1999

JOHN F. KENNEDY JR

On Friday, 16 July, a light plane carrying John F. Kennedy Jr, his wife Carolyn and her sister Lauren Bessette crashed off Martha's Vineyard; all three on board died instantly.

Some years ago when I was asked to speak to the editorial board of *George* magazine, I didn't fully appreciate the esteem in which its owner, John F. Kennedy Jr, was held by the American public. Of course, I knew he was the late President Kennedy's son, but that was the extent of my familiarity with him. Kieran Clifford, a friend, and a bright young woman who worked in our Washington office, set me right.

"If you meet John Kennedy, get me his autograph. He is something else."

As it turned out, he was actually a quiet-spoken, courteous and gracious man who welcomed me to his magazine's boardroom, listened intently as I answered all manner of questions from a large, and mainly young, group of interested and intelligent staffers, and then thanked me as he accompanied me and our group from the building.

Mairead Keane, who headed up our mission in the USA at that time, was enthusiastic about the meeting.

"He was really interested," she said.

I thought so, too. But in an extremely busy schedule, with half my head back home in whatever was happening in Ireland at that time, I had little opportunity to ponder on that particular editorial meeting. But still, the engagement with John Kennedy made an impression on me. So, some time later, despite my usual reluctance to do magazine interviews without all manner of assurances about the project, when I was asked to do an interview with him, I immediately agreed. I was pleasantly surprised to be told he was coming to Ireland for this.

That was in June, 1997. It was around the time that a Republican prisoner, Paddy Kelly, died in jail. When he was imprisoned in Britain, the refusal of the authorities to provide proper medical treatment had caused outrage in Ireland. His death came at yet another critical point in the peace process. I attended the funeral. So did John Kennedy. His interest was obviously journalistic, but I was conscious of him standing slightly apart from the main funeral party in a beautiful old graveyard on that sad summer day in County Laois. All of us were touched by the way that Paddy died, and the pipers' wailing lamentation moved everyone.

Later, John and I did our interview in the Sinn Féin head office in Dublin. He was direct and searching in his questions, and our exchanges were friendly, but robust. At the end, we arranged for him to do follow-up questions by phone closer to his publication date, and he told me he was taking up my invitation, from our first meeting at the *George* office in Washington, to visit West Belfast the following day.

Unfortunately, my schedule had me out of town, but I arranged for Richard and Chrissie McAuley to act as hosts for the visit. John insisted on travelling from Dublin by train, and Richard and Chrissie picked him up off the early morning express in Belfast, where within five minutes the three of them came face to face with heavily armed British soldiers patrolling the Nationalist markets area. It was just a month before the commencement of the IRA's second ceasefire.

One of the soldiers trained his weapon on Richard McAuley, who was driving the car, then pointed it directly at John. Momentarily startled, he jerked his head backwards. "This is surreal!" he said, once the soldiers passed on.

"Welcome to British-occupied Belfast!" Chrissie replied.

The McAuleys recall that John was curious about everything and wanted more and more detail about how they saw the political process moving forward. What were the opportunities, what were the obstacles?

They took him to Chrissie's sister's house, which was then the subject of countless sectarian attacks. Her young boys were smartly groomed and giggled when he shook their hands. He spent time making sure he'd got some of their Gaelic names right. He walked outside with Laura, their mother, and was shocked by what he saw – in this instance, the scale of the wall in her back garden, the so-called peace line. He was further perturbed by the scorch marks from petrol bombs that had been thrown at the children's bedroom windows.

2 August 1999

Returning to the living room, he put his hand on the head of her youngest son and asked her what she hoped for in the future. The McAuleys think that he didn't expect the selfless answer she gave him. She had, she said, put her trust in people like him and President Clinton to help create a better future for everyone's children, Catholic and Protestant alike.

The rest of that day they stopped off at places that, in themselves, chronologically told the story of the conflict since 1969; in and out of side streets and along the length of the "peace line". In Ballymurphy, they stopped the car and spoke at length about imprisonment, internment and the scale of the social and economic impact of the conflict, and much much more.

They stopped where my family home had been.

"Did you say there?" John asked, somewhat puzzled. "That clearing?"

He couldn't believe the house had been so badly damaged in British army raids that it had had to be demolished!

He was clearly in awe of the sprawling web of British military installations encircling the West Belfast area, but they saw the more positive sides of life here as well. In the local craft-shop John chose a large, Celtic-designed candle that he said his wife Carolyn would adore. And as he'd been raving about the home-baked wheaten bread he'd eaten during lunch, Chrissie popped across the Falls Road to a bakery and bought a selection of breads.

They then headed for Milltown cemetery. Richard recalls that it "was a muggy old day. That somehow dictated the mood. John was very quiet when we came away after spending some time going around the various graves of the hunger strikers. At the cemetery gates, he looked up at the British army observation cameras mounted on Andersonstown barracks and struck up a quicker step than we could match. Most of us, at some point, have known that feeling. For John, this was clearly another moment of deep impact that day."

"Time was drawing close to his departure," Chrissie says, "but no tour of West Belfast would be complete if we didn't treat our guests to a pint of Guinness in the local Felons [the former political prisoners] Club. Afterwards, at Central Station, John smiled warmly and kissed me on the cheek as I gave him his parcel of wheaten bread for his breakfast the next day. In such a short time, some six hours or so, it was more like seeing off an old friend until next time."

Tragically, there will be no next time for John Jr. He and I finished our interview by phone some weeks later. It wasn't long after the Royal Ulster Constabulary forced an Orange parade down Garvaghy Road. The IRA killed two RUC men in a separate incident in nearby Lurgan town. He quizzed me intensely about this. Weeks later the peace process was re-established.

We met again fleetingly a few times at various Irish-American events. I can't say I knew John Kennedy Jr well. Truth to tell, I hardly knew him at all, but I feel privileged to have met him and that he cared enough to come to Ireland and visit with people in West Belfast. In many ways, though he never to my knowledge made any political comment on the situation here, and there is no reason to suppose that he supported any particular view, his visit personifies what Irish-America is about and how it is concerned to see peace in Ireland.

The Kennedy and Bessette families have suffered mightily. These recollections are not meant to intrude upon their private grief. I hope that the knowledge that they are in the thoughts and prayers of people here in Ireland, and that John touched us by his decency and humility, will be of some small comfort for them all, and especially his sister Caroline, at this sad time.

30 August 1999

NO NEWS IS GOOD NEWS

For the last two weeks I have been entirely without knowledge of what is happening outside of the immediate or almost immediate proximity of Ballyslipnaguttery, the beautiful area where I am spending the summer holidays. My ignorance of affairs further afield is entirely self-imposed. On the eve of our departure from the fair city of Belfast, I informed my sceptical better half that I would not be reading any newspapers or listening to or watching any news programmes on the radio or television. And that is exactly what I have done.

It is easier than I imagined. In a way, I thought it would be like giving up smoking for Lent. Do people still give up smoking for Lent? When I smoked I used to try to give it up for Lent as part of my intention of giving it up for good. The notion that my abstinence was for a temporary period and that I could build up to it was a great help. Or so the theory went. It never worked out like that in practice. Even when or if I managed to stop for Lent, I rarely got past midnight on Ash Wednesday. I imagined stopping newspapers would be the same. Being determined has nothing to do with it: habits are hard to break no matter how determined the poor addict is.

By the way, I don't smoke now, and that is one of the best things I don't do, but breaking the habit had little to do with Lent. It was the look on my son's face when he caught me smoking in the toilet some days after I told him I had stopped. The shocked and disappointed look of utter disbelief and betrayal left me red-faced, ashamed and eventually nicotineless. But that's another story. Back to my news blackout.

I am a news junkie. Like many of you, dear readers? My daily fix begins with the early morning news programme on the radio. Sometimes that can be very early indeed. So by the time mid-morning comes and office hours begin, I have absorbed a few hours of recycled bulletins, interviews, debates, weather forecasts, "what the papers say" and traffic warnings. Sometimes, of course, I am part of the debates or the interviews, though only if my leader R.G. McAuley insists or I am annoyed by what I have heard. You can be on the news too much, and early morning is definitely too much.

While listening to these news programmes I usually read the morning papers. Reading in the morning is an addiction also. Sometimes when I haven't the papers at hand I find myself reading the back of Kellogg's packets or the labels on the jar of marmalade. One thing I have always avoided, and that is watching the television in the morning. I am not really a TV person. One thing I really dislike is an omnipresent, always-on-all-the-time TV. Yeuk! But I really like the wireless. Especially the every-hour-on-the-hour news bulletins, and on some stations at some times of the day you can get the news every half hour. And that's not counting the lunchtime programmes. And so the day goes by, until the evening, when the TV comes into its own. Then there is an hour or so of channel-flicking from news programme to news programme as evening becomes night and night follows the same pattern as day, with the minutes measured by the broadcasts until sleep comes with the last news of the wee small hours.

It was little wonder that my better half was sceptical when I said all this was to be off-limits for me in Ballyslipnaguttery. But it has been. I have even stopped wearing my watch. Well, actually I broke the strap, but instead of rushing to get it fixed or carrying the timepiece in my pocket, I left it to one side. Every day is now measured by hunger pangs or by the sun's journey through the heavens. Ballyslipnaguttery is like that; life here is easy and slow.

Of course, it isn't possible to avoid all the news. My better half keeps herself up to date with current affairs but loyally kept these to herself and even went without papers in solidarity with me. In the beginning I did take a peek or two at the headlines on the news-stand when I was in the local shop, but that soon passed. I began to look forward to not reading the papers. After the first few days, I would not have read them anyway even if they were about the place. I think.

As for the radio, that was no problem. My radio doesn't work in Ballyslipnaguttery. The television does but it isn't on too often, and the news is easy to avoid once you get used to the idea that walking or watching the skyscape is a better pastime. Other people give you bits of news as part of social chitchat when you meet. Thus word of the awfulness of the human dis-

30 August 1999

aster caused by the earthquake in Turkey seeped through to me in the way news must have been communicated in days gone by.

On a more local level, I also heard that my friend Belfast City Councillor Tom Hartley was arrested by the RUC, along with others, for his part in a protest against an Orange march. I was also told that the Unionists are trying to have Sinn Féin removed from the talks process. But that's hardly news, is it? Even here in Ballyslipnaguttery. Here, no news is good news. No news is bliss. And I, dear reader, am one of the blissed. For the time being anyway. Or at least until my first fix when I leave here. Funny thing is, life may never be the same again because I now know there is a life outside of the news. And that really is good news.

An Irish Journal

THE WINTER OF OUR DISCONTENT

Gerry Adams argues that the real victims as winter approaches are the growing army of drug addicts, down-and-outs and homeless.

The yellowing foliage on the hedgerows tells us that the season of summer is coming to its close and the season of autumn is coming to its opening. The Americans use an appropriate word – the fall – to describe this most mellow time of the year, and already here in the north of Ireland that's what the leaves are doing. Further south the slightly warmer clime protracts the process, but between global warming and the hole in the ozone layer it is difficult to know how long that will last. Sometimes it is possible to have all five seasons in one day. At least twice! It is little wonder that we Irish, and betimes this column, are so preoccupied with the weather.

I suppose it distracts us from politics and the drudge of a snail's pace of a peace process, but the majority of us, and that includes your columnist, are generally concerned about the elements because of how the weather affects our mood or our walk or our day off. Farmers and rural folk generally have a different concern. Bad weather can ruin crops and endanger livelihoods. For fishing communities bad weather is deadly. But country people, culchies, aren't the only ones affected in this way. One section of our people, of people everywhere, dread the coming of the fall. That section is the poor. For many of them, autumn is the advance guard of winter, and winter means death.

Street people are particularly vulnerable. At one time the only street people in Ireland were winos. We exported the rest of our human flotsam to the streets of London and Birmingham and other places. Or they went as economic exiles and fell on to the streets to become flotsam. So it was possible in recent decades to pretend that Ireland was relatively free of a sub-class, apart from the poor unfortunate victims of alcohol. Even the child beggars who litter the main streets of our capital city were explained away as the tools of unscrupulous parents who were doing well from this "business".

Nowadays we are not so naive. In these days of the Celtic

29 September 1999

Tiger, there are more homeless people than in other less-affluent times. A third of the people in the South are living below poverty level. The consequences of savage cuts in health and social services, especially in the 1980s, are coming into sharp relief. The 1980s were also the time when hundreds of young people, especially in Dublin, died from drug abuse. The poorer areas were devastated by the spread of heroin. More than a decade later we are in the midst of another crisis, with the hard drugs epidemic affecting all parts of the island from Cork and Limerick to Belfast and Ballymena, Ian Paisley's bailiwick.

It is in the South that some of the contradictions are coming into sharpest relief. It was there during the 1980s, when young people in Dublin were dying in their hundreds, when street people were being created, that the wealthiest in our society were depriving their fellow citizens of essential state services by defrauding massive amounts of tax by secreting their money in offshore accounts.

As I write, this is the main item on all the newscasts. Various tribunals and inquiries have shown that while much-needed resources were denied to communities throughout the state, a wealthy élite, with the connivance of those in successive governments, were growing richer. Wealthy people were actively encouraged by the financial institutions to evade tax, and all involved felt they could do so with impunity. And who suffered? Who always suffers? The ordinary Joe or Joanne! The Pay As You Earn worker will feel particularly aggrieved; so will lower paid employees. The elderly, particularly widows, and mothers of large families and the unemployed are on a rung below that, and they have been disadvantaged once again. But the real victims as winter approaches are our growing army of drug addicts, down-and-outs and homeless. They are the disempowered, and the gap between them and the rest of us is widening.

Is this the Ireland we want? Is this the vision that generations of patriots struggled for? It certainly is not the kind of society that the people of this island deserve. It is true that we are wealthier today. Our emigrants are returning home, and our young people have a chance of a decent job if they have the education for it. All of that is good. But in this day and age, no one in modern Ireland should fear the winter. Yet many do. And some will not survive it.

An Irish Journal

REVIEWING THE SITUATION?

On Monday, 6 September, George Mitchell, former chairman of the multi-party talks, opened the review of the Good Friday Agreement. He made clear that the review would concentrate specifically on breaking the deadlock over decommissioning and the formation of the Executive.

Discerning readers may have noticed that your columnist has not dealt in any detailed way recently with the current state of the peace process. As I am sure you are aware, Senator George Mitchell is here overseeing a review of the Good Friday Agreement, or to put it more accurately, the senator is reviewing the non-implementation of the Agreement. The review was to be short, sharp and focused, and the initial timescale envisaged it being over by about this time. But then someone somewhere suggested that the Ulster Unionist Party leader David Trimble would have little room for manoeuvre before his party conference, which is next weekend. So the timescale of the review has slipped back a little to facilitate this, which is fair enough if Mr Trimble does the right thing, but it will be a complete turn-off for everyone else if he doesn't and if his refusal to fulfil his responsibilities continues beyond the UUP conference.

I suppose a few weeks extra are of little consequence given the importance of the issue we are dealing with, but there will be a number of disgruntled people in Canada and along the east coast of the USA who made a big effort to organise events which I was to attend during this period. Now, because of the extra time added to the review, I have had to postpone most of my itinerary, so apologies to everyone affected. I will, however, if God spares us, be in New York at the first annual Friends of Sinn Féin dinner on the 20th. This will be an overnight stop, and we will catch up on the other commitments later, hopefully in November.

Meanwhile, back at the review, the only area of agreement among the parties at this juncture seems to be our mutual sympathy for George Mitchell, who is once again winging his way back and forth across the Atlantic. Ian Paisley, the obvious excep-

4 October 1999

tion, has told the senator to stay at home. Paisley, incidentally, is taking no part in the review, but he did take time out to meet with Senator Mitchell to tell him to go home. The meeting took an hour – a long goodbye. Sure, if you didn't see the funny side, you'd crack up.

Given the UUP position, and given the reality that no armed group is prepared to decommission on terms demanded by the UUP, and given the rejection by the Unionists of the decommissioning body, it is hardly surprising that there is not a great expectation that the Mitchell Review will succeed. I am asked, what is the point therefore in being involved in the review? The answer is obvious. A peace settlement is only possible through dialogue. There is no other way to find a way forward out of the protracted difficulties which have bogged down the peace process from day one. So the Mitchell review presents the best chance of achieving that. Dialogue is the only option. So we have to keep trying, because whether Mr Trimble accepts this or not, or whether he knows or cares how much his stance is disappointing and frustrating all those people who voted – North and South – for the Good Friday Agreement, the reality is that he represents the best chance, at this time, for the rest of us.

Of course the British government has a huge role – the central role – to play. Unionist resistance to change is what underpins the current difficulties, but British management of the process and Unionist tactical manoeuvring against change is the cause of the crisis. It is my view that the British government should have learned a lot in the last eighteen months. There is a clear onus on London to use this experience in order to advance the process in the time ahead, to make this review work and to do so in a way which allows all those genuinely committed to change, or those prepared to accept change, to actually manage that change in a way which people voted for in the Good Friday referendum.

One thing is certain. All the changes envisaged in the Good Friday Agreement will be secured anyway. Those of us who are resolutely committed to a complete transformation of Irish society are not going to be deflected by the shortcomings of Unionism. Furthermore, this British government could never justify its position if it failed to anchor the peace process on the foundation which is required for a truly just and lasting peace.

Mr Blair knows this. Mr Trimble probably knows this also. He and his party leadership should take their courage in their hands now and do the right thing. He should join with the rest of us in the political institutions and tackle all of the outstanding matters. He will not find Sinn Féin lacking in our willingness to do business with him and those he represents.

11 October 1999

LONDON CALLING

At the weekend of 9–10 October, David Trimble faced down his critics at the Ulster Unionist Party conference in Enniskillen, County Fermanagh. On 11 October, the British secretary of state, for the last two-and-a-half years, Dr Mo Mowlam, was replaced in a Cabinet reshuffle by Mr Peter Mandelson. Mr Mandelson's name was first suggested for the position last summer by David Trimble.

Mo must go. That's the news out of London this week as Tony Blair reshuffles his Cabinet. When Dr Mowlam was appointed to the post as Britain's first woman secretary of state in Ireland, I said I hoped she would also be the last. British secretary of state, that is. And I was only half joking. The sooner there is no longer any British involvement in Ireland could not be too soon for me and most other people on this island, and on the other island as well. And all other places most everywhere else, sez you, dear reader. I know, I know.

But even when I was saying that I knew that it is British policy which is the crucial thing, and it is that which we have to change if we are to see the changes which Ireland deserves. Implementing policy is all important. Personalities matter, of course, and I say this as someone who believes that one person can make a difference, but at this time of our history policy is what counts, and upholding policy, in this case the Good Friday Agreement, is what will decide whether the peace process stands or falls.

Having said all that, and without in any way setting aside my own well-known position on the issues at the heart of the difficulties in our country and Britain's continued responsibility for these, I also have to say that Mo Mowlam did her best and that she brought an approach to her job which was totally contrary to what existed here for as long as anyone could care to remember. This wasn't enough, and she had no right to be here anyway, but fair is fair and I am glad she survived, and I wish Dr Mowlam well in whatever else she does with her life.

Meantime, once again, back at the ranch, the Mitchell Review has moved to London. I suppose that's movement of sorts. Regular readers will recall that we were all told that David Trimble couldn't do a deal until he got the Ulster Unionist Party conference behind him. Well, the conference has come and gone, and despite all the media and political speculation of instability in the Ulster Unionist Party, their get-together demonstrated a solid, and in my view predictable, level of party unity and, most significantly, support for the party leader David Trimble.

It has often been pointed out that Mr Trimble has used a well-cultivated perception of the weakness of his leadership as his most effective negotiation strength. It is now time to use his strength in leadership to confront his critics and to implement the Good Friday Agreement. David Trimble's address to his party conference was an opportunity to show decisive leadership. Unfortunately, this did not happen. Instead, Mr Trimble adhered to his party's "no guns, no government" policy which is no part of the Good Friday Agreement. This leaves everyone else in an intractable situation, and it is a position which will, if it is maintained, cause the collapse of the Agreement.

Mr Trimble should lead the UUP into the Executive and the other institutions and let the Independent International Commission on Decommissioning (IICD) deal with the decommissioning issue, as agreed on Good Friday. As Mr Trimble knows, it is only by making politics work that we will provide the context for addressing the decommissioning issue with some prospect of success. That is what the UUP signed up for. At that time the Good Friday Agreement set out a two-year period for addressing the decommissioning issue. The UUP have wasted seventeen months of this, and in defence of their stance they have argued that this is because they are real democrats. This is particularly offensive to Nationalists and other democrats. The Unionist presumption (or excuse) is that they are qualified to judge the democratic credentials of others. Such a presumption is arrogant, prejudiced and provocative. It also ignores the fact that Unionism had decades to develop democratic credentials. It failed to do so.

Even today I have never once heard a Unionist spokesperson acknowledge the injustices sustained by the old Unionist regime, much less express any regret for them. On the contrary,

11 October 1999

Unionist spokespersons and apologists argue that discrimination and sectarianism are figments of the Nationalist imagination. And such out-dated attitudes persist. Unionism still demands the right to march over small Nationalist communities; institutional discrimination continues, and in the local government councils, political Unionism has moved away from the exclusion of Nationalists only where it has been forced to. So, too, with the peace process, wherein Unionist participation has been reluctant, tactical and at all times aimed at reducing the momentum towards change.

In short, many Unionists politicians would still prefer not to have a Nationalist or a Catholic about the place. Unless, of course, we know our place. But those days are gone. Our place is wherever we are mandated to be. As equals. There can be no more second-class citizens. That is also the potential of the Good Friday Agreement. That is what people voted for, including the majority of ordinary Unionists.

As always, the British government has the primary role to persuade the Unionist leaders of this. Let's hope that Peter Mandelson is up to the task.

An Irish Journal

BREAKING THE IMPASSE?

A statement released in Belfast at the weekend of 16–17 October by Gerry Adams reiterated Sinn Féin's commitment to the Good Friday Agreement and said Republicans needed to address the concerns of Unionists in a spirit of respect and goodwill. However, in talks under the Mitchell Review there was no progress on the substantive issues.

This is a very hectic week for this column. It started in London at Winfield House, the US ambassador's residence. Kindly provided by Philip Lader for the Mitchell Review, this house was built by the American heiress Barbara Hutton in 1936 and occupies twelve acres on the north-west side of Regent's Park, on land which was once part of a "great forest with wooded glades and lairs of wild beasts, deer both red and fallow, wild bulls and boars". Half a century before the Norman Conquest, the land belonged to the Abbey of Barking; over the years Henry VII hunted there, Elizabeth I used it for entertaining dignitaries and James I offered it as collateral to raise money to go to war.

The redbrick Georgian-style house stands behind fifteen-foot high iron gates, and this week we spent two and a half days within its walls engaging in talks with Senator Mitchell and the UUP. We were joined on Tuesday afternoon by the SDLP and on Wednesday by the other pro-Agreement parties before a one-day adjournment during which I will be flying across to New York for a very short overnight visit.

Regrettably, while the atmosphere in our conversations with the UUP is better now than at any time since they started talking to us about six months ago, as this paper goes to press, I have to report that there has been no progress on the substantive issues. The Unionists are locked into their demands around decommissioning, even though these are clearly outside the terms of the Good Friday Agreement.

I am very conscious of the challenges which Unionists face about the future and on the whole question of change. I am conscious of the difficulties that Unionists face about participating in a process of negotiations, and it has long been my view that

18 October 1999

Republicans need to address the concerns of Unionists in a spirit of respect and goodwill. This is what Sinn Féin has endeavoured to do. For our part we remain absolutely committed to the current efforts to secure the implementation of the Good Friday Agreement. At the same time, no one who is genuinely committed to change can be paralysed by the unwillingness of some less progressive elements to engage. I know that there are some within Unionism who have concluded that it is better to dig in and refuse to move rather than negotiate. Others from within Loyalism and the UUP are making the effort to engage through dialogue. They do so, in common with all other participants, within their own lights, and their efforts are to be commended. However, thus far such efforts have failed to secure the implementation of the Agreement.

I believe that the gap between the UUP demand for decommissioning and what is achievable on this issue appears to be too wide to be bridged in the context of the non-implementation of the Agreement. Their demand is also outside the terms of the Agreement, but – as I have said in a well publicised statement on Sunday last – Sinn Féin would not be dogmatic on this point if there was some way of meeting the UUP demand. The reality is that the UUP position is not do-able, and their project is not helped by their rejection over the last year and a half of a series of efforts by us to resolve this matter on their terms. This reality has to be faced up to. I say this more in sadness than in anger, and Sinn Féin will continue to do our best in the Mitchell Review because it is my conviction that it will be a huge tragedy if this review fails over this issue. This is another reality which also has to be faced up to.

Winfield House is a pleasant and hospitable venue for our deliberations. It also hosted some of the best discussions. But thus far it has not witnessed the breaking of the impasse. Maybe by the time you get to read this that will have changed. I certainly hope so. It is in all our interests to secure peace. No one will take succour from the failure of the Mitchell Review except those elements from within Unionism and Loyalism, and those on the outer margins of extreme Nationalism, who have set their faces against change. They need to be liberated from their fears and prejudices. That is the challenge facing us all, but it is especially the challenge faced by Unionism.

An Irish Journal

Mise Éire?

In Dublin multiple tribunals expose the widespread corruption of public life in the Twenty-six Counties.

I consider myself to be very lucky. This is mostly because I am often in contact with people who are less fortunate than me. So I thank God for my life and my health and for my family, and I hurry on with whatever I am doing at the time. Sometimes the hurrying – which requires some very fast running – is running fast only to avoid going backwards. Such is life. Last week I was in Dublin, London, New York and Belfast all within a few days. Many would consider that as a very exciting lifestyle. Maybe it is. Some may even envy it. I don't. Don't get me wrong. No one is forcing me to do what I do, and I know myself well enough to admit that I must be getting some satisfaction out of all this madness to sustain me. In other words, I am doing what I am doing because I want to do what I am doing. Of course, I also know that I am not indispensable. Who is?

It's not often this column descends to such a degree of navel-gazing, and I wonder as I scan these lines what brought on this mood. Maybe it's the day that's in it. Maybe it's because I got up at six thirty this morning to dash to Dublin in support of Aengus Ó Snodaigh, Sinn Féin's candidate in a parliamentary by-election, and I am on my way back to Belfast again for more talks at Stormont this afternoon. Maybe it's because I'm tired. But probably it is because electioneering gives an insight into people's thinking, and if ever I needed it this election confirms my view that people are very cheesed off indeed. And who can blame them?

Week by week for the last few years, revelation has followed revelation of dirty dealing and gangsterism in the politics of the South of Ireland. Story has followed story of collusion between some politicians, big business and the main financial institutions here so that the people have almost drowned in a sea of sleaze and corruption. Former Taoiseach Charlie Haughey is most often in the news as the main culprit, but many people feel that while he may have been the worst offender he isn't on his own.

25 October 1999

In fact, the popular view is that Mr Haughey is representative of the entire body politic. Of course he isn't. There are honourable men and women in the establishment parties, but he has sullied them all because he is seen to represent a culture of graft and hypocrisy.

I think it is the hypocrisy which most offends the ordinary punters. They recall the exhortations from successive governments for people to tighten their belts during lean times, and they learn through the tribunals which are investigating allegations of corruption that while these calls were being made, government ministers were living the high life on taxpayers' money. They read of Mr Haughey spending tens of thousands of pounds of public money on silk shirts from Paris while his government was cutting money back from hospitals, housing and schools. It is little wonder that the people are annoyed or that some of them think all politicians are tarred with the one brush. All the establishment parties are affected by these scandals. Most had senior members involved to some degree or other, but even if this were not the case, the reality is that there is so little difference ideologically between them that people cannot tell the difference in any case. All of this might be fair enough if the rest of us were in some organised or cohesive alternative. But we are not. Not yet in any case.

We are building an alternative, but it is only now slowly becoming relevant. Many people in the South were fooled for so long into believing that politics is only about voting every five years or so and that democracy is limited to this exercise, so naturally when this fails them they are cynical about all politics. They have no notion about and no wish to be involved in building an alternative. Not yet in any case. And who can blame them? The Irish people are generally sound. They want a just society. The vast majority of people do not favour a selfish system. They want the disadvantaged to benefit from the Celtic Tiger along with the rest of us. I joined nurses on the picket line this morning outside one of Dublin's main children's hospitals. The nurses are on the second week of a state-wide strike. It is a strike which never should have happened. The government should have moved early to avert it. There is huge public support for the nurses. This would not be surprising at any time, but there is a bite to it at this time. Public anger at the behaviour of the establishment has ensured that the government cannot win this dispute.

People may not see the alternative yet, but they know which side they are on. They know that a system which favours the greedy is a rotten one. They resent their disempowerment. They feel let down. It is little wonder that this causes all of us collectively to navel-gaze. So your column reflects the mood of the nation on this grey autumn day. But unlike the rest of them, your column is driving northwards to negotiate with the Unionists. Navel-gazing does not help that project. It is not enough for us to feel sorry for ourselves over events in the South. It is not enough for people in the South to feel angry at those who cause all this misery. We have to do something about it. It's up to us to stop them. Otherwise they will keep doing it.

1 November 1999

The State We're In

Gerry Adams reviews the failure of partition, north and south of the border.

When I was a young boy our family would be shushed into silence as our parents watched faltering TV news footage of a bridge wrecked by bombs. These occasional grainy images would be projected into our living room on our black and white Radio Rentals television set. While my father listened to news of the latest "outrage", stern-faced peelers looked out at us from outside sandbagged border barracks. We children had no real sense of what all this was about. Belfast was far from the border, though at one point when a posse of peelers surrounded our house and stomped loudly through the uncarpeted wooden-floored bedrooms, it was as if the border had came home. We knew instinctively that the raid and partition were interconnected.

Later when college gangs of us went on summer scholarship excursions to the Donegal Gaeltacht, we were disappointed to find no obvious signs of the border. We were only comforted by the discovery of a mysterious no man's land – a vague and questionably guessable distance of road between two states, whose existence wasn't even certain but dependent only on whether we believed Seamie Green, who first informed us about this phenomenon. Crossing the actual border was in itself an uncertain and loudly debatable event.

"We're over now."

"Nawh, we're not. It's coming now. At that big tree! Now!"

Our bus swayed gently, and Brother Beausang smiled at our dubious geographical assertions as we peered out at an unchanged and unchanging landscape.

"We're in the Free State," someone hollered.

"We're still in the North," exclaimed someone else.

"Sure, Donegal is in the North."

"I mean in the Six Counties."

"Don't be stupid. This is the Free State. Look: that post box is green."

And so it was.

Like all modern states, Ireland has its fair share of divisions – geographical, physical, religious, emotional, cultural, gender, economic and, of course, political. Some of these we are only vaguely aware of, but the border is one which imposes its presence on all aspects of our daily lives, whether we live on Rathlin Island or in Cork, in Belfast or in Galway. It is a deep scar, which meanders its way for hundreds of kilometres across our island. It is one of the most criminal of a long line of crimes committed by successive English governments in Ireland. Ireland is historically, culturally and geographically one single unit. The partition of Ireland, established by Britain's Government of Ireland Act and subsequent British acts, divides Ireland into two artificial statelets, the boundaries of which were determined by a sectarian head-count. It is only now through the constitutional and institutional elements of the Good Friday Agreement that these British acts are being dismantled.

As the English writer C.P. Scott wrote, Ireland was partitioned "to entrench the six counties against Nationalist Ireland. Its effect will not be to make a solution of the Irish question easier but harder by creating a fresh and powerful obstacle."

Within the Six Counties, a divisive, violent and sectarian system of apartheid has held sway since partition. Catholics are still two-and-a-half times more likely to be unemployed, and a recent report by the North's Statistics and Research Agency has shown that a Catholic family's average monthly income is £200 less than that of a Protestant family. Moreover 28 per cent of Catholics' average weekly income is made up of Social Security benefit, compared to 18 per cent for Protestants.

This is not to say that the Protestant working class are well off. On the contrary, sections share a common economic, as well as a class, interest with their Catholic neighbours. Inequality, injustice and discrimination permeate all aspects of the Northern state, impacting in every conceivable way on the quality of life of people.

In the Twenty-six Counties the instinct is to look at the border region, witness the economic disparity with the rest of the South and assume that the border only affects those counties which link it. But partition, and the political instability and conflict which it creates, has inhibited economic growth beyond

1 November 1999

simply the border counties; it has undermined the wider justice system and has wasted valuable resources defending a partitionist structure which all democrats and good governments should be actively seeking to dismantle. Specifically, the Southern border counties have endured decades of systematic underdevelopment by an over-centralised, narrowly focused Dublin government. A recent study by the Combat Poverty Agency on rural poverty showed that it was the border regions that were the most deprived in the Southern state.

In the North a Unionist regime at Stormont and a Unionist-dominated bureaucracy within the Northern Ireland Office have deliberately favoured development in the eastern counties. Partition has divided a natural economic region. It is on the periphery not only of the island economy, as well as the British economy, but also the European economy, making economic development even more precarious. The net result has been needless emigration, depopulation, unemployment and ongoing economic underdevelopment. It is also quite clear that economic activity and cooperation is hampered not least because of the two tax regimes that operate. This creates inefficiencies and ultimately costs jobs.

Ideologically, Sinn Féin is an Irish Republican party. We want an end to British jurisdiction in our country and a thirty-two-county-based Irish republic to replace the two states which have existed since the island was partitioned. We want an end to partition. That primary objective guides our peace strategy, determined our approach during the negotiations leading to the Good Friday Agreement, and now guides our approach to the ongoing negotiations around the efforts to implement the Good Friday Agreement.

There have been obvious attempts to breach the social, economic, and cultural barriers created by the border – most obviously through the various EU initiatives, as well as through the IFI and similar projects. Sinn Féin has argued that Ireland should be organised, and dealt with within the EU, as a single island economy. We have proposed a series of economic corridors between Donegal and Derry, or a Derry/Fermanagh–Derry link up, or a corridor between Sligo and Fermanagh/Tyrone, as well as a Belfast-Dublin corridor, as one way of redressing the imbalance.

For Sinn Féin the Good Friday Agreement is a transitional arrangement. Through those interlocked and interdependent elements of the Agreement which relate to the island as a whole, we will break down the border by bridging the political, economic, cultural and social divides. That remains Sinn Féin's focus: ending partition, dismantling a border that has divided our people and subverted our potential to create wealth and prosperity and a lasting peace. I believe we will achieve that goal.

Partition was, and remains, the main means by which equality was denied and the principal method by which self-determination was withheld from us. Partition aborted a national independence struggle in the 1920s, secured Britain a toehold in part of Ireland from which London could influence all of Ireland; it divided the people of our island into two states, and within one state it established a Unionist monopoly which divided us once more,

All that is changing. Much of it has already changed. As we go into a new century this much at least is certain: partition has failed. And the failure is not restricted to the Six Counties. There are few who will argue that the Twenty-six Counties fulfils the needs of the people of this island. Fortunately the Southern state has escaped the worst of the thirty years of conflict which has raged mostly in the North, though two bomb attacks in Monaghan and Dublin claimed thirty-three lives in one day. It is little wonder that James Connolly warned that if partition was imposed it would "mean a carnival of reaction both North and South, would set back the wheels of progress". Neither has the Celtic Tiger solved all problems. One third of citizens survive below poverty level, and the revelations emanating from various tribunals and enquiries illustrate the other end of the scale, with collusion between banks, big business, financial institutions and some senior politicians drawn from all the conservative parties who have actively conspired to defraud tax-payers and prevent the equitable distribution of wealth.

So there are lots of reasons to rid ourselves of partition. I believe we have made a real start to that job of work. The harder we work at it, the more we win people around to that position, the sooner we will achieve that goal.

8 November 1999

LAST WEEK WAS A BASTARD

This is a difficult column to write. It is never an easy chore to compress information or opinion to 800 words or so and to write a piece which will not be dated when it is published some days later. With all the twists and turns of the peace process, that is not as easy as it seems, especially because you never know who reads this stuff. Such are the problems faced by your columnist.

Last week all of this, and everything else, was put into perspective. Last week my sister Margaret's two sons were killed. Last week was a bastard.

Margaret is my oldest sister. She is a year younger than me. I am the oldest in our family. There are ten of us and Margaret is the oldest girl, which means she had the hard rearing. That's the way it was with girls, especially the oldest ones; they were expected to play a mother's role to the younger ones, cleaning and child minding and running errands amid myriad other household tasks.

Margaret was the first of us to get married. She and Mickey McCorry were childhood sweethearts. They were both politically active, and they went with the Goulding leadership and later the Workers' Party during the Republican split of 1969. In those troubled, crazy times, that made relationships between us a little difficult, but we have outgrown all that a long time ago.

Margaret and Mickey had four children: Deirdre, Mairead and then with a gap of some years Liam and Miceál. Deirdre and Mairead grew up and got married in turn and went on to have their own children. In this way, as is the way, all the rest of us followed, so that a huge clan of different generations of cousins and nephews and uncles and aunts and grannies and grandas and great-grannies and -grandas and in-laws and outlaws has grown up. All of this was accomplished against the background, and at times the foreground, of almost thirty years of war during which some of us were killed, many of us were imprisoned and most of us were subjected to house raids and daily harassment by British Crown forces.

Through it all our family remained close, though like all large families not in contact as much as we should have been. But we all stayed in touch. None of us ever fell out for very long, and we came together in sadness or anger at funerals, or in celebration at weddings or christenings and birthdays or anniversary parties or when some of us were released from prison. In other words, we survived it all. Last year Terry Enright was shot dead by Loyalists. Terry was married to Margaret's oldest daughter Deirdre. They had two little daughters, Ciara and Aoife.

Last week Margaret and Mickey's two sons Liam and Miceál were killed in a motor accident. I was at the talks building at Stormont when I got the news. It was close to midnight when I made my way from there to the Falls Road where the two boys were killed. They had been at home all evening, horseplaying in their room or generally doing boyish things. Then they did their homework and watched a soccer match on television. Before settling down for the night, Liam wanted to move his father's van so that he could park the new family car outside the front door. Liam passed his driving test a few months ago; that's when they got the new car. He treated like it was his and he was very proud of it. But Mickey had the keys of the van with him, so the two boys drove off on the five-minute journey to get the keys.

They were killed on the way home when the car was in collision with a black taxi. Margaret's two sons died instantly. Liam was eighteen. Miceál was fifteen.

Liam was quiet and dependable. He was a good student, popular with his schoolmates and teachers. Miceál was boisterous and bubbly, a keen and gutsy Gaelic footballer and hurler. They were two bright shining lights in our lives.

On Friday we buried the two of them. We are devastated by the awfulness of it all. I don't know how our Margaret can bear such a blow.

It isn't fair.

15 November 1999

EYES ON THE PRIZE

On Tuesday, 16 November, the Ulster Unionist Party and Sinn Féin issued statements committing themselves to the full implementation of the Good Friday Agreement. David Trimble recognised the legitimate aspirations of Nationalists to pursue a united Ireland and embraced the principles of inclusivity, equality and mutual respect. Gerry Adams spoke of working with, not against, Unionists. The other main political parties in the North all issued statements endorsing the Good Friday Agreement.

By the time you get to reading this column, the outworkings of the ten-week review of the non-implementation of the Good Friday Agreement will be open to public scrutiny. The No men of Unionism and the right-wing Tory press will dismiss the initiatives involved. We can be certain of that. But I hope the Ulster Unionist Party leadership will embrace these developments so that they hoist themselves and the process out of the deep hole which they dug for all of us almost eighteen months ago.

That we managed to get this far is to a large degree due to the skill and commitment of Senator George Mitchell. Throughout this marathon review he showed great tact and good humour. The two governments also played their role, as did the South African and US governments. But there should be no underestimating the limits to which Sinn Féin has stretched ourselves and our constituency. Our opponents and the British government should not underestimate the effort which that took. Neither should they exaggerate, hype, or oversell what is involved. Indeed, the success of this next phase may depend on everyone taking a measured and truthful approach in the days and weeks ahead.

Every slow, painful turn in this process has been navigated by Republicans taking initiatives which created a momentum to take the process forward. For every movement forward there has been a series of failed efforts. Most of these failed because Unionists or the Brits refused to grasp the initiative. In most cases the failure was also reinforced or hastened by the mismanagement of the situation by the British government. Short-term hype, even for benign reasons, cannot replace long-term strategy. This was never clearer than in July this year when Sinn Féin initiatives were rejected by the Unionists and hyped by London. A repeat of this type of hype at this time will undoubtedly have the same effect. In other words, it will set back the process.

In my view there was always a very good chance of this review succeeding. For one thing, it was the last chance for Unionism. A rejection by the UUP of Republican initiatives at this time would probably have led to the collapse of the Assembly. The UUP negotiating team have not rejected the conclusions of the Mitchell Report, but no one should be complacent about this. The UUP itself could still say no. In my opinion, if it is given positive leadership it will say yes. This is not to underestimate the challenges facing Unionism, but some of them have faced up to these challenges with courage. Unionism is no longer a monolith. It now needs forward-thinking leaders.

The biggest problem is that many Unionists fear change, try to minimise change and see it as working to their disadvantage. This places a huge burden on any Unionist leadership which wants to plot a course into the future. First of all, the leadership itself has to be for change. It has to be prepared to give political leadership in a way that is totally different from the leaderships of the past. The leadership of the UUP may resent me saying this. They may feel I am patronising them, but I think I have a right to say this because I am not asking them to do anything that the Sinn Féin leadership has not done.

We have our eyes fixed on the prize. We want a just and lasting peace. So, hopefully the outworkings of the Mitchell Review will receive a positive response. Hopefully the deliberations of Unionism will lead them to the only possible conclusion if they really want this process to work. And that is that the only way forward is to work with the rest of us in shaping a new future and a new beginning for all sections of our people. The only way to lead is from the front. One thing is for certain: we are all in for a bumpy ride.

22 November 1999

Always Look on the Bright Side of Life

The prospect of a reunion of former prisoners from Ballymurphy provoked this parochial response.

There were always Murph men about the prisons. From Magilligan to Mountjoy, from the *Maidstone* to Maghaberry, from San Francisco to Brixton, from Portlaoise to Parkhead and a score of places in between over the last thirty years, there were always men and women from Ballymurphy doing whack. In fact, at times it appears to me that there were two types of POWs. There were Murph men and there were those, like Gerry Kelly, who wished they were Murph men. I'm sure it was the same in Armagh for the Murph women. It seems to me, looking back on it, that Ballymurphy was a state of mind. It still is.

Not that there is a thing wrong with Dermott Hill or New Barnsley or Moyard or even Turf Lodge. Everybody knows about Springhill and Westrock and some people are vaguely familiar with the Whiterock, but I reckon nobody from any of these places ever got arrested, because when I was in jail everybody north of the Rock streets said they were from the Murph. Except the Turf Lodge ones. They were funny like that.

It was Todler who first brought my attention to this. He and I and Marshall were watching Hilary getting ready for a visit.

"Why do you say you're from the Murph, big Mick?"

Marshall was big Mick's nickname.

Big Mick didn't answer. Neither did Marshall. Or Curly.

"There's Pat Mc Clure," Todler continued. "He's from Dermotthill. He's the same. And big Ned. And Alec Crowe."

That was away back in the seventies when whack was whack. Back in the Crum and the Cages. Back when Emerson and Todler took the other escapees from other areas on their backs as the two of them exited from the *Maidstone*. That was the night when all the years of breaking the ice in the cooler paid of.

That was before Ballymurphy men burned down the Kesh. Jimmy Duff started the fire. His semaphore was broken down, and he and that well-known Murph author Jim McCann were smoke-signalling *scéal* to one another from the sentenced end to the poor internee end when big Jock accidentally fanned the flames. The rest is history.

Remember the winter of '78, when country lads froze in the Blocks? Years of living rough in the Brickie and surviving on packets of Jacobs Cream Crackers were good preparation. It was nothing to us. Hard core, how are ya?

The jail wasn't built that could hold a Ballymurphy man. After the hunger strikes it was a guy from Divismore Park who took wee Larry and Bik to one side and gave them the plan for the Great Escape. The only condition was that they take Gerry Kelly with them. Gerry is nearly as bad an escaper as me, so the Murph lads reckoned that he deserved a hand out. Or so Hugh Feeney says. He's another wannabee Ballymurphian.

Me? I'm just glad I knew all of you. All the men and women from the Upper Springfield area and everywhere else. All the rakers and latchicos and heroes and heroines. All the partners and parents who spent years in visiting boxes. All the Green Cross collectors and the transport people and the men who drove the prison bus (*Go raibh maith agat,* Fra. Ballymurphy Drive *abú*) and the RAC women and the Smash H-Block and Armagh campaigners.

All of them deserve our undying gratitude. So do the group which is organising the get-together of Ballymurphy POWs. There will probably be crowds there from the Whiterock and New Barnsley and Moyard and Springhill and Westrock as well. Oh, and Turf Lodge, too. That's the way it is.

There will be loose talk and thoughts of comrades who have passed on and memories of Brit raids and heavy whack and brewing up *poitín* and scrumpy and lots and lots of lies.

Me? I will never forget Fat Campbell after lights out in the remand wing in the Blocks as the screws prowled outside.

"Always look on the bright side of life," he would sing, his voice coming chuckling quietly up the wing.

"Do de do de do de do de do," the rest of us would join in.

He was right.

29 November 1999

No Return to Stormont Rule

On 29 November at a meeting of the Assembly in Belfast, the d'Hondt procedure for the appointment of ministers in a power-sharing Executive was triggered and ten ministers were appointed. On 30 November the British houses of parliament both approved a devolution order under the Northern Ireland Act 1998 that allowed for the transfer of power from Westminster to the Assembly at Stormont, thus ending the system of direct rule that had been in place since 1972.

This column comes to you from the Sinn Féin office at Stormont. The tricolour is unfurled in a corner, the Chieftains' *Long Black Veil* is playing on the PC speaker, Robert Emmet – a Republican leader executed by the British in 1803 – hangs in heroic pose above me, while opposite him is a tattered poster from last year's Belfast St Patrick's Day calendar. That is the carnival that the Unionists refused to fund. But that was last year. Next year there will be a Unionist minister for culture, arts and leisure, and the equality agenda is so all-pervasive that the children of the second largest city on this island could hardly be denied their national day. Ulster will have to say Yes. It could become a habit.

It's funny prattling about the corridors here. Stormont – once the seat of Unionist power for fifty years – is a pretentious building full of Africaaner architecture, long used to looking down its nose at the natives. I am here very rarely. This week is my longest stint ever. It is also probably the most important week since the partition of Ireland. It is the week, the first week, that Nationalists and Republicans got their hands on the levers of power. This is the week that the Executive was established, along with the All-Ireland Council of Ministers and the all-Ireland policy and implementation bodies.

Sinn Féin have a minister of health and social services, Bairbre de Brún, no stranger to Irish-America; and Martin McGuinness is the new minister of education. The Ulster Unionist Party and the SDLP are the largest parties, and the ultra-right-wing Democratic Unionist Party, despite protestations to the contrary, claimed their two ministries as well. The whole world is in a state of chassis.

But there's more to it than that. And there's more to it than ministries or executives or any of that. It's all about building equality and building justice. The British still have jurisdiction in this part of our island. Ireland is still partitioned. There is still huge social, political, economic and cultural injustice. Anyone listening to the DUP invective at the Assembly debate to establish the Executive can have no doubt of the strength of sectarian feeling in that quarter. I felt its breath on the way to this office as I passed some senior DUPers. "Scum!" they hissed. So there's a lot of work to be done to cure all that and to rectify all the wrongs.

This week is only the beginning. It is over 600 days since the Good Friday Agreement was concluded. There are lots more difficulties threatening this process. The securocrats haven't gone away you know. Neither have their stooges. There are still British troops on the ground in proud Republican areas like South Armagh, and Irish-America needs to be alert to the efforts to rescue the RUC and dilute the Patten Report.

So Robert Emmet on the wall or the tricolour in the corner make the place more homely and disturb Orange ghosts, but they don't and can't replace freedom. That still has to be won. Sinn Féin is very hard-headed about this process. This generation have come through the prison ships and the torture centres, the prison camps and the street protests. We stand in the tradition of the Presbyterians of the 1790s who fought for Liberty and Equality and Fraternity in Ireland and America. Our goal remains the establishment of a united, free and independent Ireland. We believe the Good Friday Agreement is the transitional structure that will allow us to achieve that entirely legitimate and desirable objective. Others in the Assembly here and throughout this state and in Britain hold a different view – that's fair enough. But what we have now is the possibility of pursuing our political goals as equals.

We have a very, very long way to go until sections of our people – the disadvantaged, the poor, the no-hopers – have a stake in society and ownership of the future. That has to become our concern as rebels at Stormont, as Irish-Americans,

29 November 1999

as individuals, as political leaders, as governments, as communities, as organisations and as businesses. Success never comes without a struggle. Struggles require risks. Struggle is risk. This week Sinn Féin took a huge risk. We have to continue doing this. This is how the challenge of change is conquered. That is the importance of this week: not just to make change but to make change in a way which gives us strength for the future.

An Irish Journal

THE ROCKY ROAD TO DUBLIN

Despite political progress, and despite the IRA's honouring of its commitments, the British military presence remains highly visible, especially in the South Armagh area.

On my way to Dublin this week I took the right turn on the road just beyond the railway bridge outside Newry. Within minutes I could see what local people have been complaining about. The beautiful South Armagh countryside is dominated by British army installations, hilltop forts and ugly watchtowers. Helicopters were omnipresent, whirring their way across this lovely Irish skyline. This was within days of the IRA leadership confirming that its representative had commenced discussions with the de Chastelain commission. When I got that news last Sunday, I could not help but feel that Sinn Féin had delivered big time on the initiatives we had taken during the Mitchell Review. And I have to agree with Deputy UUP Leader John Taylor who asserted that the IRA had honoured the commitments it had made.

You would not see this reflected anywhere in the British army occupation of the South Armagh area. If the significant headway we have seen in recent days is to be bedded in and to become a solid foundation for sustainable progress, then the British government must now address the many issues of demilitarisation which frustrate and annoy and anger Nationalists. As a prelude to its total withdrawal, the British army should return to barracks and end its patrolling on the streets and laneways and roads of County Tyrone, South Armagh, South Down and elsewhere.

The hilltop forts in South Armagh and the high-rise observation posts on top of civilian and nursing tower blocks in Belfast and Derry should be closed as a matter of priority. Their existence is a constant reminder that there are those in the British security and political establishment who still want to pursue a military strategy.

The Royal Irish Regiment (RIR), a locally recruited militia, like the B Specials and UDR that spawned it, should go. No

6 December 1999

more name changes, no more smoke and mirrors. The British government is obliged under the Good Friday Agreement to produce an overall strategy on demilitarisation. This is thirteen months overdue. The Brits have to deliver now. Big time!

The Unionist section of our people in the North is the most heavily armed of any in Western Europe. One hundred and fifty thousand weapons are in their possession. These weapons are a source of intimidation and threat to Nationalists. Demilitarisation has to embrace all aspects of our society. The RUC should be disbanded. That must be the outcome of current efforts to create a proper policing service. Its role in the killing of almost sixty people, including Robert Hamill, must be investigated. But in the short-term it should be kept out of sensitive situations and areas.

Plastic bullets are an affront to human dignity. Their continued operational accessibility and the potential for their use threatens the political process we have so painstakingly constructed. The interrogation centres which are used to torture and degrade detainees, and in hundreds of cases to set people up for long prison sentences, should be closed immediately. The use of RUC files, and British army files, by Loyalist death squads must be properly investigated. Collusion cannot be ignored and those who perpetrate it cannot remain hidden from view. Their actions must be exposed.

The existence of special units within the British security system to run counter-gangs, import weapons, and plot and kill political opponents, or human rights lawyers like Pat Finucane and Rosemary Nelson, similarly cannot be brushed under the carpet. The lid must be lifted on this sordid strategy. This will require full international and independent investigations and inquiries. The shoot-to-kill tactics of the RUC and British army, collusion, torture, the systematic abuse of human rights would not have been possible without the special laws to facilitate this behaviour and to protect the guilty. Yet on the day that the Executive and the interlocking all-Ireland bodies were established, the British government introduced yet more repressive legislation. That was stupid.

It is scandalous that new draconian legislation has been introduced or is proposed since the Good Friday Agreement was signed. For Nationalists and Republicans, justice and policing matters are the litmus test of the new political dispensation which is heralded by the Good Friday Agreement. Almost twenty months after the Agreement was reached, there has been little substantial progress on any of these issues.

In a period in which so much has been achieved, the scenic route from Belfast to Dublin, through South Armagh, shows how much more there is to be done. All of these changes are an obligation under the Good Friday Agreement. These are not new demands. The British government signed up to these changes. It is my conviction that this British government has no wish to maintain the old status quo. However, there has been too long a delay in tackling these issues. There is and there will obviously be resistance from within the system. In order to fulfil its obligations, the militarists and the securocrats will have to be challenged by London.

13 December 1999

Historic Weeks

On Thursday, 2 December, direct rule came to an end as powers were devolved to the Assembly. At a meeting in Dublin, the North-South Ministerial Council and the British-Irish Ministerial Council, as set out in the Good Friday Agreement, took effect. At the same time, the Anglo-Irish Agreement was replaced by the British-Irish Agreement. Articles 2 and 3 of the Irish Constitution were replaced by new articles. In Belfast the new Executive of the Assembly met for the first time. Present at the meeting were representatives of the Ulster Unionist Party, the Social Democratic and Labour Party, and Sinn Féin. The Democratic Unionist Party refused to attend. That night the IRA issued a statement indicating that it would appoint a representative to meet the decommissioning body.

Journalists and others who should know these things tell us that one of the most used words here recently is the word historical. That probably means that we have become a little blasé about all the goings-on of recent times. Or at least that the journalists in question have. But that doesn't mean that the word historical is an inaccurate description. In fact, it is the only appropriate adjective. That it has been used a lot is testimony to the volume of developments which have occurred this last wee while. So although I can sympathise with those who wish that a more varied vocabulary could be employed to describe unfolding events, I make no apologies myself for describing these last few weeks as historic ones.

We have still a lot to do before we get freedom, but the outworkings of the Mitchell Review, which has seen the laying of the foundation for a level playing field and the beginning of the implementation of the Good Friday Agreement over 600 days since it was agreed, have put a positive shape on the future.

This week's meeting of the All-Ireland Ministerial Council is part of all that, and the time ahead presents unparalleled challenges and opportunities. Clearly we are a society moving out of conflict, a conflict born of the British government's involvement in Ireland. The Good Friday Agreement is undoubtedly a compromise – a charter between opponents and enemies – and Irish Republicans and Nationalists see it as a transitional arrangement which needs to be built upon, but there is one thing we can be certain about: the status quo is changing and it will continue to change. All the new constitutional arrangements point up the failure of partition.

For me the most significant constitutional change is the scrapping of the British Government of Ireland Act. I take particular satisfaction from this because I raised it myself directly with the British prime minister, and Sinn Féin secured the British government's commitment to its deletion. Now, for the first time since 1920, there is an all-Ireland-wide dispensation on this island. What a good and positive way to enter the new millennium! That is something else which Irish-America can be proud of. Readers of this column and many, many more of ye can justifiably have ownership of all that has been done so far. You also need to stake your claim to the continuing effort to get a lot more done in the time ahead of us. We could never have got this far without you all. We cannot succeed in our objectives unless we go forward into the future with you beside us.

Of course, for every positive there is a negative, and the faceless men of British intelligence were exposed once again last week when I revealed that the securocrats, the spies and spooks of British covert operations here, had placed a highly sophisticated tracking and listening device in a car that Martin McGuinness and I used during the Mitchell Review. The owner of the vehicle is a private citizen, not politically active but a strong supporter of the peace process and of Sinn Féin's peace strategy. I have spoken to both the taoiseach and the British prime minister about this very serious matter. I have to say that I am not satisfied with the response from the British. I have made it clear that it is essential not only for those involved to be made accountable for their actions, but there is also an urgent need for the British government to give a clear commitment that these devices are put beyond use. I have also asked for all targets and victims of this type of surveillance, those citizens whose home, car or premises is bugged, to be informed of this.

13 December 1999

The bugging of the vehicle used by me is a clear breach of faith carried out at a very difficult and sensitive time in the effort to end the crisis in the peace process. Had the device been discovered at that time, I am sure there would not have been a successful outcome to the Mitchell Review. So, as we enter a time of great promise and potential, all this is a timely reminder of the powerful forces which are against change and against the peace process. They are clinging to the old agenda.

Me? I'm for the future and for a new agenda. That includes not letting the buggers grind me down.

An Irish Journal

Fáilte Romhat 2000

Over the last fifty-one years I have learned many many things. Good things, bad things. The flotsam and jetsam of life consciousness, a Pandora's box of experience which has sustained me all this time and which for ever encourages me to continue to try to learn more. More about life. About humanity. About almost everything. Because now I know that I know nothing. Or I have forgotten it all.

In my half century or so I must have soaked up a huge amount of information. I do not profess to being knowledgeable, even though this information must amount to a lot of knowledge. But I do know enough to know that there is a difference between having knowledge and being knowledgeable. Even so, it is as if I have learned nothing. Or I have forgotten it all.

I have met many people from all walks of life: prelates and presidents; premiers and prats; rich people and poor people; people from all nations of the world; prisoners and turnkeys; drunks and gourmets; good people and bad people; friends and foes; poetic soldiers and soldierly poets; scholarly peasants and gracious plebs; bookworms and woodworms; stupid professors and humble power-brokers; saints and sinners; reprobates and rakes; self-righteous criminals and venerable rogues; sad sacks and funny interrogators. But at the minute it is as if I have known no one.

The acoustic of my life has been filled with music, with happy music or lamentations and with jigs and reels. Arias have vied with mountain streams and symphonies have wrestled with winds whipping in over Atlantic waves. Keening at funerals has been drowned with the crack of real or plastic bullet rounds and the thud of suspect devices and the screams of terrified mourners. Or defiance in massed male voices raised in prison song and daring our gaolers to do their worst. Or the martial thump of marching feet. Or *sean nós* singing to welcome the dawn. Or Pavarotti and Leonard Cohen dueting on the words of Kris Kristofferson. Or the Buena Vista Social Club; or a gospel choir; or *Port na bPucaí* and *Ode to Joy* or Pachelbel's *Frolics*. If I was able to hear them.

Or to see all the things I used to see the way I used to see them.

3 January 2000

Because now I know only one thing. And that is that there is nothing like having a grandchild. It's as old as time itself but nonetheless true for all that.

Maybe this awesome feeling will pass and I will think of other things. Maybe? Who am I kidding? Reality is bound to intrude again... any time now. But for now, as far as I can comprehend, everything began in the last century on 27 December when a beautiful, gorgeous, wonderful wee girl came into our lives and we and another lucky couple became grandparents. And an even luckier couple became parents.

See me? I live in the future. I'm head-over-heels-besotted-silly about it all. The millennium *abú*. Our granddaughter for ever!

An Irish Journal

The Equivalence of Grief

Tom Williams was nineteen when he was executed in Belfast prison on 2 September 1942. He had been arrested following a shoot-out in which an RUC officer, Patrick Murphy, was killed. Tom Williams and five other men, including Joe Cahill, who is currently vice-president of Sinn Féin, were sentenced to death.

Following a huge public campaign, which included Irish-America, five were reprieved, but Tom Williams, as leader of the group, was sentenced to be hanged. His death had an enormous effect on Republican Ireland and particularly Belfast Republicans. A campaign started, not long after his death, to have his remains taken from Belfast prison to be reinterred in Milltown cemetery, where he had made it clear he wanted to be buried in the Republican plot.

Fifty-seven years later, last Wednesday, the respect and honour in which he is held was evidenced at his funeral when Belfast's Falls Road came to a standstill as thousands of people reached out to touch the memory of Tom Williams. At the family's request, the burial was in his mother's grave just below the Republican plot, and while some Republicans were disappointed, there was a huge, palpable sense of a chapter closing, particularly for Republicans of his generation and for the Belfast Committee of the National Graves Association who led the campaign for his reinterrment.

On Sunday, in a ceremony to mark this event, tens of thousands of Republicans gathered in Milltown cemetery. I was very privileged to be one of the speakers along with Joe Cahill. In my remarks I reflected on how I was uplifted by the great dignity of Tom's generation of Republicans as they prayed at the funeral service not just for Tom Williams but for the RUC man who was killed at the time of his arrest.

I made the point that Republicans recognise that the deaths of non-combatant civilians cause great trauma and grief for their families and friends and that we also recognise that the death of a British soldier or an RUC member has the same effect. If we are to have a real healing process, then anti-Republican sentiment in this country will have to recognise that families of IRA

24 January 2000

volunteers go through exactly the same pain and grief as other bereaved families. This is one of the realities of conflict. This is one of the matters which will have to be addressed if the healing process is to succeed.

Republicans recognise the equivalence of grief because we, too, have lost loved ones. Despite all the progress of recent years, there is still an open wound and a great hurt within Republican communities because of the lack of acknowledgement within most of the media and all the political establishments of the suffering of Republican families. Treating these families as if they don't exist and as if their pain is of no consequence is an extension of the failed propaganda lie that the IRA is an isolated terrorist organisation without popular support or approval. Those who continue to push this old agenda also refuse to accept their share of responsibility for thirty years – and longer – of conflict.

No Unionist leader has ever expressed one word of regret or acknowledged the injustice of partition and the decades of Unionist misrule. All of that, I have no doubt, will come in its own time as the old certainties fade and a truly just and lasting political dispensation is built. As part of this process, everyone will have to face up to the reality that there can be no grief more worthy than any other. There are 355 Republican activists on the Roll of Honour covering the last thirty years. Most of these are IRA volunteers. I appreciate why families and friends and communities uphold the memory of RUC and British soldiers killed in this conflict. Republicans are equally proud of those IRA volunteers who gave their lives in the struggle. The size of Tom Williams' funeral fifty-seven years after his death is proof of that.

There are brave people on all sides of any conflict, including this one. The reactionaries will reject this because it is the truth which they and, until now, the British government have for ever sought to deny. It is around these issues of legitimacy and equivalence that they fought a constant propaganda battle. It is because they understand the importance of popular support that they feel the need to dominate, to demonise and to isolate. But the truth is that Republicans like Tom Williams gave everything they had to give with no thought or expectation of personal reward. Rather they endured vilification and poverty and all sorts of hardships and anxieties, and they did all of this because they wanted freedom.

Whether you like them or not, from 1916, through the Tan and Civil War, from Tom Williams' day until now, the IRA has behaved with honour, within its own code, and with great consistency and tenacity. Whether you agree with them or not, there would not be a peace process if today's IRA had not had the courage to call and maintain a cessation which has lasted now for almost five years.

In his message from the scaffold even as he faced execution, it is remarkable that Tom Williams looked to the future. That is what we all have to do. We need to build a future which is free from the difficulties and the tragedies of the past. That is the very least that our bereaved families deserve. All of them.

31 January 2000

The Process Can Be Saved

The demand for decommissioning continues to retard and damage the peace process. But with the de Chastelain Report due to be published, the possibility exists for positive responses and the full implementation of all aspects of the Agreement.

To the casual observer, or even those who should know better, the current difficulties in the Irish peace process appear simple enough. It is all down to why the IRA has not decommissioned by now. This has been the hypnotic, all-pervasive drumbeat now rising to deafening loudness and drowning out all other logic.

In a review of the process, chaired by Senator George Mitchell, certain agreements were made which led to an unprecedented move by the IRA to engage with the Independent International Commission on Decommissioning and led also to the Ulster Unionist Party participating in institutions which they had boycotted since the Good Friday Agreement in May 1998.

The Mitchell Review was actually set up because the Unionists, in a bizarre but successful attempt to face down the British government, boycotted the new Assembly in July last year when London triggered the mechanism by which ministers could be appointed. By their actions and their rejection of what was a Sinn Féin initiative, the Unionists successfully scuttled yet another effort by us and others to implement the Good Friday Agreement. It is not surprising, therefore, that there was a huge welcome when, as a result of the Mitchell Review, the Unionists were eventually persuaded, eighteen months late, to go into the institutions. David Trimble did the right thing. But as always, like the cow that gives the good milk and then kicks over the bucket, the UUP, at the last minute, and totally outside the terms of the Mitchell Review, announced its own unilateral deadline for IRA disarmament.

So what's it all about? There are undoubtedly problems within Unionism, which finds it difficult to come to terms with the changes that are required if the Good Friday Agreement is to become a reality and if a transformation of the political landscape here is to be achieved. Some of those within Unionist activism have opted for the rejectionist anti-Agreement demand for the Good Friday Agreement to be scrapped. These include the DUP who, despite their rhetoric of outright opposition, have nonetheless taken up their ministries and committee chairs and are working within the Assembly and the institutions and with the other, pro-Agreement parties. The anti-Agreement clique also includes elements within Mr Trimble's UUP. In my opinion, despite the opposition within his own party, David Trimble's leadership would have won majority support in the UUP for participation in the institutions at any time in the last eighteen months if he had put such a proposition. True, he would not have won unanimous support, but what party leader enjoys such a mandate?

The truth is David Trimble never put such a proposition because his tactical approach to the Agreement, unlike the rejectionists, was to constantly renegotiate it, to whittle it down, to minimise and to protract the process. It wasn't Sinn Féin who persuaded the UUP leadership to enter into the institutions in December. We tried and failed. It was the British government, and particularly Peter Mandelson, who persuaded the UUP leadership to do the right thing. On Remembrance Sunday weekend at the end of the Mitchell Review, Mr Mandelson conducted an intensive lobby of the UUP. This followed the rejection by David Trimble of propositions contained in the Mitchell Review.

The result of this work and of persuasive arguments by others, including US President Bill Clinton, was that the institutions came to life. Now Mr Trimble is saying that Sinn Féin is in default of that review because the IRA did not decommission by 31 January. Mr Trimble is wrong and he knows it. I can provide chapter and verse of the detail of Sinn Féin's position, and it is the same position we have argued publicly and privately with successive British and Irish governments and others, including the Unionists, for almost as long as I can remember. So, I repudiate absolutely any accusation of bad faith by us. On the contrary, we acted in good faith and we continue to do so.

Even now, at the time of writing, as Mr Trimble threatens to resign his position unless the British government pulls down the

31 January 2000

institutions, Sinn Féin is working away trying to save the process. We are in intensive discussions with all sides to avert disaster. In my view the whole issue of arms can be satisfactorily resolved, and I am committed to resolving it, but proving that politics does not work is not the way to persuade armed groups. In other words, this issue can be resolved and in my view will be resolved, but only if everyone plays their part in a constructive and positive way.

The IRA cessation has lasted five years. At its outset, the leader of Unionism, James Molyneaux, described it as the most destabilising thing to have taken place in seventy years. The demand for decommissioning came after this cessation and was no part of it. It has been used to cripple and retard and may indeed eventually hole this process below the waterline. Of course, it would be simpler if the armed groups would just do what is demanded of them, but it was never going to be that easy. Yet there are positives. On Tuesday the IRA, in an effort to reassure Unionism, has said that it is committed to the peace process and that there is no threat to the process from it.

So guns that are silent, that are out of commission for five years, which belong to an organisation whose representative is engaged with the decommissioning body, are going to be the reason or the excuse to tear down institutions which are barely eight weeks old. Why?

Could it be that this is not about decommissioning at all? Could it be that the Unionists want a different agreement? That they imagine they have some short-term advantage over Sinn Féin? That they can bring down this agreement and renegotiate another one more satisfactory and acceptable to them? Could it be that Peter Mandelson will facilitate them in this?

One thing is for certain – within the next thirty-six hours or so the process can be saved. The de Chastelain Report – essentially a progress report – will be published by then. There is no reason why it cannot be a positive report and why it cannot be taken up positively by the British government and by the UUP. That way the full implementation of all aspects of the Agreement is guaranteed.

There's another thing for certain. If the Unionist game plan spooks the British government into suspending or collapsing the institutions – and there is no difference between suspending and collapsing – then like Humpty-Dumpty all of this will be very difficult to put together again, and decommissioning, which the Unionists make such a great fuss about, is unlikely ever to be achieved.

Some political leaders see this peace process as about winners and losers. There will be no winners, and the only losers will be the plain people of Ireland and our friends and supporters throughout the world. I say there will be no winners. That's wrong. Because of course the anti-Agreement clique, those who are against the change, the reactionary bigots, will have succeeded in dragging Unionism back to their agenda.

21 February 2000

THE BAD FRIDAY AGREEMENT?

At midnight on 11 February the new devolved government was suspended and direct rule was reintroduced. The suspension covered the Assembly, the Executive, and other institutions.

An old cynic once remarked to me: "The more things change the more they remain the same." I disagreed with him then and I still disagree with him now. His out-of-the-side-of-the-mouth observation is an excuse for doing nothing. But after the British government's decision, on 11 February, to collapse the institutions and the political processes which were put in place here only a short eight weeks before, I know what he meant.

In one arrogant, unilateral and illegal move, an international treaty was swept aside, the Good Friday Agreement was torn up and the duly elected institutions were torn down. Why? Because the Ulster Unionist Party had demanded this. If the IRA don't meet our demands on the arms issue or you don't suspend the institutions, the UUP told the British government, the UUP ministers are going to resign by six o'clock on Friday, 11 February.

So what could the Brits do? Stand by their international agreement with the Irish government and the rest of us? Tell the Unionists that their demands were outside the terms of the Good Friday Agreement? Assert the integrity of the British government's own position on all these matters? Spell out London's commitments to all the changes involved in the Good Friday Agreement and tell the Unionists and the world that these changes were going ahead anyway, no matter what the UUP did? Uphold the independence of the Independent International Commission on Decommissioning (IICD) and tell the world and the UUP that this was the body which deals with the arms issue?

Nope. The British government did what it has always done when the Orange card is played. It reinstated the Unionist veto. Peter Mandelson's suspension of the institutions was the outworking of his understanding with the UUP. It was the Bad Friday Agreement.

Mr Mandelson has defended his position in a number of

ways. He has also shifted his position considerably and has engaged in a confusing series of media briefings in Belfast, London and Dublin and now in the USA. The British secretary of state has also claimed that he did not know of the IRA position or the content of the de Chastelain Report before he suspended the institutions. Let me say that both the British and Irish governments knew exactly what Sinn Féin was trying to do. They were part of this. And they knew the detail of each step as the situation progressed, including the Independent International Commission on Decommissioning and the IRA positions.

I was in contact on a daily basis and sometimes a few times daily with officials from both governments. On a number of occasions I had detailed discussions with them around the evolving IRA position and the commission's view of this. And I was also in contact with senior ministers, including the taoiseach and the British prime minister, with the de Chastelain commission and with the IRA and others. As the de Chastelain Report makes clear, the IRA was also in regular contact with the commission. And, of course, British officials and Irish officials were all the time in touch with the commission also. Peter Mandelson knows this.

He also knows that as part of Sinn Féin's very intense shuttle diplomacy, an advanced IRA position was secured. I have since described this as a major breakthrough. We gave this to the Irish government on the morning of Friday the 11th. Subsequently this position was passed to the British government. The British prime minister and I discussed this on the phone before noon. In the course of the afternoon I also spoke to the taoiseach and to Peter Mandelson, while Martin McGuinness and I were also in contact on a number of occasions with both British and Irish officials. Martin also met with David Trimble at my request and with the IICD.

By this time the commission had received the IRA's position. Martin McGuinness discussed these matters with the IICD for a short time and then contacted me by telephone. He and I formed a clear view that a second report was imminent and would be positive. I spoke again to Mr Mandelson, and on the basis of the new initiative I asked him not to collapse the institutions. He told me that there was not enough for the UUP. I also

21 February 2000

spoke to Mr Trimble by telephone and asked him to withdraw his resignation on the basis of this new initiative. He also told me that it was not enough.

In this context and in an effort to forestall Mr Mandelson's move to suspend the political institutions, I issued a public statement saying:

- There was an initiative capable of resolving this matter.
- There was a second and very positive IICD report.

For Peter Mandelson to say that he was not aware of the IRA's or the de Chastelain commission's position is nonsense. The reality is that he was working to another imperative, and that was the UUP threat to proceed with Mr Trimble's resignation unless an announcement about suspension was on the 6pm news. So, despite being aware of the IRA position, of Sinn Féin's view of it, of the Irish government's view and a positive de Chastelain Report, Mr Mandelson proceeded with suspension.

Why did he ignore the report? Because the report said: "The representative indicated to us today the context in which the IRA will initiate a comprehensive process to put arms beyond use, in a manner as to ensure maximum public confidence. The Commission believes that this commitment, on the basis described above, holds out the real prospect of an agreement which would enable it to fulfil the substance of its mandate."

The UUP demand on IRA decommissioning or of the suspension of the institutions was untenable in the face of such a report. So Peter Mandelson moved before the report was published.

Since then the process has been in crisis. That's hardly surprising.

Before Mr Mandelson suspended the institutions, I asked him, "What next?" I am still waiting for an intelligible answer.

Over to you, Peter!

A New Phase?

Having suspended the institutions and caused a political vacuum, the British government shows no sign of knowing where the process is to go next.

In the course of a speech to a recent Sinn Féin conference, I made the point that a phase in the process to implement the Good Friday Agreement has come to an end. A week or so later, and a month after Peter Mandelson unilaterally and illegally suspended the political institutions, I see no reason to change my mind.

I made other points in that speech as well, which are equally valid and which have been misrepresented by some of our political rivals, but that is a subject to which I will return to on another day. For now I want to concentrate on the new phase in the process which is opening up. It is my view that how this phase is managed will be critical to the success of the overall process.

I feel very strongly that what Peter Mandelson did on 11 February was to give British government support to the closure of one phase of the process. Of course, it may not be if Mr Mandelson moves speedily to restore the institutions. However, I see no sign of that. From my discussions with the British government and its officials, it is my view that they really don't know how they are going to proceed from here. I have no doubt that they want the institutions back in place and that the political leadership is concerned about a lengthy vacuum. But having suspended the institutions and caused the vacuum, London thus far has no real notion of where the process is to go from here.

For its part, the Irish government, which stood against the suspension of the institutions, is also in difficulties. It is faced with a British government which has behaved in an illegal way, a British government with which it enjoys good relations and with which it wants to restore those relations as soon as possible, for reasons I understand and support. The Irish government also faces the possibility that it may have to introduce legislation to amend the British-Irish Agreement Act 1999 and the related British-Irish Agreement (Amendment) Act in order to

6 March 2000

remedy the defective legal basis of the Southern leg of the all-Ireland institutions. I am advised that this would be seen as a huge international rift. Dublin is also, for obvious reasons, gravely concerned about the consequences of a vacuum.

So how can the process be saved? Some parties are calling for round-table talks chaired by the two governments. Sinn Féin is not opposed to this, but changes in the format of meetings will not on their own save the process. A change of mind-set and a return to the Good Friday Agreement is required. But because there is no sign of that from the Unionists, it is difficult to see how any variations of meetings can succeed.

The only way we can get an answer to how the process is to be saved is by establishing why it is in jeopardy. The process was always in jeopardy, as any process of change will be, because Unionism is against change. It is in jeopardy at this time because the decommissioning section of the Good Friday Agreement was turned on its head and allowed to become an obstacle to progress as opposed to an objective of a peace process. The arms issue became now an issue of tactical political management. That was the downfall of the process.

It may be worthwhile briefly recapping some of the things that we know about decommissioning:

- It is not a security issue.
- Silenced weapons are not a threat.
- Decommissioning was no part of the cessations.
- None of the armed groups are committed to decommissioning.
- There will be no decommissioning in the absence of political progress.
- There seems to be no possibility that any armed group will decommission by 22 May.
- Decommissioning is not a precondition in the Good Friday Agreement.
- No political party can be held in default over the failure or refusal of any armed group to decommission.
- The decommissioning issue has bogged the process down since the Good Friday Agreement, almost two years ago.
- The arms issue can be resolved in an acceptable way if it is dealt with as an objective of a peace process.

The British government may have a different view. Indeed, the Ulster Unionist Party obviously wants to continue as it has until now, and it probably feels strengthened by London's support. For a week or so, some elements of Unionism may feel they had a victory of sorts. But if they had it was a pyrrhic victory. A successful peace process is about more than that.

It is my view that this is the phase of the process which has come to an end. Of course, I can only speak for Sinn Féin, and I have made it clear that I see no merit in our chasing our tails again on this issue. If that has indeed become clear and if an acceptance that tactical short-term gesture politics is not the way to deal with this issue, then that can become the one powerful positive in an otherwise bleak situation. Because it is in that context that the issue can be dealt with strategically. For our part, Sinn Féin remains committed to taking all the guns out of Irish politics.

The Unionists will have lots of reasons to deal with the arms issue on a tactical basis. Remember the UUP, including the then First Minister David Trimble, voted against Patten in the British House of Commons. So this is a battle they intend to continue. They also will obviously oppose the long overdue report of the Review of the Criminal Justice System.

The Orange parades are once again an issue, and the UUP and DUP have set their faces against demilitarisation and the equality agenda, so we really can't blame them if they see merit in tactically using and abusing the decommissioning issue for their own narrow ends. We have to dissuade them from this course, but the big challenge, as always, about bringing about change in this part of Ireland is for the British government.

Is it prepared to think strategically? Is it prepared to abandon the short-term tactical approach it has adopted thus far on the arms issue? Or is it prepared to restore the institutions, to assert the primacy of politics and uphold the section in the Good Friday Agreement on decommissioning?

18 March 2000

THE WORK BACK HOME

St Patrick's Day in the White House highlights the fact that President Clinton's policy on Ireland has been a pivotal influence in the search for a lasting peace.

On this beautiful, blue-skied, bright spring morning, the metroliner thunders its route from Washington to New York. Your columnist is enjoying the relative anonymity and relaxation of a rare train journey. The countryside is greening itself on all sides, the trees in bud as we rush through small towns with shabbily impoverished railtrack-side housing allotments and random empty and litter-infested warehouses and work-yards. It is the morning after the night before. The promise of spring and growth and the future, cheek by jowl with decay and shabby remnants, almost mirrors the current state of the Irish peace process.

Last evening we celebrated St Patrick's Day in the White House, hundreds of us from all over Irish-America and from Ireland itself. It was the last St Patrick's Day of this US president's term, and he and the first lady and their daughter Chelsea were about enjoying themselves. The celebrations were as good-humoured, with as much *craic* as any of the other years, even though everybody knew that back home the grim consequences of the British government's illegal and unilateral suspension of the institutions was steadily deepening the current crisis.

The president was in good form. At the Speaker's lunch the Chieftains lifted Capitol Hill in their frenzy of fiddles, pipes, flute and Derek Bell. From their barnstorming version of *Cotton-Eyed Joe* to *Mo Ghile Mear* to the lightning feet of the dancers, the room jigged and reeled. Did I see David Trimble's feet tapping? No, perhaps not. But Bill Clinton could barely stay in his chair. Little wonder later that night he would say, "I love Ireland – I love its music. I love its dance. I love the Irish people."

Clinton's policy on Ireland has been a pivotal influence in the search for a lasting peace. He is miles ahead of any of the principals in Ireland and Britain in his strategic grasp of what needs to be done. That was clear once again from our meeting with him. Growing up in the segregated South has imbued him with a sense of the changes which are required if equality is to become the birthright of citizens here, or in Ireland. At the American Ireland Fund dinner, the great and the good hung on to every word of the brilliant, unscripted speech he delivered at the end of the evening.

Despite the spin from British Secretary of State Peter Mandelson that real work would be done here in the USA, it was always obvious that the work is back at home, waiting for us all, and especially for him, when we return.

The president's role – in his own words – is that of a "friend" – in my view a good and loyal friend of the peace process in Ireland. Irish-America knows that. Irish-America also knows the enormity of the set-back arising from the British government's suspension of the institutions. Ireland voted – Britain vetoed. Over a month later, with the dust settling, Irish-America has seen beyond the British embassy-inspired rash of editorials critical of Sinn Féin and is angry at the superficiality of London's tactical approach. How many British secretaries of state does it take to change a light bulb? One, but he needs the Unionists to tell him when and how to do it.

So what do the rest of us do? What can we do? Well, we can give up or we can refuse to give up. That's what we can do. We can take a deep breath in the knowledge that the naysayers and the No men, the bigots and the chancers can only win if we give up. Yes, they have been encouraged by the British government's cave-in to Unionism. Yes, the process is in the worst crisis so far. And yes, the Republican well is dry and the arms issue has been successfully exploited to bring everything to this critical point. But change cannot be prevented. Unless we give up. It can be delayed and it can be frustrated, but it cannot be stopped.

Two things are for certain. The way the arms issue has been handled thus far is the wrong way. The British government needs to get down now to handling it the right way. London is in breach of the Good Friday Agreement. This needs to be set to rights. As soon as possible.

Another thing is for certain. This Irish Republican isn't for giving up. Not when so many people back home are depending on people like us to win a future for them and their children.

18 March 2000

Tony Blair holds the key to unlock that future. We have to persuade him to turn it so that the people of one small island can go forward to freedom, justice and peace.

An Irish Journal

A False Spring?

Two years on from the dawn of the new dispensation of the Good Friday Agreement, there is no celebration or consolidating of its implementation, because Peter Mandelson has caved in to Unionist demands and suspended the institutions.

I am writing this column on the Monday morning after the Sinn Féin Ard-Fheis. It is also the second anniversary of the Good Friday Agreement. It's a beautiful spring morning, quite warm, unlike the historic 10 April two years ago. But even this column, which tries always to look on the bright side of life, has come to learn that every silver lining has a cloud. Our spell of good weather does not match the political climate.

A week or so ago a countryman told me that unseasonal warmth like this is called a false spring. It confuses the plant life and the wild life.

"Watch the crows," he said. "They're pulling the sheep's wool off the fences to line their nests. That's a sign that they are expecting bad weather."

"Cast ne'er a clout till May's out?" I queried.

"Exactly," he said.

He could have been talking about the political situation. It, too, is confusing. And I have a sense of extreme foreboding.

The signs and utterances from Peter Mandelson are all positive, but like a false spring they are also confusing. Mr Mandelson issues more statements than your average fax machine, but I have given up trying to read the signs. For politicians, influencing public opinion is a very necessary thing. Trying to make politics work is another thing entirely. It's the difference between shadow and substance.

And where does Tony Blair sit in all of this? The majority of delegates at the Sinn Féin Árd-Fheis have given up on Mr Blair.

In my presidential address I tried to rationalise this. In my view, many Republican activists, despite themselves perhaps, and contrary to the history of Anglo-Irish relations and the last thirty years, had come to hope that this British government was different from the rest and that it was really going to keep to its

10 April 2000

commitments. So when London caved in to the Unionists and suspended the institutions, many Republicans, though they may never admit this, were hurt.

I don't know if the British government accepts this, though I have said this both to Tony Blair and Peter Mandelson, but I'm sure they understand why this is the case. I am also certain that they know that the entire Sinn Féin peace strategy is predicated upon movement and progress. It has to be seen to work, particularly by the activists. But at the moment the activists, like the crows, are working on deeper instincts.

Peter Mandelson defends his action of suspending the institutions by claiming that he did so in order to save David Trimble. But has he done so? It can be argued that Mr Trimble's position is worse than before because he now has nothing at all to show for all his perambulations. The only good bit in this is that David Trimble needs the institutions back in place if he is to survive. As a delegate told the Ard-Fheis, without the institutions David Trimble will run out of time.

Another interesting aspect of the inner machinations of the UUP is that it is now obvious, for those who want to see, that Trimble's leadership has had a consistent 60–40 per cent majority since the day he became leader. It is clear that had he acted at any time from the Good Friday Agreement to put a positive proposition to his party that he could have relied on this support. In other words, if in January he had responded positively to the de Chastelain Report, a majority of the UUP would have supported him.

Now, instead of encouraging David Trimble to go forward on a positive basis, Peter Mandelson is making public suggestions that perhaps elements of the Patten Report into policing could be changed to make it more acceptable to the UUP. So much for consistency or for a long-term strategic view! Everything becomes hostage to the short term, and thus far there is no strategic or tactical merit in what I have come to understand of the British approach to the question of bringing change to this part of our island.

"Maybe," a long-time activist confided in me in a corner of the conference hall, "maybe if you look at the way they handled the contest for the Labour nomination in the London mayoral election, you see what this government is about. They have the most popular candidate in the field, Ken Livingstone. Instead of enlisting him and at last having some control of him, they get involved in silliness and end up all over the place. The Good Friday Agreement could be suffering from the same problem. What do you think?"

What do I think? I'll tell you after May.

I haven't given up yet on Tony Blair. He, too, is probably pondering this morning on what could and should have been. But if we're to prove that it's nothing like the same old story, then Mr Blair will have to accept that he holds the key to progress here.

There is no easy way forward. Either the British government is committed to the Good Friday Agreement and to the measures contained within it or the Agreement will have signalled nothing more than a false spring. Will there be negotiations between now and Easter? Maybe. Will they be real negotiations? I don't know.

As I told a sceptical Ard-Fheis, the Good Friday Agreement can be saved, but it will take Mr Blair to face up to his responsibilities. The British government cannot pass the buck on this issue or make this opportunity for peace conditional on the whims of rejectionist Unionism or Brit securocrats. Two years on we should have been celebrating or consolidating the implementation of the Agreement. Instead, following fifty years of one-party rule under the old Unionist regime, and thirty years of conflict, we had a mere eight weeks of inclusive institutions.

Maybe the real problem was that the institutions worked and they were popular. Maybe the real problem was that, alongside their ministerial colleagues, Sinn Féin Minister for Health Bairbre de Brún and Minister for Education Martin McGuinness behaved with honesty, magnanimity, fairness and impartiality. They were good ministers. Everyone accepts that. Maybe that's the real problem.

If the decline of the Good Friday Agreement is to be reversed before it become terminal, Mr Blair must steer the process out of the current wobble. He has to face up to those within his own system, and within rejectionist Unionism, who don't want change. He must order the reinstatement of the institutions.

17 April 2000

FOREIGN DEBT IS KILLING MILLIONS

Gerry Adams supports the cancellation of developing countries' debt.

On the eve of a Tony Blair visit to Ireland, I see from my television screen that Washington was under siege for much of last weekend, and the start of this week, as thousands of protesters took to the streets in protest at the World Bank and International Monetary Fund (IMF), who were meeting in the US capital with finance ministers from the leading industrial countries. The protestors demanded the cancellation of developing countries' debt.

This column has long supported this demand. Institutions such as the World Bank and the IMF have acted for too long without accountability to the people their programmes affect. The time for the cancellation of developing countries' debt is long overdue, and action cannot come soon enough. In recent months I have met with Jubilee 2000, which is the leading campaign group against world debt. In meetings with President Clinton, Tony Blair and Bertie Ahern, I urged them to maintain the momentum by supporting this call and taking the transparent action necessary to cancel all debt. During the St Patrick's Day celebrations at the White House, I talked for some time with President Clinton about this huge issue, and I have to say that he appeared to me to be well disposed to doing more.

The urgent need for this was highlighted recently in Mozambique. While thousands of men, women and children clung desperately to trees and roof-tops, their government was being forced to send $1.4 million a week to its debtors in the G7 countries.

After Hurricane Mitch, Honduras and Nicaragua were spending over half their government revenue on debt repayments. In Nicaragua, government funds that could have been used to meet the basic needs of the unemployed, the malnourished and the poor went instead to pay off a debt that is considered unpayable. The government of Nicaragua, where over half the population is under sixteen years old, is sacrificing a generation to pay its debt.

Without a natural disaster to draw the attention of international media, the same tragedy and suffering goes on daily away from the television cameras. This week sixteen million people again face starvation in the Horn of Africa. Thirty-seven African countries owe a total of $354 billion. About half of this is owed directly to individual governments – mainly Japan, the US, Britain, Canada, France, Germany and Italy – the G7. Most of the rest is "multilateral" debt – owed to the World Bank and the IMF, which are effectively run by the G7 governments. Only about 10 per cent is owed to private banks.

The UN estimates that if funds being used to pay off debt were diverted back into health and education from debt repayment, the lives of seven million children a year could be saved. That is two million people more than live in the island of Ireland. That is 134,000 children a week.

The United Nations Sub-Committee on Nutrition (ACC/SCN) Commission chair, Philip James, said recently: "The nutritional health of children and adults often deteriorates as a result of cutbacks and austerity programs imposed by international institutions like the IMF. IMF-negotiated structural adjustment programs normally focus on an immediate balancing of the budgets even at the cost of human hardship. It is evident that this seemingly temporary sacrifice prejudices the lives of future generations – balancing budgets at a cost of unbalancing children's lives."

He continues, calling for "pro-poor structural adjustment". The World Bank and IMF should be required to show "how progress towards nutrition goals could be maintained and supported as a priority during programs of structural adjustment and debt repayment, especially of the heavily indebted poor countries". We must heed this call as well as cancelling all existing debt immediately.

Another issue that needs to be addressed is that of lending to dictators and corrupt leaders. Lenders have a history of lending money to prop up dictators. In a new report, the Jubilee 2000 Coalition estimates that 22 per cent of debt was given to dictators during the Cold War, totalling more than $451 billion. The biggest loans were $126 billion to Suharto in Indonesia and $100 billion to the military governments of Brazil. Indeed, the

17 April 2000

west reduced its lending to Brazil after the advent of democracy fifteen years ago, so the loans to the military juntas still account for 56 per cent of Brazil's debt. South Africa is still paying loans given to the apartheid state to help it block majority rule. Loans were knowingly given to Marcos in the Philippines and Mobutu in Zaire, even though the lenders knew they were corrupt.

At its first international conference in Rome on 17 November, Jubilee 2000 delegates called for the cancellation of debt incurred by repressive regimes. Banks should not be able to make loans to repressive regimes which misuse money and violate human rights and then force the victims of those regimes, many of whom were not even alive when the loan was taken, to repay the loans.

All of this puts the problems in the Irish peace process in context. Yet even this Easter week, as we labour to save the process, we have to stand up for others in other parts of the world. We cannot continue this way. Too many people are suffering because of the lack of concern of a few at the top. Enough is enough. Loans made by the lending institutions and countries are coming at too high a cost. The case for Third World debt cancellation is too great to be ignored any longer.

An Irish Journal

THE HEARTBEAT OF THE PEACE PROCESS

On Saturday, 6 May, the IRA issued an historic statement.

On Saturday last I unveiled a monument to IRA volunteers killed in action from the Lenadoon area of Belfast. It is a very fine monument in the form of a large life-sized sculpture of Cúchulainn. The monument is in the grounds of the Roddy McCorley Society on the lower slopes of the Black Mountain, on an elevated site overlooking Belfast and its lough. Saturday was a beautiful day. The unveiling was scheduled for 1.30pm, and when we arrived there was a large throng of people assembled. There were the families of the dead volunteers, their comrades, neighbours, friends, and all those who had helped raise the money for the monument and organise the event.

They were, for various reasons, a crowd of people who had one thing in common: they were supporters of the IRA who had suffered much for their commitment over the last three decades. Unbeknownst to them, half an hour earlier the IRA leadership had issued a statement which is now acclaimed as historic and unprecedented. I decided both to tell the gathering about this development and to explain it to them. As I spoke I watched the faces all around me. That the IRA was going back to meet the de Chastelain commission was obviously a surprise. Given the way that the positive report from the Independent International Commission on Decommissioning (IICD) had been treated by the British government in February, this was very much a natural and widespread reaction. By suspending the institutions the British not only binned the IICD report but they undermined the commission itself.

Little wonder then that my audience were taken aback. But that wasn't all. The IRA were also prepared to set in place a confidence-building measure which involves international statespersons Cyril Ramaphosa and Martti Ahtisaari inspecting a number of arms dumps on a regular basis. I explained the detail of all of this, the imperative of the peace process and the need for Republicans not to be confused or confounded by all the various spins and twists that would be put on this latest IRA initiative.

8 May 2000

I asked them to get a copy of the statement and to read it themselves and to discuss it calmly and strategically. I explained and read to them the context in which the army leadership will put arms beyond use. The IRA said: "The full implementation, on a progressive and irreversible basis by the two governments, especially the British government, of what they have agreed will provide a political context, in an enduring political process, with the potential to remove the causes of conflict, and in which Irish Republicans and Unionists can, as equals, pursue our respective political objectives peacefully."

The crowd was focused and intent, and it struck me that of all those who have a stake in the issues involved, apart from the IRA itself, that my audience was representative of that great sward of Republican activism which really has given its all, and would do so again if it had to, for the cause of freedom and justice on this island. They are the heart of the Republican struggle and the heartbeat of the peace process.

I had some sense then of the difficulties facing the IRA leadership and of the magnitude of the IRA's initiative. That leadership, this latest initiative and the way that it is managed will be scrutinised closely by the Republican base. The tolerance threshold amongst Republicans for messing by the British government and/or the Unionists is now very low. In better circumstances, inadvertent mistakes, mishaps, could be tolerated, but given the amount of messing over the last number of years, I doubt very much that this is part of the current mood. That is not to say that most Republicans will not give this initiative a fair wind, but I cannot overstate the internal pressures on the IRA leadership.

So why did they do what they did? Clearly because they want the peace process to succeed. And also because they want to give some assurance to those Unionists who want to be assured of Republican intentions.

Could it all come to naught? Yes. The British government could yet do some side deal on some other issue, probably around the future of the RUC, in a tactical manoeuvre which will be outside the conditions which led to the IRA initiative. Or the UUP could seek so many concessions around the IRA initiative that they will fritter away the potential for progress that now exists. Or both.

On the other hand it strikes me that thinking Unionism will embrace this offer and the peace process could be saved. The Sinn Féin leadership gets some credit for all of this, and that's fair enough, but the real credit goes to the IRA. Sinn Féin put together the package, but it was the IRA leadership which had to take the hard decisions. I think the crowd at the unveiling last Saturday realised that. They also knew that however this latest development works out the struggle for freedom and justice has to continue. That's if we are to build the only proper monument to those who died, and that's as much the responsibility of good and decent people in the USA as it is for people here.

22 May 2000

PATIENCE

The British government's reaction to the IRA initiative provokes a backlash amongst Republicans.

My last piece, written immediately after the IRA initiative of 6 May, raised the question of whether this latest effort to save the peace process could come to naught. And while I outlined my view that thinking Unionists would embrace the opportunity, I also said, and I quote: "The British government could yet do some side deal on some other issue, probably around the future of the RUC, in a tactical manoeuvre which will be outside the conditions which led to the IRA initiative. Or the UUP could seek so many concessions around the IRA initiative that they will fritter away the potential for progress that now exists. Or both."

Since then I and others in the Sinn Féin leadership have been engaged in a fire-brigade exercise trying to manage the Republican and Nationalist base. Because, of course, not only did David Trimble seek concessions and reopen negotiations, but he was actively encouraged to do so by the attitude of the British government. So until last Friday, the UUP leader poured cold water over the IRA initiative, sought to have the recommendations of the Patten Report into policing set to one side, and demanded that the Union Jack be flown on public buildings and that local ministers (that is, Sinn Féin ministers) would have no discretion on this matter.

In an effort to be measured about all of this, I won't comment even at this stage on the last two elements on this wish list, but there is a need to point up how the British government's dilution of the Patten recommendations on policing has seriously undermined the IRA move. What was first seen by many Republicans and others as a bold and brave effort to reassure Unionism is now being seen as a well-intended going-too-far step in the wrong direction. In all my years of engaging with the Republican base, I have never experienced such a backlash. And most of the anger, frustration and downright annoyance was created not by the Unionists but by the British government. Whatever the effect this has on the IRA, the clear message from the broad Republican base is that the British government have changed the context in which the IRA made their offer. All of this is hugely problematic. And this is especially the case because when the Sinn Féin leadership moved to create this latest opportunity we attempted to legislate for all of this. Our motive was to save the peace process.

It is clear now that the suspension of the institutions did not hurt Sinn Féin. In fact, our vote doubled in two by-elections since the institutions were collapsed. So there was no party political imperative on us to stretch ourselves. Neither was the IRA required to do what it did. But the alternative to taking an initiative is to see the process slide back into conflict. In seeking to prevent this, the senior Sinn Féin negotiators sought commitments in the first instance from the two governments so as to create a context in which to get commitments from the IRA leadership. We wanted to avoid the pitfalls of the Mitchell Review last autumn and of the nonsense which followed it. We wanted to make sure that there was clarity, certitude and certainty, so whatever the view of what was produced, there could be no doubt about what it represented.

As it turned out, the IRA initiative was universally welcomed, and there is no doubt whatsoever that it is a genuine, real and unprecedented contribution which should have been seized upon by anyone interested in anchoring and advancing the peace process. It is little wonder then that efforts to whittle this away or devalue it have been met with incredulity by supporters of the process.

Is the IRA initiative at risk? Well, we will see. Sinn Féin's objective is to see all of the institutions restored and the IRA initiative maintained. But the answer to that question will only be found after Saturday when we discover the basis of the Ulster Unionist Council (UUC) acceptance of this initiative. If they accept it. In my view they will, but really no one knows. What is for sure is that the focus for Nationalists and Republicans won't only be about whether the UUC agrees to move forward; it will be about the terms and conditions that they or the British government may add to this.

One casualty of all the recent machinations has been the Patten Report. The British government's emasculation of the

22 May 2000

Patten recommendations, as contained in the current legislation published just last week, has made it impossible for any Republican or Nationalist to join or support the police force envisaged in the British government bill. Whether it has been fatally wounded or not remains to be seen, and there is a job here for Irish-America and for friends of the Irish peace process throughout the USA. We still need, and we are entitled to, a decent policing service.

An Irish Journal

TREES

I love trees. Small trees. Big trees. Tall trees. Short trees. Wee one and big ones. I'm in awe of the truly big ones, the old giants which have been about for centuries. It must be the druid in me, but I have always looked up to trees, and even now I like to clamber up into the friendly branches of a great oak, an ash or a chestnut. I prefer deciduous trees. Conifers are not to be sneered at but I wouldn't plant one. Broadleafs are my favourites. They change with the seasons, and their bark and shape and seed are a joy to behold as they slowly evolve through the year.

For a very long time now I have collected the seeds of trees and grown them on. It isn't such a big deal, but it is really rewarding if you are lucky with your harvest. Trees have their own story to tell, especially the hand-reared ones. A tree can mark the birth of a baby, an anniversary, the death of an old friend or a family member. A young tree makes a lovely present.

There are not enough trees in Ireland. They, too, were victims of colonisation, felled to furnish wood for the Empire. That's not why I am so fond of them. Even if I lived in a place with lots of trees, I would still try to add to their numbers. I especially like native species. They sustain native insects, which in turn provide food for native birds and other creatures. It is my ambition to grow a forest: not all in one place but here, there and everywhere.

I am already well advanced in my endeavours. I have beech trees in Dublin and Tipperary. I have ash trees everywhere. A wise man and a friend of mine, Paddy McGeady, is a noted tree man. He has planted acres of trees, and he and I have slipped offshore each year for the last few years to plant, so far unsuccessfully, on our western islands. The wind is the big problem there. Methinks we will have to plant shelter belts if we are to prevail. Someone told me once that when people came out of Conamara during the Great Hunger, they were frightened when they saw trees. It was the first time they had seen such things.

Chestnuts are my speciality. From where I am typing this column, I can see that my very first chestnut, now in its late teens, is already starting to form this year's "cheesers". God spares

12 June 2000

me, this autumn I will collect them and dozens more from a secret place and try to grow them on for transplanting near and far. The Belfast Mountains will be home for some of my little saplings and even more, mostly oaks, brought there by a friend of mine. In the next month or so I hope to plant some hazel. For the fairies. I also have a rowan, which is a wonderful tree. Did you know that the birds get drunk eating the fermented seeds of some of our native trees?

Two years or so ago I collected a copious amount of such seeds and gave them to the local Conservation Volunteers, at their request. They included some oak. Some time after that the British army withdrew from Fort Jericho, a huge sprawling and unsightly military structure from which troops used to venture out to attack local people. The fort overlooked Turf Lodge and Ballymurphy. Now another more modern one half a mile away does the same job, but that's another story.

Fort Jericho had blighted the Upper Springfield area for almost three decades, so local people were understandably delighted at its demise. When the British commandeered the land, it included a local cooperative project, the Whiterock Industrial Estate. That estate was the only provider of employment in the locality. It was owned by the people themselves. The British army closed it down. When they eventually vacated the place, I am pleased to say that this column was part of the effort to get the industrial estate reestablished. And we succeeded! Now the local people have a stake once again, and this time the area for development is bigger than it used to be. From little acorns...

Which brings me back to where I started. Remember the seeds I gave to the Conservation Volunteers? Well, last week I was invited to join local school children, including some with learning difficulties, and we went to where Fort Jericho used to be, to where the British army used to be, and we planted some of my oak trees on the site of the new Whiterock Industrial Estate.

An Irish Journal

CLEAKY CLARKE: OUR UNIQUE FRIEND

As I finished last week's column I was tempted to add a little postscript asking *Irish Voice* readers to think of Cleaky Clarke. Cleaky who? you may ask. Well, you might if you weren't among those who met him on his last visit to the USA. Friends in Irish Republican America will know Cleaky. He died last week. I knew he was going to die because he told me so the night I wrote last week's column.

Cleaky (Terry) Clarke is a friend of mine. He is looking at me now from a framed photo on the wall above me. There's him and Todler and the Dark and Bobby Sands and Tom Cahill and me and Jimmy Gibney and Tomboy enjoying the sunshine in Cage Eleven. He had hair then, a wispy thatch of ginger which receded in the years after that. Little wonder. Cleaky did twenty-one years in gaols North and South. Twenty-one and a half years to be exact. I have known him for all those years and for almost a decade more. Most of this time he got me into trouble of some kind or other. In gaol and out of gaol. Even when we were in or out at separate times. He was one of my heroes. A mixer. A raker. A winder-upper. But a hero nonetheless. In fact, when I think of it, we are surrounded by heroes and heroines.

Cleaky's love of life shines through all his exploits and difficulties. These commenced insofar as politics is involved in 1971. In October he was arrested and sent to Crumlin Road Prison. A few weeks later he escaped. He was not part of the original escape plan. He was asked to help, saw his opportunity and went over the wall with eight others. The Crumlin Kangaroos were born.

Cleaky headed south. He described this as his long-rifle phase, but he remained steadfast in his commitment to the struggle. Consequently, he and fifteen others, or if you believe Cleaky's life-long friend Martin Meehan, he and his right-hand man took on the British army at Drumgooley in South Armagh. According to media reports, in the ensuing four-hour gun battle the British fired 20,000 rounds. The only casualty was a prize pig. Cleaky and several others were arrested later that evening. They were charged and taken to Mountjoy Gaol in Dublin, from which he unsuccessfully tried to escape. This was probably very fortuitous because they were all released after several weeks.

Later that year, in October, he was arrested again in Belfast. At his trial he refused to recognise the court and told the judge that he had no right to try him for defending his country and that the day would come when their roles would be reversed. The judge promptly doubled his sentence.

He then went to the cages. There he again tried to escape, along with others including another Ardoyne legend, Larry Marley. They were captured and charged. Several months after the Long Kesh prison camp was destroyed, twelve wannabe Republican escapees were taken to Newry Courthouse to face various escape charges. The bars in the holding cells were not up to scratch, and once again Cleaky, with eleven others in tow, was off at the gallop.

While the others got away, himself and big Deuce were caught before they could reach the border. It was back to the cages again. Below us the H-Blocks were taking shape. Soon it was the end of political status for newly sentenced Republican prisoners. Cleaky was a PRO in the cages. He helped to organise a very effective letter-writing campaign, as well as working closely with the newly formed Relatives' Action Committees.

Some time later and a few weeks before his release, he rushed to the aid of a comrade who was being assaulted by prison officers outside the gate of the cage. Several prisoners and screws were hurt, but it was the prisoners, including Cleaky, who were charged. When he was sentenced, the administration stripped him of his political status and moved him to the H-Blocks where he joined the blanket protest. He was eventually released in 1984.

A year later, in 1985, he was arrested on the word of a paid perjurer and was held for some months before the case collapsed. On 19 March 1988, at the funeral of IRA Volunteer Caoimhín Mac Bradaigh, who had been killed three days earlier at the Gibraltar funerals by Loyalist killer Michael Stone, two British soldiers drove into the funeral cortège. They were armed, and those, including Cleaky, who saw them believed them to be Loyalists trying to repeat Stone's actions.

Cleaky, who was chief steward, demonstrated enormous

courage and great selflessness by tackling an armed man. The subsequent show trial against those who defended the mourners that day was a travesty, and Cleaky received another jail sentence. Back in prison he became ill, and it was during this time that he was first told that he had cancer. The distress of that for him and his family was compounded by the conditions under which he received medical treatment.

Cleaky was released in December 1992. For a short time he worked in the Sinn Féin press office in Belfast. He was enormously effective, especially when challenging the frequent media misrepresentation of our point of view.

The 1980s and early 1990s also saw an increase in Loyalist attacks on Republicans. He was asked to take on the difficult job of providing security for Republicans at risk. He went on to do so with few resources. To tell the truth, his ability to scrounge doors, lights, intercoms, security grills, toughened glass, bullet-proof vests and anything else that he could get his hands on undoubtedly saved lives.

It was a job he took very seriously, right up to close to the end; even from his sick bed. None of that surprised me: it was in the nature of the man. But what did overawe me was the way he faced his death. He did so with grace and dignity and a touch of black humour. He didn't want to die, of course. His big ambition was to live in a free Ireland and his big regret about dying was for Mary Doyle and Maire and young Seamus.

I have never believed in iconising the dead. Or the living for that matter. We are all of us human. Terry was a good and decent human being. He told me that he believed that as long as your friends don't forget, you will always be remembered. The thousands at his funeral, including friends from the USA, and all the people at the wake house is testimony that there are many of us who will always remember.

Those who cared for him, the hospital staff and others, have our gratitude. So, too, do Mary Doyle and Maire and Seamus. Colette and I and Gearóid and Roisín will never forget Cleaky, and our Drithle, whom he nursed last week a short time before he died, will hear all his stories. He would have enjoyed that. He got a great send-off. He would have enjoyed that also.

7 August 2000

A NEW POLICE SERVICE: THIS IS OUR GOAL

British Secretary of State Peter Mandelson engages in double-dealing on the policing issue as fundamental and substantive aspects are gutted from the Patten Commission recommendations. Gerry Adams calls for a new civic policing service which is democratically accountable, working in partnership with all citizens, and upholding international standards of human rights.

Why has this British government made such a mess of the policing issue? Is it Perfidious Albion? Is it cock-up or conspiracy? Incompetence or double-dealing? The answer to those questions depends very much on who is asking the question. But one question will meet with a unanimous response. That question? Is the British government's handling of the policing issue good for the peace process? The answer? No!

So how did it get like this? Let's begin at the beginning. During the negotiations which led to the Good Friday Agreement, there was acceptance of the need to create a new policing service. A commission was established to make recommendations on how this could be achieved. The commission, headed by former British Tory Chairman Chris Patten, was made up of a range of quite conservative individuals. Hardly radical or revolutionary cadres. Notwithstanding this, their report was a progressive and serious attempt to create a new beginning for policing. While Sinn Féin's policing policy goes much further than the Patten recommendations, we welcomed the positive elements of the Patten Report, but we made it clear, wisely as it turned out, that we would withhold our judgment until the British government had dealt with the recommendations. When he received the report, Tony Blair said that he was going to implement the Patten recommendations, but he seems to either have underestimated the resistance there would be within his own system to these recommendations, or else having given that commitment he left it with others who did not share his view. Or maybe he has changed his mind? We have seen all this happen in the past with other British governments on other issues.

The faceless men within the sub-committees which managed British rule in the North of Ireland for the last thirty years have lots of good reasons for resisting the advent of civic policing. The state apparatus which coordinated the counter-insurgency drive of the last few decades has wielded unprecedented power on a range of judicial, military, political, economic, social and planning matters, and will not easily give up that power. Yes, the more long-sighted insiders will know that there will have to be changes. They are prepared to go along with some of these, but only if an instrument of civil control is retained. In other words, they want to maintain ownership of policing. A genuinely open, depoliticised or politically neutral civic policing service would not permit this.

So, who had the first trawl through the Patten recommendations? The faceless officials who make up the Patten Action Committee and the RUC's own Change Management Team. The very people representing the very system which will have to be turned around by modernising political leaders, particularly the British prime minister or his secretary of state, if the Good Friday Agreement is to succeed. And what did these officials do with the Patten recommendations? They did what they have been paid to do for years. The result? They gutted fundamental and substantive aspects of the report.

It was their recommendations that formed the basis of Peter Mandelson's statement on policing in January of this year to the British House of Commons, and the subsequent Mandelson Policing Bill. This bill has been rejected by all shades of Nationalism in Ireland, by the Catholic Church, by the Irish government, by a range of justice and human rights organisations, by those members of the Patten Commission who have spoken on it, and by mainstream political opinion in the USA. And, of course, the Mandelson Bill did not satisfy Unionism, including the UUP. And herein lies another element of the British government's implementation of the Patten recommendations. The Unionists tended to concentrate very much on the symbolic and other trappings connected to the RUC, including issues that the Patten Action Team and the Change Management Team were prepared to concede. However, faced with a *rí-rá* within Unionism, the British government sought to placate the "pro-Agreement" element

7 August 2000

under the leadership of David Trimble by making concessions on the name of the RUC and other issues. So at Hillsborough during the negotiations leading to 5 May, while the British government gave private commitments to Sinn Féin, and repeated these in a joint public statement and letter with the Irish government, Peter Mandelson gave a different commitment to John Taylor about the name of the RUC. Of course, the difficulty with this bit of double-dealing is that it quickly becomes public, not least because there is intense rivalry among Unionists vying to become saviours of the RUC.

So what did the British government do then? In briefings which are reminiscent of the bad old days, it went back to blaming Sinn Féin, and there was a crude PR and lobbying exercise to drive a wedge into the wider Nationalist consensus that the Mandelson Policing Bill is inadequate. This has involved letters from Peter Mandelson to US elected representatives selectively quoting the SDLP and public statements and private briefings which accuse the SDLP of running scared of Sinn Féin. It also involves high-level briefings by senior British officials in the USA that Sinn Féin "are never going to sign up for a new policing service anyway. Sinn Féin are never going to be satisfied and they are dictating the pace"; that the "Irish government understands this and are on board but that Fianna Fáil is worried about Sinn Féin's electoral challenge"; and that "we [the British] are confident that we will get Seamus Mallon back on side". Mr Mandelson also took the unusual step last week of writing to the leader of the opposition in Dublin. His letter was in similar vein to the arguments he and his colleagues have been pursuing in Washington and in the media in Ireland..

At the heart of this spin is the lie that Sinn Féin will never sign up to a new policing service anyway. That is not the case. Sinn Féin want a new policing service and we will not settle for something less than this. Republicans want and need the security of a decent, democratic and accountable policing service. Sinn Féin had produced a comprehensive policy on policing long before the Good Friday Agreement. We will consider and give a fair wind to alternative policing policing proposals. The Patten Report, if fully implemented, may give us the opportunity to do that. The Mandelson Policing Bill does not. We are continuing to work hard to ensure that there is a new policing service. We have produced more amendments, held more private and publicised meetings with the British government, and others, on this issue, and produced more detailed assessments as Mandelson's bill progressed through the British parliament than anyone else. We have done this because one logical outcome of the peace process, if it is to be successful, must be a policing service which Republicans can join and encourage others to join. Currently we have a paramilitary police force which is 100 per cent Unionist.

What is required is a new civic policing service which is democratically accountable, working in partnership with all citizens and upholding international standards of human rights. A policing service that reflects the goals set within the Good Friday Agreement and which is supported by the whole community. The British government has turned the policing issue into a political battleground. It didn't need to be like that. It doesn't need to be like that. It is still possible to secure a policing service that attracts and embraces Republicans, Nationalists and Unionists. This is our goal. It should also be the goal of the British government. It is their stated public objective. But to achieve this Mr Blair will have to face up to and turn around his own system. There is no other way.

28 August 2000

Belfast Is a Planet Away

In the course of a Loyalist feud on Belfast's Shankill Road, the UVF killed Bobby Mahood and Jackie Coulter on 21 August; two days later Samuel Rockett was killed by the UDA. Explosives and arms finds were reported, and Britain's secretary of state ordered Johnny Adair of the UDA to be returned to prison.

This column is officially on holidays. Holidays are very good days indeed, especially holidays with people you love. Holidays in heaven. These last few weeks have been like that. They have been better than that. The weather here in this wee bit of Ireland has been tropical. The food has been terrific. (This column is also the holiday cook.) The company has been gorgeous, the music magical. Every day has been an adventure. Even Oscar and Cara, the dogs, are laid back. That's the way it is.

So the thoughts of going back to whence we came are daunting thoughts indeed. Back to the drudgery of a battle a day. I had forgotten all about it until I bumped into a non-activist friend of mine yesterday.

"I'm sure you're looking forward to going back to all that ****," he said sympathetically and with no sense of irony.

Last year, regular readers will recall, I cancelled all newspapers and ceased listening to or watching news broadcasts. I did the same this year, but not as successfully given that I had to break the holidays twice, by arrangement, once to make an important speech and then to do a party meeting.

So I picked up on the convulsions within Loyalism, and for a few days I felt compelled to listen to a daily newscast. One of the sad things about the funerals of those killed in what is essentially sectarian gang warfare was the number of young men at one of the UFF funerals. The UFF is nothing less than a machine for killing Catholics, at times deployed by anonymous men in British military intelligence, at times exploited by corrupt little neighbourhood thugs for their own ends. The attendance of young working class Loyalist males – the cannon fodder of their generation – is proof of the strength of the sectarianism which grips that section of our people and of the challenges facing us all.

Here where I am, amid spectacular western skies and wide ancestral landscapes, it is easy to be daunted by all that and to wonder what any of this has got to do with life. Here on the edge of the world, with beauty everywhere, it is better not to dwell on the sad, sordid mess which still has to be dealt with and cleared up if there is to be a decent future for as many people as possible. And that includes the young Loyalist men of the Shankill Road and other once-proud Loyalist areas. They, too, must have their place in the scheme of things. Whether they accept their place and take ownership of it is a matter for them, but the only real way to defeat the scourge of sectarian division is to build an alternative society.

That means starting by accepting that places like the Shankill do not have a monopoly on sectarianism. It is not the province of the Protestant working class and they should not be demonised or caricatured. Bigotry is to be found in the highest reaches of the system, in government departments, in the churches and in the drawing rooms of the middle classes of "respectable" Unionism. It has to be stamped out. How? By making sure that sectarianism doesn't pay, either in politics or business, or anywhere else for that matter. And that's a tall order, because the very existence of a status quo in the northeast of this island depended on sectarianism. And as a new status quo evolves those who benefited from the old order will seek to inculcate themselves in the new one. They will not give up easily. Why should they? That's what the *rí-rá* over the Patten Report is about. That's why the British government have been unable so far to fulfil the commitments it made back in May.

It is relatively easy for a British secretary of state to face down a Johnny Adair. He looks and performs and fits everyone's stereotype of a sectarian thug. It's a different matter when the force against change is clothed in mohair suits and soft accents. When it has plausible arguments. When the system depends on it. When it has power. It takes real courage to face that down.

But maybe that's enough for today. This column has other important things to do. Like prepare lunch. There are hungry

28 August 2000

funny people clamouring downstairs. The sun is shining outside. The sky is blue. Belfast is a planet away. Why should I let reality trespass on my space. I have a life.

At least until this time next week. The **** can wait till then!

An Irish Journal

CRISIS! WHAT CRISIS?

In the South Antrim by-election of 21 September, two anti-Agreement candidates compete for the Unionist vote.

This column spent some time this week canvassing in South Antrim, a mainly Unionist constituency where a by-election is being held following the recent death of the UUP MP Clifford Forsyth. The victor will come from either Ian Paisley's DUP or David Trimble's party. If I was a betting man, my money would be on Trimble's man, but as I'm not a gambler the issue doesn't arise.

It is also not a straightforward contest between pro- and anti-Agreement Unionism. You see, the UUP candidate, David Burnside, is not really Trimble's man. He is a No man. The difficulty, therefore, is that some pro-Agreement Unionists won't bother to vote, thus allowing the DUP's singing bigot, the Rev. Willie McCrea, in as the South Antrim MP, with all the ramifications which that will create for the political process and everything else.

Sinn Féin's effort in the area is about building the party structure locally and growing our vote through to next year's local council elections and on into the Assembly elections in a few years' time. For obvious reasons, the risks involved for local people have retarded our organisation in Unionist constituencies like South Antrim. But nowadays more and more brave people are raising their heads above the barricades, and in three recent council by-elections in the South Antrim area, the Republican vote has doubled on each occasion. Martin Meehan is a candidate this time out, and from the response we got on the doorsteps he will do well.

In any case, the results will be known by Friday, and whatever the outcome one thing is certain: the focus of the British government will continue to be about bolstering David Trimble. And therein lies the underlying weakness in British strategy, because every move they contemplate, including the delivery of their own commitments, is decided on how it will effect Mr Trimble's position. Or that, at least, is the reason given. So be sure that even if Mr Trimble's UUP win the by-election, the mes-

18 September 2000

sage will be that he is still in trouble. For example, he has a party conference early next month and that will be the next new problem.

Now let me be clear about where I stand on this issue. I recognise the need to bolster support for the Good Friday Agreement within Unionism. But for the British government to reduce this to a question of the political state of health of one political leader, notwithstanding Mr Trimble's importance and the centrality of his role, reduces British strategy to filtering the rights and entitlements of Nationalist and Republican citizens through a Unionist prism. Or, even worse, our rights and entitlements as citizens are made conditional and dependent on the state, or the perceived state, of Mr Trimble's leadership within Unionism. Or that becomes the excuse for British action or inaction on many fundamental issues.

Therein lies part of the explanation of the current state of the peace process. Because, of course, such a tactical approach is unacceptable by any ethical or democratic standard. It also gives an advantage to any leader in Mr Trimble's position, and any leader like him and worth his or her salt will exploit this. So, too, will other elements, including some within the British establishment itself, who are against change. The British government's current tactical approach puts these people in the driving seat. It also reduces a strategy for conflict resolution to one-day-at-at-a-time crisis management. The No men of Unionism know this. Their strategic aim, therefore, is to build political strength for their position; tactically they do so by creating or deepening the difficulties which threaten Unionism unless it reshapes itself to manage the process of change which the Good Friday Agreement entails. So at a time when the British government has up-ended the recommendations of the Patten Commission on Policing, at a time when it has failed to keep its commitments on demilitarisation and other issues, and at a time when Loyalists are slaughtering each other and anyone else who gets in the way, what is a crisis being created around?

Yes! Right first time. The IRA. No matter that IRA guns are silent, that despite all the difficulties, including those created by the British government, the IRA took the unprecedented step of opening up arms dumps to regular inspection by outsiders. No matter that the IRA has always honoured its commitments and that it has consistently taken risky initiatives to enhance the peace process. No matter about all of this, what is the growing issue?

Right again! The big issue is IRA arms, and the demand that the international statesmen Cyril Ramaphosa and Martti Ahtisaari are brought back *now* to do another inspection will grow more and more in the days and weeks ahead.

This column is satisfied that the IRA will bring the inspectors back. But it will do so in its own time and in line with the commitments it made in May, not at the behest of others, especially those whom it deems to have broken their commitments. So my concern is not about the IRA. Its commitment to the peace process is clear, and its record of keeping commitments is absolute.

But I am concerned. My concern is that there is an effort to create a public crisis around this issue of IRA arms inspections. The excuse for all of this? Mr Trimble needs another arms inspection. *Now*. Of course, he could say that he is satisfied that the inspections will proceed as outlined by the IRA. He could claim credit for progress on this issue. But we cannot expect him to minimise his problems. Not when a British government has shown him the benefits of a tactical approach.

25 September 2000

Taking a Deep Breath

In the South Antrim by-election Rev. William McCrea of the DUP won the seat from the UUP candidate, David Burnside.

And so it came to pass. The singing bigot William McCrea is now the MP for South Antrim. It was a No contest. Faced with the choice of two No men, pro-Agreement Unionists stayed at home. The UUP campaign is a lesson in how not to fight an election. But that's all history now. The Sinn Féin percentage share of the vote increased modestly and we're well pleased with that. All of the parties suffered grievously from the gloomy wet day that was in it, but it was a failure of political leadership by the UUP which handed the seat to Paisley's DUP.

Now it's impossible to talk about any aspect of the Good Friday Agreement without being faced with a question about David Trimble's future as leader of the UUP. And Mr Trimble himself, in a number of blunt and highly publicised remarks, has warned that the Agreement faces collapse if the British government makes any concessions on the policing issue. What he means, of course, is that the Patten recommendations should be scrapped. That's been the UUP position since the Patten Commission published its report. No doubt Mr Trimble will hammer that message through when he meets the taoiseach this week. And we can be sure in the next few weeks that there will be lots of wheeling and dealing between the two governments and all the political parties.

So what's to be done? Everyone who wants to see proper policing and the full implementation of the Good Friday Agreement should take a deep breath. This is the time for steady nerves and for strategic and long-headed thinking. It is not the time for short-term tactical manoeuvring. The Good Friday Agreement is more important than any political leader. If I quit politics tomorrow morning, there would still be a need for democratically accountable civic policing. If David Trimble quit politics tomorrow, ditto.

The policing issue is in a mess at the minute because the

British government has not honoured its obligations under the Good Friday Agreement and because it has failed to implement the Patten recommendations. It now has to move its Policing Bill forward if it wants to create a new beginning to policing. This column has rehearsed the core areas of concern many times. Great work has been done in the USA by a wide range of people across the political spectrum. Some of the critical areas under the British Policing Bill are:

- Excessive powers are assigned to the British secretary of state and the chief constable. Democratic accountability is dumped.
- The Policing Board is stripped of power, especially in the vital area of inquiries.
- The recommendations for district community and policing arrangements have been emasculated.
- There is no provision for Nationalist and Republican representation in the police service.
- Provision on name, flags and emblems is not as prescribed by Patten.
- The new oath for all officers, the Patten mechanism for compromise between disbandment and undifferentiated continuation of the RUC, has been dumped.
- The role of the ombudsman, an essential means of modifying police behaviour, has been subverted.
- The role of the Oversight Commissioner proposed by the British government has little resemblance to that in Patten.
- No action is proposed in respect of Patten's recommendations on the Special Branch – the "force within a force" – and the Full-time Reserve.

As we go to press there is no sign that the British government is going to deal with these issues properly, so as well as keeping our nerve, all of us who want to see a new beginning to policing must also redouble our efforts to impress upon London the folly of it reneging on one of its stated objectives. This is not a matter of making concessions to either Nationalists or Unionists. It is about implementing an international agreement. And policing isn't the only issue that London has to catch up on.

As Peter Mandelson positions himself to push ahead with London's Policing Bill, we could well see some limited progress

25 September 2000

on other issues. He may well seek to make concessions to Unionism on the issue of flags or issues like that while doling out concessions to Nationalists or Republicans on other matters. This is no way to resolve conflict. He will have reduced the necessary and agreed programme for change to a scoreboard with so many points for the UUP and so many points for the rest of us. The victors, of course, will be the anti-Agreement forces. The losers will be the people – the vast majority of people on this island who voted for the Agreement. This will guarantee only one outcome to the policing debate, and that will be that Nationalists and Republicans will refuse to have anything to do with the police force envisaged in his proposals.

But all is not lost. Not yet anyway. There is still the time for the British government to get it right. Of course, this will create problems for Unionism, but that was always going to be the case. The British government's historical responsibility has to include the need for it to create conditions which will help Unionists to face up to the reality of the twenty-first century, and that is that there can be no second-class citizens. Policing can be got right if Mr Blair has the political will to do the right thing.

An Irish Journal

PLAYING THE GAME

Following the drawn All-Ireland Football Final of 24 September, Kerry triumphed over Galway in the replay on 7 October.

Some people say that Gaelic football comes a very poor second to hurling. They obviously never had to play at today's level of athleticism, but I know what they mean. Hurling is a game of the gods. But football isn't bad either, especially last Saturday. Last Saturday was the replay of the All-Ireland. I was there. There were other things happening on Saturday as well. The Ulster Unionist Party was holding its annual conference in Belfast. The Ard-Chomhairle of Sinn Féin was holding its monthly executive meeting in Dublin. And Kerry was playing Galway in Croke Park.

Saturday's Ard-Chomhairle meeting was a particularly heavy one. It has been a busy year thus far. Sinn Féin is also facing into the possibility of three elections in the months ahead. There is a local government election in the North. There is speculation about a British general election. And the taoiseach can call a contest at any time in the South. There's also the matter of the Ard-Fheis in March. So there were lots of party things to be discussed.

There was also the current state of play of the political process. David Trimble was to address his conference at about 11am, and some of us would have to respond to that. So you can see the kind of Saturday that was in it: get to Dublin for 9am in the morning; find out what's happening at the UUP conference; figure out an appropriate response to that; all the while ploughing through the Ard-Chomhairle agenda in order to be in the Hogan Stand in time for the throw-in at 3.30pm.

Usually when I go to an All-Ireland I start the day before by catching up on all the up-to-date details about both teams. I watch the "Up for the Match" programme on RTÉ the night before and generally talk nonsense about how the game will go with anyone who is interested. This follows through into early Sunday morning when a squad of us voyage forth to Dublin for an early lunch and into Croke Park in time to catch most of the

9 October 2000

minor match and the Artane Boys Band and all the other atmospherics.

But on Saturday there was no preparation time. My head was still filled with politics as I took my seat ten minutes before the throw-in. The Ard-Chomhairle meeting was being abandoned around that time for those without tickets to get to the nearest pub and TV screen. Another meeting has had to be called to catch up on unfinished business. Back in Belfast, David Trimble had made a good speech to his conference. He had actually challenged the No men and women and showed – what had always been obvious – that he has the support of the majority of his party.

Party politics and Gaelic football have some things in common. In both the role of the men on the bench is crucial. The manager and his advisers are becoming increasingly central to whether a team wins or loses. It isn't just down to the players, to their skills or stamina. It is how they are positioned and directed. It is in the preparation. It is how they are motivated. It is how a team's character is shaped. It is about whether a team is satisfied to play the game, whether it is mesmerised by the big occasion or whether it really wants to win the championship.

Of course, some of the difficulties of party politics or of peace process politics are more fundamental than that. On Saturday in Croke Park everyone was agreed that the game was to be Gaelic football. If Kerry or Galway for that matter had turned up to play hurling, we would have all been in a bit of a fix. No amount of clever tactics, match plans or field craft would have sorted that out.

That's the difference between an All-Ireland and the peace process. The peace process is supposed to be a partnership. There is supposed to be some sense of pursuing common, agreed objectives and of building a shared peaceful and just future for everyone on this island. That has to take precedence and priority over any other objective. And there's the rub. The crisis within Unionism is because the activists either don't want to play the game, or they want to play a different game, or they want to play the game by their rules, or they don't want to play at all.

The vast majority of their supporters – the spectators – have voted and know what they want. They are like the people last

Saturday who didn't really mind whether Galway or Kerry won as long as it was a good match and everyone enjoyed themselves. As it turned out, Saturday's game was like that. It was hugely enjoyable and satisfying. Maybe the Galway supporters were disappointed, but someone had to lose, and the final was a great advertisement for Gaelic games. On the day the best team won.

David Trimble won also on Saturday, but now he faces a replay. Another one. The rest of us, the vast majority of people on this island, want him to win, but we can't play the game for him, nor can we change the rules. They are well established, agreed by the two governments and endorsed by the people of this island. We just want the Unionists to get on with it. It's all about change and managing that change collectively and in a shared way. We want the Unionists to be part of this. We want them to play the game.

30 October 2000

There Can Be No Unionist Veto

On Saturday, 28 October, the peace process was again thrown into turmoil when the Ulster Unionist Council endorsed proposals by David Trimble to prevent Sinn Féin ministers from attending North-South Ministerial Council meetings.

This column goes to press in the midst of the latest storm in the unpredictable, spontaneous and often frustrating Irish peace process. The current upset is the result of the Ulster Unionist Council resurrecting the issue of arms once again in a stupid and unattainable demand for IRA decommissioning on a Unionist timetable.

It did this only days after the IRA had once again given evidence of its commitment to the peace process by honouring commitments it made in May when the Irish Republican Army had undertaken to open up some of its arms dumps to regular inspection by two international statesmen. This happened a week ago even though the British government has yet to honour its commitments.

The UUP decision, in support of proposals from its leader David Trimble, can only be described as an ungracious rejection of the IRA initiative.

The IRA initiative had two parts. One, which involved the inspection and reinspection of IRA dumps, was a confidence-building measure aimed at reassuring Unionist opinion and without doubt at the cost of serious difficulties within Republicanism. The other issue of putting IRA weapons verifiably beyond use is, it seems from the IRA statement, seen by the IRA as an issue between the IRA and the British government with a context outlined by the army leadership in which this could be accomplished.

While the responsibility and indeed the credit for all of the recent IRA initiatives lies with the IRA itself, some of the progress that has been made was because this Sinn Féin leadership sought, through engagements with the British and Irish governments, the Unionists and others, to develop ideas to keep the process moving on.

The UUP has arrogantly failed to take any of this into

account. Mr Trimble's propositions to the Council differ from those of his opponents, led by Jeffrey Donaldson, only with regard to timing. The attention being paid to Mr Trimble's victory over Mr Donaldson has sidelined the more important issue, which is the consequences all of this has for the political process.

David Trimble should have faced down his opponents by pro-actively promoting the Good Friday Agreement. Instead he has chosen to step outside that agreement, and if he follows through on his threat to try to exclude Sinn Féin or to disempower Sinn Féin ministers, he will be in breach of the Agreement and in contravention of his pledge of office and of his ministerial code.

Sinn Féin does not hold executive position by dint of patronage from the UUP. We have a mandate, and the citizens whom we represent must have exactly the same rights as all other citizens. Could it be that Mr Trimble's move today is tacit acknowledgement that Unionism isn't up to the challenge of working alongside other citizens or of developing and sustaining a peaceful future based upon equality? Could it be that he is unable to rise above the role of a party leader, the leader of the UUP, to be a first minister for all the people?

I have been in touch with both governments and I have told them of the need to preserve the political process and the peace process through upholding and implementing the Good Friday Agreement. They cannot allow a Unionist veto.

The job of responsible political leaders, but especially of the British Prime Minister Mr Blair, must now be to provide effective political leadership, to fulfil outstanding commitments, and plan the programme of change that is essential for the full implementation of the Good Friday Agreement.

While we all have a role to play in this, and the Irish government also has a central role, the primary responsibility for advancing peace and justice and democracy rests with the British government. And at this time, as we face into another crisis caused by the refusal of Unionism to accept the democratic imperative of agreements and responsibilities entered into by them, Irish Republicans have serious concerns about the focus and intent of Mr Blair and his colleagues. London has to

30 October 2000

stop pandering to Unionism.

The time ahead will present challenges for everyone. The battle within Unionism is a tactical one, but it is restricted to political Unionism. Civic Unionism, the business community and the broad bulk of ordinary Unionism, want this process to work. Are they to be let down once again?

An Irish Journal

SEE YOU IN COURT!

In November Sinn Féin Ministers Bairbre de Brún and Martin McGuinness initiated legal proceedings to challenge the ban imposed by David Trimble on their attending meetings of the North-South Ministerial Council.

This column has cried wolf so many times that I'm almost afraid to mention "crisis in the peace process". In contemplating the subject of this week's piece, I thought of giving you my view of the ongoing presidential election, or even the commendable visit by President Clinton to Vietnam. That truly was a wondrous event, and the huge coverage here given to the photographic imagery of the president of the United States with a huge bust of Ho Chi Minh behind him shows how far it is possible to go. I couldn't help but think of my friend Jack, who lost many of his buddies in that war, and wonder what he thought of it all. But Jack's a good guy and I'm sure, painful though it may be for Vietnam vets, that he would agree with me that Bill Clinton did the right thing. Whatever about the results of the count for the presidency, one thing's for certain: Bill Clinton is going to be sorely missed.

Which brings me back to where we are. Back to the future? Back to crisis! Because even though we have managed thus far, and even though you may be crisis fatigued, and even though the festive season beckons, for this column not to tell it how it is would be the easy option. And there are no easy options in this process.

Last week Minister for Health, Social Services and Public Safety Bairbre de Brún initiated legal action against First Minister David Trimble because of his refusal to make nominations to the North-South Ministerial Council sectoral meeting on health and food safety, which was scheduled for 3 November.

Regular readers of this column will recall that I spent the time since the Ulster Unionist Council meeting on 28 October, which authorised David Trimble's action, trying to ascertain whether or not the British government had the political will to resolve these issues. My consultations involved lengthy and detailed discussions with the two governments, including Taoiseach

20 November 2000

Bertie Ahern and British Prime Minister Tony Blair. I also spoke to David Trimble. At the end of that period I formed the view that the British government is more concerned at this time with its management of Unionism and with pandering to rejectionists within its own system than it is with the full and proper implementation of the Good Friday Agreement and the commitments it entered into last May.

When Bairbre de Brún announced her legal action, she described David Trimble's action as both "discriminatory and anti-democratic". She accused the first minister of being in breach of his pledge of office, the ministerial code, and the Good Friday Agreement. She also pointed out that British Secretary of State Peter Mandelson has the power to direct the first minister to fulfil his obligations and that she has a responsibility as a minister for all the people here to challenge any action which prevents her from fulfilling her responsibilities as a minister.

Bairbre's case is about a meeting which should have taken place at the beginning of this month. A similar meeting is scheduled for Minister of Education Martin McGuinness for the end of this week. Martin is also lodging judicial review proceedings. The difference between his case and Bairbre's is that his could end up in court before Friday with David Trimble in the dock.

So, what is all of this about?

At the very least it is about the failure of the political process, and particularly the British government, to deal with a clear breach of the Good Friday Agreement by the very man elected to protect, defend and implement that agreement. That in a way is a matter for all of us, but as we see from the legal proceedings so far, it is a matter that the Republican ministers want sorted out as a matter of urgency.

But it is about more than that. Sinn Féin also has the option of taking a separate case. David Trimble's position was outlined by him in a comprehensive letter to members of his party. He said that he intended to increase pressure progressively on Republicans and Nationalists by creating a crisis around the Executive and the Assembly. He said that he wanted to achieve the suspension of the Agreement while placing responsibility for this on Republicans.

Peter Mandelson, the British secretary of state, protests that he does not endorse Mr Trimble's position, yet he refuses to intervene. This is at odds with his record so far when he abused his power at the beginning of the year, unilaterally and illegally, to collapse the institutions and more recently, in contradiction of the Good Friday Agreement, when he ordered the flying of the British flag on designated days. Today as this column goes to print is one such day.

So, is this just a matter of Sinn Féin ministers upholding people's democratic rights and entitlements? Have Republicans suddenly gained confidence in the legal and judicial system here? No and no again. Speaking for myself – and I drew the media's attention to this when I concluded my range of meetings with the two governments – it is about the fact that I have little confidence in the British government's management of this process. I told Mr Blair that when I spoke to him by phone on my return from the USA early last week.

In America the courts may decide the outcome of the race for the White House, and that is a new and historical experience. But the one important difference between that court action and the court actions here is that, for all the discontent in Florida and Washington, the American system remains remarkably stable. Ours on the other hand is remarkably unstable. How could it be otherwise when the first minister behaves as he does and when the British government panders to him?

11 December 2000

And Whatever You Are Having Yourself

On Tuesday, 12 December, Bill Clinton visited Ireland for the last time as president of the United States of America.

I'm penning these lines on the eve of Bill Clinton's arrival in Dublin. When the US president's visit was first announced, there was a mad outburst of media speculation about how much work would be done to ensure that the president's visit would lead to a "breakthrough" in the present impasse in the peace process. All the media-speak was about how the president's visit would put Irish Republicans under pressure and how Sinn Féin was being leaned on.

As a visit came closer the spin slowed down, with only the UUP and the British government holding to this hackneyed line. There was going to be major movement, they briefed. But even though it is they who are in default of their obligations and commitments under the Good Friday Agreement, the major movement wasn't from them. On the contrary, they were latching on to the US presidential visit and spinning it up as an occasion for major movement by the IRA. This was despite the IRA's recent historic initiatives on the arms issue.

The White House itself was sanguine about all of this. While the administration obviously would like a breakthrough and is, as always, prepared to assist the search for such an advance, senior spokespersons made it clear that President Clinton's role was not a negotiating one. So David Trimble, who had been saying that the IRA owed President Clinton "big time" and that they needed to do some decommissioning as a thank you to the president, rowed back into safer waters with a comment to the effect that "I don't expect any great breakthrough."

Downing Street sources, which had briefed the media about an expectation that the IRA would "pour concrete over its dumps", chimed in with a press briefing which reduced expectations to "the President's visit will remind people of how much has been achieved".

In the face of this it would be little wonder if this column had become the complete cynic.

Are the British government burning the midnight oil to get

movement? Are they making the effort? What is happening?

Nothing. Well, that's not quite true. There's a big effort being made to get Sinn Féin, the SDLP, the Irish Catholic bishops and the Irish government to acquiesce to Peter Mandelson's Police Act. All the effort is about getting us to accept that the changes which were recommended by Patten and rejected by the British government and not included in the Police Act are now going to be put in an implementation plan.

Everybody in the British government, Sinn Féin, the SDLP, the Irish government and the Irish Catholic bishops know that this is impossible. All the King's horses and all the King's men can't put Humpty together again.

Why not? Because at this time they don't want to. If the British government really wanted to implement the Patten recommendations, they could do so. And no one who is truly committed to a genuinely new beginning to policing can or should give up on this objective. We should not be bullied, or coaxed or cajoled or pressurised by the British government, or anyone else, into accepting less than our entitlements.

The point is: does the British government's plan meet the prescribed requirements of the Good Friday Agreement in respect of a democratic, accountable policing service capable of attracting the membership and support of the community as a whole? That is, Nationalists, Republicans and Unionists? This is an issue that is central to any society. It has to be got right.

The British government's Police Act is not the last word on the issue of policing. The last word will come from the people. Without their support the British Police Act is useless. Others may consider that this is as good as it gets and argue for a tactical approach. But it is a strategic and not a tactical approach that is required at this time. Short-termism is out. All decisions on policing have to be based on a long-term view of where the platform provided by the British government will bring the policing issue.

There is no doubt that if the British government did the right thing Irish Republicans would have to engage positively, even if the outcome did not meet our requirements at this time. Republicans want and need the security of a decent, democratic and accountable policing service.

11 December 2000

So, the British government must go back to the drawing board. The Irish government, the SDLP, the Irish Catholic bishops and Sinn Féin know this. So does the British government. That is why they are trying to fracture the consensus on this issue. That is why in press briefings they tried to utilise the presidential visit.

Of course, whether the consensus is fractured, whether elements of it acquiesce in what Seamus Mallon described as "chicanery" by the British government, will be crucial factors in whether the people of this part of the island get the policing service we deserve.

What's happening on the other issues?

Nothing.

What are the other issues? Demilitarisation is probably the big one. There are five major British army/RUC bases in South Armagh alone. There are also fourteen hilltop forts, thirty-one hilltop spy posts, and 3,000 troops.

The British government says it cannot remove any of these because its army won't let them. The world knows what happens in countries where armies run governments. I have no doubt that in due course Tony Blair will face up to his responsibilities on these matters. In the meantime there has been another outbreak of killings and attempted killings by Loyalists. For a number of families this will be a bleak Christmas.

So there you are. President Clinton's visit will undoubtedly provide a timely reminder of how far we have all come. I have no doubt in that context that it will be a huge success and that it will create a dynamic at popular level for the continuation and the development of this process. But amongst those who are against change, both inside and outside the British system, it will be an incursion which they have to put up with.

An Irish Journal

Game, Set and Match

My first love is hurling. That includes camogie. Although there are those who will argue that the camogs play a different game, I think they play a better game. Then comes football which is mostly a kind of sport to keep hurlers fit.

Hurling is over 4,000 years old. If ancient manuscripts are to be believed, hurleys or hurling sticks have been made from many different materials. Setanta, or Cúchulainn, is said to have had a *camán* or hurley of red bronze. That is not as widely used today, and the best material is ash with, according to Gerard Rogan, that well known craftsman and former hurler, the best ash coming from an ash tree between twenty and twenty-five years old. Hurling is said to be the fastest field game in the world. It is one of the most spectacular and skilled of all games. It is also uniquely Irish.

Handball is much under-rated, and I am too out of condition now to even think of competing though I know some aged Belfast men who are still up to championship standard. Recently I was told, though I can't vouch for this, that rounders is also a Gaelic game. Maybe someone, somewhere out there in Gaeldom will confirm this.

So what does it all mean? How important are Gaelic games? What part do they play in our lives?

To suggest that one particular sport is better than another simply because it is a native game borders on xenophobia. So Gaelic games are not necessarily better than other games simply because they are Gaelic. They are better simply because they are better.

Soccer is a pedestrian sport, hyped by big money, more entertainment than athleticism. An odd time you would see a good match. Rugby isn't too bad. In fact it can be very good, and I wouldn't mind getting more time to learn more about it. Croquet and tennis and ice-skating are okay as far as they go, but they are not exactly team sports. Golfing is less élitist than it used to be, and I presume that even bad hurlers could be good golfers and that a half decent hurler could be a great golfer. Tiger Woods' people come from Dunloy.

18 December 2000

There is merit in all sport, and I can't think of one that I would be against. Not on principle anyway, though poorly trained or badly managed boxers battering each other's brains out has never appealed to me. At the same time, Muhammed Ali is one of my sporting icons. Him and Sambo McNaughton.

Cricket is popular in Derry City. The least said about that the better. It just goes to show that everyone has their own taste. And that is how it should be.

But Gaelic games are special not only because of the skills, the degree of athleticism, team work and sheer commitment involved. In this context, even a sceptic would concede that they compare favourably with any other sport, and a neutral would agree that they outclass all alternatives. I know other ball players who have been amazed at how far and how accurately a senior footballer can kick a dead ball, and hurling still bewilders visitors from other disciplines.

But Gaelic games are special because they are firmly rooted in local communities and open to all who support the Gaelic code. Because they bring drama and excitement, *craic* and huge enjoyment to players and spectators alike. Because everyone can be an expert. Because they are part of what we are. Uniquely Irish. No better on that basis than anyone else, but special nonetheless.

An Irish Journal

Fáilte Romhat 2001

I am emerging from a Christmastide stupor after an unprecedented layoff which has stretched almost since my last column until now. It was wonderful. We had our worst snow in almost twenty years. That was wonderful also. I was supposed to be away, but on account of the weather conditions we couldn't travel. However, because everyone thought we were away it was almost as good as being away. We had family time, big time.

I love Christmas. Not the mad commercialism which threatens to replace the magic of that wonderful story of the birth of the baby Jesus in a stable in Bethlehem. No. I love the story of Christmas. That and the quiet time and all the rituals involved. And the sense or the hope that there is something more to life than... well, than life. That's not to say that life is bad. As this column has testified many times, life is good. It's all a matter of perspective. And there is certainly the need for a lot of that around here.

The last column of last year came, you may recall, from Mayo. You should know that this column dashed back from there to continue the intense discussions which the British government had opened up with Sinn Féin on the eve of the visit to Ireland by President Clinton. These discussions basically went nowhere, but when the president returned to the USA the British indicated a willingness to recommence dialogue. I spoke at some length with Tony Blair about this, and we quickly agreed on the issues which needed to be resolved.

Senior British officials along with senior Irish government representatives then took up the dialogue. I had kept the taoiseach fully informed of developments, and there was a focused effort from our side to establish if the issues involved could be cracked before Christmas. The aim of Sinn Féin in these discussions was, as it has been the case for some time now, to get the British government to face up to its responsibilities and to honour the commitments it made on Good Friday and at Hillsborough last May.

After some days of concentrated discussions it was clear that many obstacles remained. In my opinion there was no way this

3 January 2001

was going to be sorted out before Christmas. I told the two governments that. I also briefed the White House on the up to date situation.

On 21 December there was an adjournment to allow the people from the British side to confer with their bosses and to amend some text. When they returned there was no sign of a mood change, but in the draft papers offered there was a definite clawback from positions already discussed. I challenged this and things rapidly went downhill. Without warning, and from my knowledge of the man involved, in an uncharacteristic display of bad manners, the senior guy got up, put on his coat and proceeded to leave. And that's how our discussions ended. Mumbled and awkward wishes for happy Christmas were proffered all round and away the British representatives went, leaving the rest of us to wonder what it was all about.

So, as the cat said to the mouse, there you are.

In the meantime another year passes. A new one beckons. Some say this is the real millennium. Who knows? Who can tell? I hope all of ye had a nice Christmas. Among other things, between the beginning and the end of these words, the snow vanished and this column took itself off to Donegal. That's where I am writing to you now.

Yesterday a funny thing happened. Well, not really funny haha. Nicer than that. I overheard a man of obvious Asian extraction shouting *"Bliain Úr faoi mhaise duit"* to a passer-by in a village street not far from here. And so say all of us, said I to myself. Thons a sign of the times.

So here's looking forward to another bout of talks, of delays and crisis, of efforts to manage and produce change while others manage to prevent it. Back to porridge tomorrow. Back to Belfast. Back to the future.

Bliain Úr faoi mhaise daoibh go leir.

An Irish Journal

Chronology

1997
September Multi-party talks open at Stormont.
October Gerry Adams and Martin McGuinness meet Tony Blair for the first time.
December Sinn Féin delegation meets the British government in Downing Street.

1998
January Multi-party talks at Lancaster House in London.
February Sinn Féin temporarily expelled from multi-party talks.
March George Mitchell sets deadline of 9 April for finding agreement between the parties.
April On Friday, 10 April, all parties in multi-party talks at Stormont sign the Good Friday Agreement.
May Sinn Féin members vote to change their constitution to allow candidates to take their places in the proposed new Northern Assembly. There is a huge turnout throughout the island of Ireland as people vote in a referendum on the Good Friday Agreement: Yes 85.46 per cent, No 14.54 per cent.
June In Assembly elections UUP win 28 seats, SDLP 24, DUP 20, Sinn Féin 18, Alliance 5, UKUP 5, PUP 2, Women's Coalition 2, Independent Unionist 1, UU 1, and the UUU 1.
July Drumcree Orange parade again a focus for conflict. Three young Catholic boys killed after their home is petrol bombed by Loyalists.
August Twenty-nine people die as a result of an explosion on 15 August in Omagh, County Tyrone, including one woman pregnant with twins; hundreds of people injured.
September David Trimble invites Gerry Adams to round-table meeting. Bill Clinton pays his second visit to the North.
October Deadline is missed for the formation of the Executive, the Assembly and the North-South Ministerial Council.
November Tony Blair and George Mitchell in Belfast for talks with political leaders.
December Six new North-South administrative bodies and an increase from six to ten ministries agreed.

1999
February Amidst growing concern for the peace process, David Trimble warns that he will press for transfer of powers to new Executive while excluding Sinn Féin.

Chronology

March British Secretary of State Mo Mowlam indicates her willingness to delay the triggering of devolution. Rosemary Nelson, a human rights lawyer who had complained of Loyalist and RUC threats against her, is killed by a booby-trap car bomb.

April Multi-party talks at Hillsborough end on 1 April with a "Hillsborough Declaration" agreed by Tony Blair and Bertie Ahern.

May Tony Blair announces an "absolute" deadline of 30 June for formation of an Executive and devolution of power to the Assembly.

June In European Elections the UUP's Jim Nicholson, DUP leader Ian Paisley and John Hume of the SDLP retain their seats; the Sinn Féin vote significantly increases. The 30 June deadline set by Tony Blair passes without the establishment of the Executive.

July The attempt to form the Executive of the Assembly collapses when David Trimble and the other UUP Assembly members fail to attend the sitting.

September Senator George Mitchell opens the review of the Good Friday Agreement. The Patten Commission on Policing releases its recommendations for a new beginning to policing.

October David Trimble faces down his critics and defends the Good Friday Agreement at the UUP conference. British Secretary of State Mo Mowlam is replaced by Peter Mandelson. George Mitchell announces that his review of the Good Friday Agreement will be extended.

November George Mitchell issues a report on his review, concluding that the basis now exists for devolution to occur and the formation of an executive to take place. At the Assembly on 29 November ten ministers, including two from Sinn Féin, are appointed to the power-sharing Executive. The British parliament approves a devolution order for the transfer of power from Westminster to the Assembly at Stormont.

December Direct rule ends on 1 December and the North-South Ministerial Council and the British-Irish Ministerial Council, as set out in the Good Friday Agreement, take effect. The Anglo-Irish Agreement is replaced by the British-Irish Agreement. Articles 2 and 3 of the Irish Constitution are replaced by new Articles. The new Executive of the Assembly meets for the first time. The IRA issues a statement indicating that it will appoint a representative to meet the decommissioning body.

2000

January Unionists demand IRA decommissioning by 31 January, and David Trimble threatens to resign if the British government do not suspend the new institutions.

February On 11 February the first (31 January) de Chastelain Report on decommissioning is made public followed some hours later by the second (11 February). The new devolved government is suspended by the British government and direct rule reintroduced.

May The British government announces on 5 May that it will enable the Assembly and Executive to be restored by 22 May and commits itself to implementing the Patten Report and achieving demilitarisation by June 2001. On 6 May the IRA issues a statement indicating that it will put arms beyond use in the context of the full implementation of the Good Friday Agreement and announces its intention to allow two international statesmen to inspect a number of its arms dumps. The British government publishes legislation on policing which is described by many as an emasculation of the Patten Report recommendations.

June The Independent International Commission on Decommissioning (IICD) reports on its inspection of IRA arms dumps: "This is a genuine effort by the IRA to advance the peace process."

August A Loyalist feud erupts in the Shankill Road area of Belfast and several people are killed by the UDA and UVF; many are also forced from their homes.

September In the South Antrim by-election the anti-Agreement UUP candidate is defeated by the anti-Agreement DUP candidate.

October The IRA leadership announces that it "has decided that the reinspection of a number of arms dumps will be repeated to confirm that our weapons remain secure". The UUP adopts proposals by David Trimble to prevent Sinn Féin ministers from attending North-South Ministerial Council meetings.

December Bill Clinton visits Ireland for the last time as US president.

Biographies

Adair, Johnny UDA leader.
Ahern, Bertie Taoiseach and leader of the Fianna Fáil party.
Ahtisaari, Martti Former Finnish president, one of two statesmen acting as arms inspectors.
Breathnach, Lucillita Ard-Rúnaí (general secretary) of Sinn Féin.
Cahill, Joe Republican activist since the 1940s; current honorary vice-president of Sinn Féin.
Clegg, Lee British soldier, sentenced to life for the murder of a teenage girl in West Belfast, who was released by the British government after serving only two years.
Davitt, Michael Fenian born in 1846, died 1906; leading Land League and National League activist and influential author.
de Brún, Bairbre Sinn Féin member of the Assembly and minister for health in the Northern Executive.
de Chastelain, General John Canadian chairperson of the three-member Independent Commissioning on Decommissioning.
de Klerk, F.W. President of South Africa 1989–94.
de Valera, Eamon Commandant in the Irish Volunteers in the 1916 Rising; president of Sinn Féin in 1917 and president of the Dáil in 1919; led the anti-treaty forces in the Civil War of 1922–23; founded Fianna Fáil in 1926; taoiseach 1932–48, 1951–54, 1957–59; president 1959–73.
Ferris, Martin Member of the Sinn Féin negotiating team, from County Kerry.
Finucane, Pat Civil rights lawyer shot dead in 1988 by the UDA amidst allegations of collusion with the British army's Force Reaction Unit (FRU).
Gildernew, Michelle Member of the Sinn Féin negotiating team.
Hamill, Robert Nationalist kicked to death in Portadown while RUC looked on.
Hartley, Tom Head of the Sinn Féin group on Belfast City Council.
Holkeri, Harri Former Finnish prime minster is a member of the Independent Commissioning on Decommissioning.
Hume, John Leader of the SDLP, Westminster MP for Derry, MEP.
Keane, Mairead Sinn Féin Ard-Chomhairle member; former head of Women's Department.
Kelly, Gerry Sinn Féin Assembly member for North Belfast; senior party negotiator and spokesperson on policing.
McAuley, Chrissie Sinn Féin representative on Belfast City Council; former head of Education Department.

McAuley, Richard Sinn Féin press officer.
McGuinness, Martin Leader of the Sinn Féin negotiating team, minister for education in the Northern Executive and Westminster MP.
McManus, Sean Mayor of Sligo and Sinn Féin Ard-Chomhairle member.
Meehan, Martin Sinn Féin representative in South Antrim.
Mac Stiofain, Seán Former chief of staff of the IRA.
Mallon, Seamus Deputy leader of the SDLP and deputy first minister of the Northern Executive.
Mandelson, Peter Labour MP who was British secretary of state in the North from October 1999 until his resignation from government in January 2001.
Mayhew, Sir Patrick Former British secretary of state in the North.
Meyer, Roelf Chief negotiator for the apartheid regime in South Africa.
Mitchell, Senator George US senator and former Senate majority leader who played a crucial role in the peace process as chairman of the multi-party talks.
Mowlam, Marjorie ("Mo") Labour MP who was British secretary of state in the North from May 1997 until she was replaced by Peter Mandelson in October 1999.
O Caolláin, Caoimhín Sinn Féin TD for Cavan.
O'Dowd, Niall Publisher of *The Irish Voice* and *Irish America* who played an important role in encouraging US support for the peace process.
O'Hanlon, Siobhán Member of the Sinn Féin negotiating team.
O'Hare, Rita Former editor of *An Phoblacht/Republican News* and former national publicity director of Sinn Féin.
Parnell, Charles Stewart Elected Irish Parliamentary Party MP in 1875, founding president of the Land League in 1879.
Patten, Chris Former Tory government minister and former governor of Hong Kong, he chaired the Patten Commission on Policing.
Ramaphosa, Cyril Former secretary general of the ANC in South Africa, one of two statesmen acting as arms inspectors.

Glossary

Abú For ever.
Agus And.
Alliance Party A small Northern moderate political party represented in the Assembly which wishes to maintain the Union with Britain.
Ancient Order of Hibernians Irish Catholic organisation.
Ard-Chomhairle National executive, usually of a political party.
Ard-Fheis National conference, convention.
Arís Again.
Assembly The parliamentary body set up in the North under the terms of the Good Friday Agreement.
B Specials Unionist state militia first formed in 1920; replaced by the Ulster Defence Regiment (UDR) in 1970, which was itself replaced the the Royal Irish Regiment (RIR) in 1992.
Bliain Úr faoi mhaise duit/daoibh Happy New Year to you/ye.
Camogie Women's hurling.
Ceilí Dance session.
Ceol Music.
Clann Family.
Comhghairdeas Congratulations.
Craic Conversation, a good time.
Crown The British government and all the forces, such as the British army, and institutions that compose the British state, whose constitutional head is the queen.
Culchie Country person.
Cumann na mBan The women's IRA.
Dáil Seat of Irish parliament in Dublin.
d'Hondt procedure The electoral mechanism agreed by the governments and parties in the multi-party talks to ensure equality of representation within the new institutions.
Drumcree From the Protestant church in Drumcree, Orangemen seek to force their march down the Garvaghy Road in Portadown.
DUP Democratic Unionist Party – right-wing Unionist party; fiercely anti-Republican, and led by one of the most controversial party leaders in the country, the Rev. Ian Paisley.
Eile Other.
Fáilte romhat Welcome.
Féile an Phobail People's festival held annually in West Belfast.
Fenian A term, usually pejorative, for a Catholic that implies that he or she is a Republican. The original Fenians were an Irish-American revolutionary group in the 1860s.

An Irish Journal

Fianna Fáil The largest political party in the South, founded by Éamon de Valera in 1926; its present leader is Bertie Ahern.
Fleadh Festival.
Gaeltacht Irish-speaking area.
Garvaghy Road A nationalist suburb of Portadown which has been placed under sectarian siege by the Orange Order.
Go ndeana Dia trócaire ar a anam/anamacha God rest his/their souls.
Go raibh maith agat. Thank you.
Gorta Mór Great Famine.
Grá Love.
H-Blocks Colloquial name for the buildings in Long Kesh where most political prisoners were held.
INLA Irish National Liberation Army.
IRA Irish Republican Army. The IRA's goal is a united Ireland.
Joxer Character in Sean O'Casey's *Juno and the Paycock*.
Leaba Bed.
Loyalist Someone who is resolutely opposed to a united Ireland and who favours maintaining the Union with Britain.
Lughnasa August, and the harvest festival.
LVF Loyalist Volunteer Force – paramilitary group formed in 1996; its first leader, Billy Wright, was murdered by the INLA in December 1997.
MP Member of the British parliament.
Mé féin Myself.
Nationalist Someone who aspires to a reunited Ireland.
Nolan, Gypo Title character in *The Informer* by Liam O'Flaherty.
Ól Drink.
Orange Order A sectarian order of Protestant men characterised by ritualistic pageantry and supremacist celebrations.
Poitín Illicit whiskey; moonshine.
PUP Progressive Unionist Party – small fringe Unionist party associated with the Loyalist paramilitary group, the Ulster Volunteer Force (UVF).
Referendum A vote by all citizens over eighteen on a proposed amendment to the Constitution.
Republican Supporter of a united Ireland.
RIR Royal Irish Regiment: see B Specials and UDR.
Rí-rá Hullabaloo.
Rounders Game with a bat and ball, similar to baseball.
RTÉ – *Radio Telefís Éireann* – Irish public broadcasting.
RUC Royal Ulster Constabulary – paramilitary state police force in the North.

Glossary

Sam The Sam Maguire Cup – trophy for winners of the All-Ireland Football competition.
Scéal Story, news.
Saville Enquiry Set up in 1998 to enquire into the circumstances of Bloody Sunday in Derry.
SDLP Social Democratic and Labour Party – Nationalist political party in the North.
Sean nós Old style.
Sinn Féin The major Republican political party in both the North and the South.
Sliotar Hurling ball.
Slógadh Hosting.
Stormont The seat of government in the North and the principal location of the multi-party talks.
Tá Yes.
Tá mé buioch duitse. I am grateful to you.
Taig, teague Pejorative name for Catholics.
Taoiseach Prime minister; currently the leader of the Fianna Fáil party, Bertie Ahern.
Taoisigh plural of taoiseach
TD Teachta Dála (member of the Dáil).
UDA Ulster Defence Association – Loyalist organisation which also fronts for the Ulster Freedom Fighters (UFF).
UDP Ulster Democratic Party – small fringe Unionist party with few elected councillors. It is linked to the UDA/UFF.
UDR Ulster Defence Regiment – branch of the British army, set up in 1970 to replace the discredited B Specials. Composed mainly of Protestants, it was considered by Nationalists to be a sectarian organisation. Some of its members have been jailed for paramilitary activities. After disbandment in 1992, the UDR was replaced by the Royal Irish Regiment (RIR).
UFF Ulster Freedom Fighters – Loyalist paramilitary group synonymous with the UDA.
Unionist Someone who believes in maintaining the North's political Union with Great Britain.
UTV Ulster Television – independent commercial television channel serving the North.
UUC Ulster Unionist Council of the Ulster Unionist Party.
UUP Ulster Unionist Party – the largest political party in the North, it supports the governance of the North from Westminster. It is led by David Trimble.
UVF Ulster Volunteer Force – Loyalist paramilitary group with links to the Progressive Unionist Party.

UKUP United Kingdom Unionist Party – small Unionist party represented in the Assembly.
Widgery, Lord Former British Lord Chief Justice whose report sought to whitewash the British army killings in Derry on Bloody Sunday in January 1971.
Women's Coalition A cross-community women's organisation represented in the Assembly.
Ye plural of you.

INDEX

Adair, Johnny, 245, 246
Adams, Annie, 87–8
Adams, Colette, 67, 69, 73, 74, 108–11, 240
Adams, Gerry
  birth of granddaughter, 206–7
  death of mother, 87–8
  fiftieth birthday, 85–6
  love of dogs, 73–4, 121–2, 245
  threats to life, 129–30
  on trees, 117, 236–7
Adams, Sean, 87, 88
African National Congress (ANC), 151–2
Agnew, Paddy, 142
Ahern, Bertie, 65, 82, 227, 261
  and Good Friday negotiations, 52–8, 83, 92–3, 103, 104, 131–2, 134, 135–6, 158, 159, 161, 164
Ahtisaari, Martti, 230, 250
Albright, Madeline, 46
Ali, Muhammed, 267
Alliance Party, 22, 44
All-Ireland football finals
  of 1997, 15, 17
  of 2000, 254–6
All-Ireland hurling final, 78
All-Ireland Council of Ministers, 55, 63, 64, 65, 79, 101, 102, 104, 134, 135, 139, 144, 197, 203
  Unionists ban Sinn Féin from, 260–2
Ancient Order of Hibernians (AOH), 80
Angel Orensanz Foundation, 27
Anglo-Irish Agreement, 203
Armagh Women's Prison, 141, 195
  campaign, 110
Artane Boys Band, 255
Arts Council, 71

Assembly, 53, 55, 59, 64, 66, 78, 81, 93, 101–4, 128, 144, 203, 261
  ministers appointed to Executive, 65, 197
  suspension of, 215–20, 222, 224–6, 234
Australia visit, 117, 123–5

Balkan crisis, 133–4, 138–9
Ballina Union and Workhouse, 16
Ballymoney children die, 75
Bangor Erris (County Mayo), 16
Beausang, Brother, 187
Belfast, 21, 26, 36, 78
  Ballymurphy, 78, 121–2, 169, 195–6, 237
  Conway Mill, Falls Road, 18
  Duke of York pub, 41
  Felons Club, 169
  festivals in, 71–2
  Fort Jericho, 237
  hunger strikes rally, 140–1, 142
  Milltown Cemetery, 169, 208
    attack in, 114
    monument to IRA volunteers, 230
  Ormeau Road bookmaker's shop attack, 114
  presidential visit to, 25
  Shankill Road, 245, 246
Belmullet (County Mayo), 15, 16
Bessette, Lauren, 167, 170
BinLids, 26–7
Blair, Tony, 11, 14, 127, 158, 159, 227, 241, 244, 253, 258, 261, 262, 265, 268
  and Bloody Sunday inquiry, 89
  Cabinet reshuffle, 179
  and Good Friday negotiations, 52–8, 83–4, 92–3, 103, 104, 131–2, 134, 135–7, 139, 145, 161, 162–3, 164, 166, 178

279

Index

Blair, Tony *(cont.)*
  meets with Bertie Ahern, 52–3
  meets with Sinn Féin at Downing Street, 32–4
  meets with Sinn Féin at Stormont, 18, 19–23
  and Nelson case, 115
  and suspension of institutions, 223, 224–6
Bloody Sunday, 22, 40, 105
  commemorations, 38, 105
  "Hidden Truths" exhibition, 89–91
  independent inquiry demanded, 33
  inquiry reopened, 89–90
Bloody Sunday Justice Campaign, 90
Bohola (County Mayo), 66
BookMarks (London), 31
Breathnach, Lucillita, 31, 59
Bridge to the Future, A, 47
British army, 37, 51, 265
  Force Research Unit, 113, 114
  gun battle at Drumgooley, 238
  Palace Barracks interrogation centre, 120
  see also collusion of security forces in atrocities
British government, 10, 19–23, 31–4, 36, 37, 46, 61, 76, 83–4, 127–8, 144, 159, 177, 233, 263
  bug Gerry Adams' car, 204–5
  censorship policies of, 146–7
  close *Maidstone* prison ship, 119
  criminalisation of political prisoners, 141–2
  establish commission to inquire into 'disappeared', 148
  exclusion of Sinn Féin from talks, 39
  and Finucane case, 136
  indicted by European Court of Human Rights, 120
  and Nelson case, 115, 136
  on policing issue, 234–5, 241–4, 246, 249, 250, 252–3, 264–5
  reject Widgery Report, 43
  suspend devolved government, 215–20, 222, 224–6
British-Irish Agreement, 203, 218
Broadcasting Act (Section 31), 146
Brown, Ron, 47
B Specials, 200
Burnside, David, 248, 251
Business Committee, 14

Cahill, Joe, 59, 208
Cahill, Tom, 238
Campbell, Alaister, 32
Campbell, Brendan, 43
Campbell, Fat, 196
Castlereagh, Lord, 79
Catalpa, 124
Celtic Tiger economy, 174–5, 185, 190
censorship, 146–7
Chieftains, the, 197, 221
Civil Rights Association, 70
Civil War, 210
Clarke, Terry (Cleaky), 238–40
Clegg, Lee, 144
Cleland, John, 78–9
Clifford, Kieran, 167
Clinton, Bill, 57–8, 147, 169, 221–2, 227
  and implementation of Agreement, 83, 92, 93, 212
  meets Sinn Féin delegation, 46–8
  visits to Ireland, 76, 263–5, 268
  visits Vietnam, 260
Clinton, Chelsea, 221
Clinton, Hilary, 48, 76, 221
Cold War, 228
collusion of security forces in atrocities, 22, 51, 105–6, 113–15, 137, 201, 245
colonisation, 95
Columbine High School tragedy, 138
Combat Poverty Agency, 189
Connolly, James, 190
Coulter, Jackie, 245

Index

Crumlin Road prison, 238
Cumann na mBan, 110
Cumaraswamy, Param, 136

Dalton, Patrick, 90
Davitt, Michael, 16
de Brún, Bairbre, 14, 60, 197, 226
   legal challenge to Unionist ban, 260–2
de Chastelain commission *see* Independent International Commission on Decommissioning
decommissioning issue, 13, 49, 50, 57, 62, 75, 76, 82, 126–8, 134, 135, 138–9, 182–3, 200, 203, 211–14, 215–17, 219–20, 230–2, 249–50, 257, 263
   see also Independent International Commission on Decommissioning
de Klerk, F.W., 49–50, 127
demilitarisation issue, 44, 53, 54, 57, 61, 63, 65, 144, 159, 200–2, 249, 265
Democratic Unionist Party (DUP), 9, 64, 101, 203, 248, 251
   boycott Stormont talks, 9
   elected to Executive, 65
   take up Executive ministries, 197–8, 212
Derry *see* Bloody Sunday
Devine, Micky, 140
d'Hondt procedure, 197
Dillon, Seamus, 36
'disappeared', the, 131–2
   search for bodies in the South, 148–50
Dobson, Mike, 123
Doherty, Kieran, 140, 142
Doherty, Pat, 19, 22, 31, 59
Doherty, Tony, 105
Donaldson, Jeffrey, 10, 258
Donnelly, Josie, 67–9
Dougan, Robert, 43
Doyle, Mary, 240
Drogheda (County Louth), 29

drugs epidemic, 175
DubbelJoint Productions, 26, 27, 71
Dublin bombing, 105, 190
Duff, Jimmy, 195

elections, 153–4, 248, 254
   to Assembly, 64–5, 153, 248
   parliamentary by-election, 184
   South Antrim by-election, 248–9, 251
emigration, 16, 174
Emmet, Robert, 197
Enniskillen (County Fermanagh), 67, 179
Enright, Deirdre, 35, 191, 192
Enright, Terry, 35, 38, 192
equality agenda, 20, 22, 33, 36, 44, 53, 54, 55, 56, 57, 61, 63, 65, 79, 159, 165, 188, 197
European Union, 189
   calls for independent enquiries, 137
   European Parliament elections, 153, 154
Evers, Medgar, 35
Famine, the, 16, 80, 236
Feeney, Hugh, 196
Féile an Phobail, 71

Ferris, Martin, 31, 59
Finucane, Geraldine, 114
Finucane, Pat, 113–15, 136, 144, 201
Fitzgerald, Garret, 18
Fitzgerald, Maurice, 15
Flannigan, Ronnie, 39
Flying Column, The, 108
Flynn, Bill, 29
Forced Upon Us, 71
Forsyth, Clifford, 248
Forum for Peace and Reconciliation, 49
Framework Document, 43
Friends of Sinn Féin, 176

Gaelic games, 266–7

281

Index

Gaeltacht areas, 15, 187
Gaoth Saile (County Mayo), 15
Garvaghy Road Residents' Association, 106
George magazine, 167, 168
Ghosts of Mississippi, 35
Gibney, Jimmy, 238
Gildernew, Michelle, 31
Glengannon Hotel attack, 36
Glenmore (County Louth), 67–8
Good Friday Agreement, 52–8, 60–1, 64, 65, 75, 76, 77, 79, 81, 130, 131–2, 156, 188, 189, 198, 201, 202, 203, 204, 212, 215, 219, 224, 225, 226, 241, 249, 251, 252, 258, 261, 262, 264, 268
   delays in implementation, 82–4, 92–4, 101–4, 126–8, 134, 135–7, 138–9, 143–5, 150, 158–60, 161–3, 179, 211–12, 263
   endorsement of, 193–4
   Strand One, 54, 55, 56
   Strand Two, 53–4, 55, 56
   Strand Three, 54
   "Validation, Implementation and Review" section, 93
   see also Mitchell, George: review of Agreement; referenda
Goulding leadership, 191
Government of Ireland Act, 188, 204
Green Cross, 110, 196
Guiney, Jim, 38

Hamill, Robert, 144, 201
handshake issue, 18–19, 29, 75, 76
Hartley, Tom, 173
Haughey, Charles, 184–5
"Hidden Truths", 89
Hillsborough Castle meetings, 131–2, 133, 243, 268
   Hillsborough Declaration, 135–6
Holmes, John, 32
holy wells, 116–17
homelessness, 174–5
Hope, Jimmy, 79

Howard, John, 125
Hume, John, 10, 22, 25, 45, 56, 138, 154
hunger strikes (1981), 140–2, 169
Hurricane Mitch, 95, 227
Hurson, Martin, 140
Hutton, Barbara, 182

Independent International Commission on Decommissioning (IICD), 161, 180, 200, 203, 211–14, 215, 216, 217, 230
   de Chastelain Report, 211, 213, 216, 217, 225
   Unionists reject decommissioning body, 177, 180
INLA *see* Irish National Liberation Army
International Monetary Fund (IMF), 96, 227, 228
internment, 26, 70–1
Irish Constitution, 53
   Articles 2 and 3 replaced, 203
Irish government, 10, 13, 33, 36, 39, 43, 45, 61, 83, 144
   censorship policies of, 146–7
   establish commission to inquire into 'disappeared', 148
   Sinn Féin present IRA position on decommissioning, 216
   and suspended institutions, 218–19
Irish language issue, 53, 54, 55, 56, 57, 65
Irish National Liberation Army (INLA), 35, 36
Irish Republican Army (IRA), 31, 106, 208–9
   accused by RUC of killings, 43–5
   cessations, 9, 21, 45, 168, 210, 213
   and decommissioning, 76, 126–8, 134, 135, 138–9, 200, 203, 211, 212, 215, 216, 217, 230–2, 249–50, 257, 263
   execute Tom Oliver, 69

282

Index

and graves of 'disappeared',
   131–2, 148–50
kill two RUC men, 170
split of 1969, 191

James, Philip, 228
Jubilee 2000 Coalition, 227, 228, 229
Just A Prisoner's Wife, 27
JustUs Community Theatre, 26, 27,
   71

Keane, Mairead, 46, 59, 167
Kelly, Gerry, 31, 195, 196
Kelly, Paddy, 167–8
Kenneally, Thomas, 124
Kennedy, Caroline, 170
Kennedy, Carolyn, 167, 169
Kennedy, John F., 48
Kennedy, John F., Jr, 167–70
King, Martin Luther, 156

Lader, Philip, 182
Lake, Tony, 47
Lancaster House talks, 40, 41–2, 43
Largey, Eamonn, 108–9
Lincoln, Abraham, 90
London, 31–2, 42, 182
Long Kesh, 36, 39, 70, 110, 119,
   195–6, 238
   fire in, 195–6
   H-Block campaign, 110, 239
   see also hunger strikes
Loyalists
   attacks on Catholics, 35–7,
      38–40, 114, 136, 138, 245
   break cessation, 35–7, 39, 43
   sectarian gang warfare, 245–6,
      249
Loyalist Volunteer Force (LVF), 38,
   39
Lynch, Kevin, 140

McAuley, Chrissie, 168–70
McAuley, Richard, 31, 168–9, 171
Mac Bradaigh, Caoimhín, 239
McCann, Jim, 195

McCarry, James, 131
McCarry, Valerie, 131
McCartney, Bob, 10, 13
McCaughley, Eamonn, 31
Mac Cionnaith, Breandan, 106
Mc Clure, Pat, 195
McConville, Jean, 148
McCorry, Liam, 191, 192
McCorry, Margaret, 191, 192
McCorry, Miceál, 191, 192
McCorry, Mickey, 191, 192
McCrea, Willie, 248, 251
McCready, Kathleen, 108–112
McCreesh, Raymond, 140
McCullough, Colleen, 124
McDonnell, Joe, 140
McElwee, Tom, 140
McGeady, Paddy, 236
McGrady, Eddie, 103
McGuinness, Martin, 11, 13, 14, 59,
   60, 204, 216
   appointed minister of education,
      197, 226
   and decommissioning body, 75,
      82
   and Good Friday negotiations, 56,
      57, 103, 131, 161
   legal challenge to Unionist ban,
      260–2
   meets Clinton, 46–7
   meets Tony Blair at Downing
      Street, 31, 33, 34
   meets Tony Blair at Stormont, 18,
      19–23
   reports to Ard-Fheis, 52
McLoughlin, Mitchel, 59, 153–4
McManus, Sean, 10–11, 59
McNaughton, Sambo, 267
Mac Stiofain, Seán, 109
McVeigh, Fr Joe
   Crying Out for Justice, 18
Maginnis, Ken, 12, 13
   reads indictment of Sinn Féin,
      10–11
Mahood, Bobby, 245
Maidstone prison ship, 118–20, 195

Index

Major, John, 21, 22, 46
Mallon, Seamus, 22, 82, 101, 126, 265
Malloy, Eamon, 148
Mandela, Nelson, 22, 151–2
Mandelson, Peter, 179, 181, 212, 213, 222, 261–2
  and policing issue, 241–4, 252–3, 264
  suspends Assembly, 215–20, 224–6
Marley, Larry, 239
mass rocks, 116–17
Mayhew, Patrick, 29
Mbeki, Thabo, 152
Meehan, Martin, 238, 248
Meisner, Chuck, 47
Mexican-American War, 89–91
Mexico visit, 89–91
Meyer, Roelf, 21–2
Milošević, Slobodan, 133, 139
Mitchell, George, 49, 50
  and Good Friday negotiations, 52, 53–8, 93
  review of Agreement, 176–8, 180, 182–3, 193–4, 200, 203, 204, 205, 211, 212, 234
Molyneaux, James, 21, 34, 213
Monaghan bombing, 105, 190
Morgan, Arthur, 69
Mountjoy Gaol, 195, 238
Mowlam, Marjorie (Mo), 19, 32, 36, 39, 57, 114, 115, 126, 127, 179
Murphy, Patrick, 208
Murphy, Paul, 19, 32

National Graves Association, 110, 208
NATO bombing of Belgrade, 133–4, 139
Nelson, Brian, 22, 51, 113, 114–15
Nelson, Rosemary, 130, 136, 144, 201
Northern Ireland Act (1998), 197

O'Byrne, Cathal, 79

Ó Caolláin, Caoimhín, 59
O'Donnell, Liz, 135
O'Donoghue, Lowitja, 123
O'Dowd, Niall, 28, 29, 30, 73
O'Dowd, Orla, 29
O'Dwyer, Paul, 66
Ó Fiaich, Cardinal, 141
O'Hanlon, Siobhán, 19, 22, 31
O'Hara, Patsy, 140
O'Hare, Rita, 46, 59, 80
Oliver, Tom, 69
Omagh (County Tyrone) bombing, 73–4, 75
One Man's Hero, 71
Orange parades, 20, 63, 136, 144, 155–7, 159
  Drumcree, 65
  on Garvahy Road, 75, 106, 136, 144, 156, 159, 170
  "Long March", 155–6
Ó Snodaigh, Aengus, 184

Paisley, Ian, 10, 13, 136, 154, 176–7, 248, 251
  and Orange parades, 65
partition, 21, 24, 187–90, 197, 198, 204
Patten, Chris, 130, 198, 220, 225, 233, 234, 235
  recommendations undermined, 241–4, 246, 249, 252–3
Patten Action Committee, 242
policing issue, 53, 54, 55, 56, 57, 61, 63, 65, 130, 137, 165, 200–1, 225, 233–5, 241–4, 246, 249, 251–3, 264
Policing Bill/Act, 242, 252–3, 264
Portadown, 106
  bombing, 45
  Garvaghy Road siege, 75, 106, 144, 156, 159, 170
poverty in Ireland, 174–5, 188, 189, 190
Powell, Jonathan, 32
presidential election (1997), 24, 25

Index

prisoner release issue, 43, 44, 54, 55, 56, 57, 61, 63, 65
Progressive Unionist Party (PUP), 38
Propositions of Heads of Agreement, 40, 43

Radio Ulster, 146
Ramaphosa, Cyril, 21, 152, 230, 250
referenda
 on Good Friday document, 62–3, 143, 177
 on local government in South, 153
Relatives' Action Committees, 110, 239
Republican Prisoners' Welfare, 110
Restorick, Mrs, 32
Riley, John, 90
Robben Island prison, 152
Robinson, Mary, 25
Rockett, Samuel, 245
Roddy McCorley Society, 230
Royal Irish Regiment (RIR), 200
Royal Ulster Constabulary (RUC), 37, 43, 61, 63, 71, 113, 140, 144, 165, 170, 198, 201, 208, 231, 233, 252, 265
 Change Management Team, 242
 and Loyalist killings of Catholics, 38, 39, 137
 and Orange parades, 173
 warn Adams of threat to his life, 129–30
RTÉ, 146

Sands, Bobby, 67–8, 140–2, 238
San Patricio Battalion, 71, 89, 90
Saville Enquiry, 105
Scott, C.P., 188
Second World War, 134
Sinn Féin, 19–23, 24, 31–4, 36, 38, 39, 48, 49, 50, 52–8, 76, 216, 257–8
 Ard-Fheiseanna, 52, 58, 59–61, 143–5, 224–6, 254
 church leaders refuse to meet, 37
 differences with SDLP, 42
 in elections, 64–6, 153–4, 248, 251, 254
 expelled from talks, 43–5
 return to multi-party talks, 49
 Slógadh, 15–16
 stance on plenary motion, 12
 Unionist indictment of, 9–11
Sisulu, Walter, 152
Slovo, Joe, 152
Social Democratic and Labour Party (SDLP), 36, 44, 49, 50, 138, 197, 203, 243, 264
 differences with Sinn Féin, 42
 elected to Executive, 65, 103
 and Good Friday negotiations, 52, 53, 54, 56, 57, 182
Soderberg, Nancy, 47
South Africa, 151–2
Statistics and Research Agency, 188
Staunton, Ciaran, 29
Steele, Jimmy, 110
Stephens, Jonathan, 19
Stone, Michael, 239
Stormont estate, 78–9
Sunday Telegraph, 51
Sutton, Malcolm
 An Index of Deaths from the Conflict in Ireland, 113

Taylor, John, 30, 103, 200, 243
Tempo (County Fermanagh), 18
Thatcher, Margaret, 147
Third World Debt, 95–7, 227–9
Thomas, Quentin, 32
Thornley, Sir Arnold, 78
Tory government (Britain), 20
Trainor, Edward, 39
tribunals into corruption in South, 175, 184–6, 190
Trimble, David, 30, 47, 48, 49–50, 56–8, 60, 64, 65, 82–3, 101–4, 145, 162–3, 164–6, 176–8, 179, 193, 225, 243, 248–9, 251, 256
 bans Sinn Féin from Council, 260–2

Index

Trimble, David *(cont.)*
  and decommissioning issue, 76, 82–3, 126–8, 139, 182, 211–13, 216, 217, 233, 250, 257–8, 263
  first meeting with Gerry Adams, 75–6, 78–9
  indicts Sinn Féin, 9–11
  and party conferences, 176, 178, 179–80, 254
  and plenary motion, 12–13
Trinity College Dublin, 18
Turkey earthquake, 173

UK Unionist Party (UKUP), 9, 36, 64, 101
  boycott Stormont talks, 9
Ulster Defence Association (UDA), 113, 114, 245
  end cessation, 38–9
Ulster Defence Regiment (UDR), 10, 11, 200
Ulster Democratic Party (UDP), 36
  expelled from talks, 38, 39
Ulster Freedom Fighters (UFF), 38, 245
Ulster Unionist Council (UUC), 234, 257, 260
Ulster Unionist Party (UUP), 10, 21, 38, 56–8, 64, 82, 83, 101–4, 154, 163, 164–6, 177, 182–3, 197, 203, 211–12, 231, 233–5, 253, 257–8, 263
  ban Sinn Féin from Council, 260–2
  elected to Executive, 65, 197
  endorse Agreement, 193–4
  have Assembly suspended, 215–20, 225
  joins Stormont talks, 9
  meetings with SDLP, 49–50, 56

  party conferences, 176, 179, 180, 254
  and South Antrim by-election, 248–9, 251
  supports plenary motion, 12–13
  see also Trimble, David
Ulster Volunteer Force (UVF), 245
UNICEF, 96
Unionists
  extremism of, 13–14, 180–1
  veto, 33, 37, 57, 163, 164, 166
  see also individual Unionist parties
United Nations Sub-Committee on Nutrition Commission, 228
USA, 27, 66, 124–5
  Friends of Sinn Féin dinner, 176
  Gerry Adams visits, 28, 80–1, 147, 221–2
  International Relations Committee, 136–7
  Lawrence (Massachusetts), 80
  Sinn Féin's Washington office, 167
  weather, 155

War of Independence, 190
"Way Forward" document, 161–3
weather in Ireland, 98–100, 155, 174
Widgery Report, 43, 89, 105
Williams, Tom, 208–10
Winfield House (London), 182
Workers' Party, 191
World Bank, 96, 227, 228
Wright, Billy, 35, 36, 38

Ziff, Trish, 90

Also by Gerry Adams

An Irish Voice
The Quest for Peace

A unique insight into the Irish peace process, this collection of articles from the New York newspaper, *The Irish Voice*, provides a revealing chronicle of political events between June 1993 and August 1997. A companion volume to *An Irish Journal*.

"*An Irish Voice* is a good read. For the humour as much as the philosophy or the politics." Tim Pat Coogan, *The Irish Times*

ISBN 1 902011 01 5 1; 288 pages, original paperback £9.99

Selected Writings

"Adams writes fluently and observantly. . . He displays a hard-edged compassion for the silent poor, the old and the down-at-out." *Financial Times*

"Should be read by all who wish to take the measure of the man." *The Times*

ISBN 0 86322 233 1; 352 pages; paperback £8.99

Falls Memories

"This nostalgic and very personal account of a working-class community deeply steeped in Republicanism is especially valuable because it has been written by someone who has strong and deep-rooted ties and involvement in both the class and the Republican struggles." *Irish News*

ISBN 0 86322 013 4; 156 pages; paperback £6.99